Anis Charfi

Aspect-Oriented Workflow Management

Anis Charfi

Aspect-Oriented Workflow Management

Concepts, Languages, Applications

VDM Verlag Dr. Müller

Imprint

Bibliographic information by the German National Library: The German National Library lists this publication at the German National Bibliography; detailed bibliographic information is available on the Internet at http://dnb.d-nb.de.

Cover image: www.purestockx.com

Publisher:
VDM Verlag Dr. Müller Aktiengesellschaft & Co. KG , Dudweiler Landstr. 125 a, 66123 Saarbrücken, Germany,
Phone +49 681 9100-698, Fax +49 681 9100-988,
Email: info@vdm-verlag.de

Zugl.: Darmstadt, TU, Diss., 2007

Produced in USA and UK by:
Lightning Source Inc., La Vergne, Tennessee, USA
Lightning Source UK Ltd., Milton Keynes, UK
BookSurge LLC, 5341 Dorchester Road, Suite 16, North Charleston, SC 29418, USA

ISBN: 978-3-8364-5638-8

Contents

CHAPTER 1

Introduction

1.1 This Book in a Nutshell

The Workflow Management technology [87, 175] has its origins in office automation systems, which emerged in the seventies with the promise to automate office work and eliminate paper.

The main focus of Workflow Management is *process automation*. This technology has been used in the traditional business domain [126, 87] and more recently in science and engineering [133, 200]. Moreover, advances such as the Internet and the Web have sustained the interest of academia and industry in the workflow technology, which is a suitable vehicle to automate complex processes even in distributed, cross-organizational, and heterogeneous environments.

Workflow Management systems provide software support for modeling and coordinating the flow of work and information between several participants [183]. Two main concerns are addressed by these systems: the *workflow specification* using workflow languages and the *workflow execution* using workflow engines.

A workflow process specification is a description of the workflow process in a form that supports its automated execution by the workflow engine. It consists of units of work called *activities*, transition information that defines the control flow between them, data declarations for the workflow process and its activities as well as data flow information, declarations of the participants that can perform the activities, and declarations of the IT applications that support them.

Workflow process specifications are complex by nature. They are even more complex than procedural and object-oriented programs because they address not only control flow and data flow aspects but also organizational and technical aspects. In addition to the inherent complexity of workflow specifications, today's organizations are characterized by a large number of workflow processes, which often need to be adapted or customized. As a result, having modular workflow specifications becomes necessary to master the complexity and the frequent change requirements of workflow processes.

1

However, the modularity support provided by current workflow languages is limited. When expressing crosscutting concerns (i.e., concerns that cut across the modular structure of workflow processes) and workflow changes (i.e., modifications of the workflow processes) in current workflow languages and workflow management systems the following problems are observed:

First, the workflow constructs, which implement crosscutting concerns such as data collection for billing and measurement of activity execution time are *scattered* across the workflow specifications of several processes. In addition, the workflow specifications are *tangled* as the workflow constructs that implement the process business logic are intertwined with the workflow constructs that implement other crosscutting concerns. Thereby, scattering and tangling span not only the activities, but also the data variables, the participant declarations, and the application declarations. This leads to complex workflow specifications that are hard to understand, to maintain, and to reuse.

Second, state of the art workflow languages and workflow management systems lack a construct for expressing workflow changes modularly. The modular expression of changes is needed especially when the workflow changes define variations that should be switched on and off flexibly and when the changes should be applied to running workflow process instances.

In fact, when expressing a workflow change in static workflow management systems such as current implementations of the Business Process Execution Language (BPEL) [61], the change has to be integrated directly in the workflow process specification. In such an approach, the change is not expressed in a separate module. Moreover, the change is not treated as a first-class entity because it looses its identity when it is integrated in the workflow process specification.

Like static workflow management systems, adaptive workflow management systems such as ADEPT [162] and WASA [198] also lack a module concept for encapsulating the activities, the variables, the participants, and the applications that are necessary for a dynamic change. ADEPT and WASA merely provide low-level change operations for adding/deleting activities and/or transitions to/from the workflow graph at runtime. That is, these systems do not support a declarative high-level expression of workflow changes as first-class entities. Consequently, understanding, tracing, and managing workflow changes becomes a difficult task.

The goal of this work is to design workflow languages that support the modularization of crosscutting concerns and workflow changes. To show the feasibility of these languages, they will be demonstrated by a prototype implementation. The central thesis of this work is that Aspect-Oriented Software Development can be applied in the context of workflow management to solve the problems that were mentioned above.

In the context of programming languages, crosscutting modularity problems were solved by Aspect-Oriented Programming (AOP) [121]. AOP supports a multi-dimensional decomposition of software applications [180] and separates crosscutting concerns from the business logic by providing new language constructs such as aspects and pointcuts. So far, Aspect-Oriented Software Development [56] has been used mostly in the context of programming languages.

This book introduces *aspect-oriented workflow languages*, which incorporate the application of the aspect-orientation paradigm to workflow modeling and workflow specification. These languages support a *concern-based decomposition* of workflow process specifications. Moreover, they provide language constructs that allow the modularization of crosscutting concerns and workflow changes. To illustrate the concepts of aspect-oriented workflow languages, this book presents three aspect-oriented workflow languages.

First, a visual graph-based language called *aspectual workflow graphs* will be presented to illustrate the concepts of aspect-oriented workflow languages in an understandable and graphical way.

Second, the *AO4BPMN* language for business process modeling will be presented. This language, which is an extension to the Business Process Modeling Notation (BPMN) [144], supports aspect-oriented business process modeling and aspect-oriented workflow modeling.

Third, the *AO4BPEL* language for Web Service composition will be introduced. This language, which is an extension to BPEL, supports aspect-oriented workflow specification. The design and implementation of this language can be considered as a proof-of-concept for aspect-oriented workflow languages.

With AO4BPMN and AO4BPEL, the necessary means for a novel and holistic aspect-oriented workflow management approach are provided. This approach supports the modularization of crosscutting concerns from process design to process implementation.

This book shows how AO4BPMN and AO4BPEL aspects allow the modularization of several crosscutting concerns and workflow changes. In addition, it presents two important applications of AO4BPEL to emphasize the value and usefulness of workflow aspects.

In the first application, aspects are used to implement a light-weight process container that provides support for security, reliable messaging, and transactions to BPEL processes. In the second application, aspects are used to implement business rules in BPEL processes in a modular way according to the principles of the Business Rules Approach.

1.2 Contributions

The contributions of the work presented in this book can be summarized as follows:

- *Identification of the limitations of current workflow languages w.r.t. crosscutting concern modularity and workflow change modularity*

  This book is the first work that identifies the lack of means in current workflow languages for modularizing crosscutting concerns and for expressing workflow changes as separate first-class entities.

- *Introducing aspect-oriented workflow languages*

  This work is the first to introduce aspects to workflow languages. It does not simply transfer constructs from Aspect-Oriented Programming to workflow languages. It rather considers the particular needs and properties of workflow languages and workflow management systems when defining join point models, pointcut languages, advice languages, and composition mechanisms of aspects and processes. Aspect-oriented workflow languages show that Aspect-Oriented Software Development is applicable in other contexts beyond programming languages.

3

- *Introducing aspectual workflow graphs*

  This book introduces *aspectual workflow graphs*, which illustrate the concepts of aspect-oriented workflow languages graphically.

- *Design of the AO4BPMN language*

  This book presents an aspect-oriented extension to BPMN supporting the modularization of crosscutting concerns in business process models. AO4BPMN supports aspect-oriented business process modeling and aspect-oriented workflow modeling.

- *Design and implementation of the AO4BPEL language*

  The AO4BPEL language and its implementation can be considered as a proof-of-concept for aspect-oriented workflow languages.

  This book shows how AO4BPEL aspects allow to modularize several crosscutting concerns such as data collection for billing, security, and transactions. Moreover, it shows how aspects modularize workflow changes such as replacing a partner Web Service and how appropriate composition techniques support treating workflow changes as first-class entities.

- *Supporting dynamic changes in BPEL processes*

  A major limitation in BPEL is the lack of support for dynamic changes. As the AO4BPEL engine supports the dynamic composition of aspects and processes, AO4BPEL aspects enable dynamic changes. Thus, AO4BPEL improves the flexibility and adaptability of BPEL processes in a significant way.

- *Survey of support for non-functional requirements in current engines*

  This book studies the non-functional requirements of BPEL processes w.r.t. security, reliable messaging, and transactions. Moreover, it proposes a classification of non-functional requirements and it presents a survey of the support for these requirements in many BPEL engines.

- *Design and aspect-based implementation of a process container for providing middleware support to BPEL processes*

  To support the non-functional requirements of BPEL processes, this book presents a generic, modular, and extensible process container framework, which consists of three main components:

  - An *XML-based deployment descriptor* to specify the non-functional requirements of the process activities declaratively.
  - A *process container* to intercept the execution of activities at well-defined points and plug in calls to middleware services.
  - *BPEL middleware services* to provide the necessary middleware functionality for enforcing the non-functional requirements.

The process container is implemented as a light-weight container using a set of AO4BPEL aspects that are generated automatically from the deployment descriptor using XSLT. This book shows that container architectures are also feasible in the context of workflow processes and that an aspect-based implementation of the container brings several benefits.

4

- *Implementation of three middleware Web Services for BPEL*

  As part of the implementation of the process container framework, three middleware Web Services were developed respectively for security, reliable messaging, and transactions. These Web Services extend Open Source implementations of WS-* specifications from Apache to support advanced non-functional requirements such as secure conversations and multi-party ordered message delivery. These Web Services can also be used independently of the process container framework.

- *Design and aspect-based implementation of a hybrid approach to business rules in BPEL*

  This book proposes a hybrid approach to Web Service composition, which lies between workflow-based approaches and rule-based approaches. This approach separates the business rules that are implemented with AO4BPEL aspects from the BPEL implementation of workflow processes. This book shows that AO4BPEL aspects can implement all types of business rules modularly according to the principles of the Business Rules Approach.

1.3   Structure of this Book

This book consists of an introduction in Chapter 1, three main parts, and a conclusion.

I. The first part provides some background knowledge and presents the problem statement of this book.

   Chapter 2 provides a brief introduction to three technologies that are relevant to this work: workflow management and workflow languages, the Web Service protocol stack including the BPEL language, and Aspect-Oriented Programming.

   Chapter 3 presents the problem addressed in this book. It shows the lack of crosscutting concern modularity and change modularity in current workflow languages by means of a travel agency scenario and two workflow languages: a visual graph-based language and the workflow-based Web Service composition language BPEL.

II. The second part presents the solution to the modularity problems outlined in the first part and introduces specific languages incorporating the solution concepts.

   Chapter 4 introduces aspect-oriented workflow languages and presents their core concepts. This chapter illustrates how aspect-oriented workflow languages solve the modularity problems that are mentioned in Chapter 3 by using aspectual workflow graphs .

   Chapter 5 presents AO4BPMN and shows how this notation modularizes the crosscutting concerns and workflow changes that were presented in Chapter 3.

   Chapter 6 presents the AO4BPEL language and its implementation. Moreover, it shows through examples how AO4BPEL solves the modularity problems related to crosscutting concerns and workflow changes that were presented in Chapter 3.

5

III. The third part presents two applications of AO4BPEL.

Chapter 7 presents a process container framework for supporting the non-functional requirements of BPEL processes such as security, reliable messaging, and transactions.

Chapter 8 describes an aspect-based implementation of the process container framework that is proposed in Chapter 7. Moreover, it presents BPEL middleware Web Services for reliable messaging, security, and transactions.

Chapter 9 presents a hybrid approach to Web Service composition and shows how AO4BPEL aspects implement the different types of business rules in a modular way.

Chapter 10 summarizes the results and contributions of this work. Moreover, it outlines several directions for future work.

In the framework of the research done in this work, the following papers were published.

1. Anis Charfi and Mira Mezini, *Aspect-Oriented Web Service Composition with AO4BPEL*. In Proceedings of the 2nd European Conference on Web Services (ECOWS), Volume 3250 of LNCS, pp. 168–182. Springer, 2004.

2. Anis Charfi and Mira Mezini, *Hybrid Web Service Composition: Business Processes Meet Business Rules*. In Proceedings of the 2nd International Conference on Service Oriented Computing (ICSOC), pp. 30–38. ACM Press, 2004.

3. Anis Charfi and Mira Mezini, *Using Aspects for Security Engineering of Web Service Compositions*. In Proceedings of the 3rd IEEE International Conference on Web Services (ICWS), pp. 59–66. IEEE Computer Society, 2005.

4. Anis Charfi and Mira Mezini, *Application of Aspect-Oriented Programming to Workflows*. In Proceedings of the 5 èmes Journées Scientifiques des Jeunes Chercheurs en Génie Electrique et Informatique (GEI), pp. 117-122, 2005.

5. Anis Charfi and Mira Mezini, *An Aspect-based Process Container for BPEL*. In Proceedings of the 1st Workshop on Aspect-Oriented Middleware Development (AOMD), pp. 1-6. ACM Press, 2005.

6. Anis Charfi, Benjamin Schmeling, Mira Mezini, *Reliable Messaging for BPEL Processes*. In Proceedings of the 4th IEEE International Conference on Web Services (ICWS), pp. 293–302. IEEE Computer Society, 2006.

7. Anis Charfi and Mira Mezini, *Middlware Support for BPEL Workflows in the AO4BPEL Engine*. Demo paper at the 4th International Conference on Business Process Management (BPM), 2006.

8. Anis Charfi and Mira Mezini, *Aspect-Oriented Workflow Languages*. In Proceedings of the 14th International Conference on Cooperative Information Systems (CoopIS), Volume 4275 of LNCS, pp. 193–200. Springer, 2006.

9. Anis Charfi, Benjamin Schmeling, Andreas Heizenreder, Mira Mezini, *Reliable, Secure and Transacted Web Service Composition with AO4BPEL*. In Proceedings of the 4th European Conference on Web Services (ECOWS), pp. 23–34. IEEE Computer Society, 2006.

10. Anis Charfi and Mira Mezini, *AO4BPEL: An Aspect-Oriented Extension to BPEL*. World Wide Web Journal: Recent Advances in Web Services (special issue). Springer, 2007.

11. Anis Charfi, Benjamin Schmeling, Mira Mezini, *Transactional BPEL Processes with AO4BPEL Aspects*. In Proceedings of the 5th European Conference on Web Services (ECOWS), pp. 149–158. IEEE Computer Society, 2007.

Part I

Background and Problem Statement

CHAPTER 2

Background

2.1 Introduction

This chapter provides the reader with background knowledge about the relevant technologies for understanding the work presented in this book. In particular, a short overview of Workflow Management, Web Services, and Aspect-Oriented Programming will be given.

The remainder of this chapter is structured as follows. In Section 2.2, an introduction to workflow management and workflow languages is provided. In Section 2.3, the Web Service protocol stack is presented. In Section 2.4, the Web Service composition language BPEL is introduced. In Section 2.5, Aspect-Oriented Programming is presented. Section 2.6 concludes this chapter.

2.2 Workflow Management

The *Workflow Management Coalition (WFMC)* [183] is the main organization in the area of workflow standardization. In the following, the core concepts in Workflow Management are introduced using the definitions of the WFMC [201].

A *business process* is "a set of *activities* that collectively achieve a business objective". A *workflow* is "the automation of a business process, in whole or part, during which documents, information or tasks are passed from one participant to another for action, according to a set of procedural rules "[201]. Each execution of a workflow process is called a *workflow instance*.

A *workflow schema* is "the specification of the workflow process in a form that supports automated manipulation, such as modeling or enactment by a workflow management system". The workflow schema consists of a set of activities and their relationships, criteria to indicate the start and termination of the process, and information about the individual activities, such as participants, data, and the associated IT applications. The term workflow schema and the term workflow process specification are used as synonyms in this book.

In [132], the following three types of workflows are distinguished:

- *Administrative workflows* are repetitive and structured processes, whose execution can be effectively automated, e.g., bureaucratic processes such as travel expense processing or car registration. They are generally not mission-critical and are characterized by simple information processing that involves few information systems [87, 176].

- *Production workflows* are repetitive and structured processes like administrative workflows. However, they involve several heterogeneous information systems and pose high requirements w.r.t. throughput, transaction, reliability, and security. Production workflows implement critical processes and are characterized by a high number of workflow instances [87, 176].

- *Ad hoc workflows* are unstructured and non-routine processes, where the workflow is not fully predefined, e.g., sales proposal processes, design processes, etc. Ad hoc workflows require human interaction not only for performing the activities but also for coordinating them [87, 176].

For this book, only administrative and production workflows are relevant.

2.2.1 Workflow management systems

A *workflow management system* is "a system that defines, creates, and manages the execution of workflows through the use of software. This software is running on one or more workflow engines, which are able to interpret the workflow schema, interact with workflow participants and where required invoke IT tools and applications" [201].

Workflow management systems consist of two main components: a *build time component* and a *run time component*. The build time component is used to model, define, and analyze workflow processes. The run time component is concerned with coordinating the various activities, supporting their execution in a given organizational and technical environment by interacting with human users and software tools, and managing the workflow instances.

Workflow management systems enable a new kind of application development paradigm, in which a *workflow-based application* [127] consists of a workflow process and a collection of software tools that support the execution of the process activities.

This *two-level programming paradigm* [127] separates the activity specification level from the activity implementation level: workflow processes are specified in the upper level (programming in the large) and functional algorithms and activity implementations are specified in the lower level (programming in the small).

The separation of these two levels brings several benefits. It makes the process flow explicit instead of being buried in the code of several applications. Thus, workflow-based applications become more flexible because changes to the workflow process have no impact on the activity implementations. Moreover, this two-level programming paradigm increases the reusability of the workflow process and the activity implementations.

2.2.2 Workflow languages

Unlike programming languages, which describe computations, workflow languages describe processes. In [131], workflow languages are classified based on the underlying methodologies into the following classes:

- *Graph-based languages*: They are the most traditional and intuitive way for specifying workflows. They use directed graphs, whereby *nodes* represent activities and *edges* represent the flow of control and/or data between them.

- *Petri-net based languages*: Petri-nets [156] were originally developed to describe and analyze concurrent systems. In several works [94, 185, 186] enhanced Petri-net models were used to specify workflows.

- *State and activity charts*: State charts are an extension of finite state machines [97]. In this model, a *transition* moves the workflow from one *state* to another. State charts are complemented by activity charts to describe the events that trigger state transitions. State charts and activity charts were used to specify workflows in several works [101, 172, 203].

- *Workflow programming languages*: They are used either to directly specify workflow schemes or to provide an internal representation of a workflow process. MOBILE [113] is a such a workflow language.

The WFMC process definition meta-model

The WFMC defined a meta-model for process definition as shown in Figure 2.1. This meta-model provides a common method to access and describe workflow process specifications in a vendor-independent way. Thus, it gives a good overview of the constructs that are typically found in workflow languages.

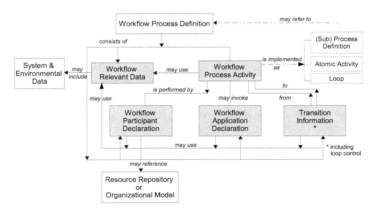

Figure 2.1: The process definition meta-model

The different entities of this meta-model are:

- *Workflow Process Activity:* Each activity comprises a logical, self-contained unit of work that will be processed using a combination of a resource (participant assignment) and a software application (application assignment). An activity may also specify the usage of some *workflow relevant data.*

- *Transition Information:* Activities are connected to one another via transitions. Each transition has a source and a target activity in addition to an optional transition condition. If an activity has more than one incoming transition a *join* is used to specify the semantics of those transitions. A *split* is used to specify the semantics when an activity has multiple outgoing transitions.

- *Workflow Relevant Data:* The workflow relevant type declarations specify the user-defined data types. The workflow relevant data specifies the workflow variables, which can be either used for decision data (e.g., to evaluate conditions), for the input and output data of the activities, or for system data.

- *Workflow Participant Declaration:* The participant declarations describe the resources that perform the different activities. The participant assignment attribute associates an activity with the resources that perform it.

- *Workflow Application Declaration:* This includes the tools that will be invoked by the workflow engine to execute the activities. The application assignment attribute associates an activity with the applications that execute it.

Workflow perspectives

The entities of the WFMC process definition meta-model correspond to different dimensions in workflow specification that are known in the literature as *workflow perspectives.* According to [64, 175], there are five workflow perspectives:

- The *functional* perspective specifies which activities have to be executed within the workflow process. This perspective also covers the functional decomposition of workflows into activities (what does the workflow do).

- The *behavioral* perspective focuses on the ordering, the control flow dependencies, and the pre- and post-conditions of the process activities (when and under which conditions are the activities executed).

- The *informational* perspective specifies the workflow data, the input and output data of the workflow process and its different activities, and the data flow between those activities (which data will be used by which activities).

- The *organizational* perspective describes the organizational environment, in which the workflow process is executed. In addition, it specifies the assignment of activities to participants within the organization (who will perform the activity).

- The *operational* perspective covers technical issues such as the external software tools that implement some activity and how they are invoked (*which application will be used*).

Workflow patterns

To compare the expressiveness of workflow languages, a set of twenty workflow control patterns has been identified in [188]. These patterns address the behavioral workflow perspective. They are classified into *basic* patterns and *advanced* patterns [188].

The basic workflow control patterns are supported by most workflow languages. In the following, these patterns are presented shortly:

- *sequence* refers to a set of activities in the workflow process that are executed in sequential order.

- *parallel split* refers to a point in the workflow process where a single thread of control splits into multiple threads of control, which can be executed in parallel.

- *synchronization* refers to a point in the workflow process where multiple parallel activities converge into one single thread of control, thus synchronizing multiple threads.

- *exclusive choice* chooses one execution path from several alternatives based on some decision.

- *simple merge* refers to two or more alternative branches that come together without synchronization.

A simple graph-based workflow language

In the following, a simple graph-based workflow language is introduced. This language, which was presented in [166], will be used in the next chapter to illustrate the problems of crosscutting concern modularity and change modularity. This language provides two kinds of process modeling objects: *nodes* and *transitions*.

A node can be either an *activity* node that represents a workflow activity, or a *choice/merge* node. Activity nodes are represented graphically by a rectangle and choice/merge nodes are represented by a circle.

A transition links two nodes and it is represented graphically by a directed edge. A transition defines the execution order of its source and destination nodes. A workflow process can be modeled by connecting nodes with transitions into a directed acyclic graph.

This language provides other workflow modeling constructs as shown in Figure 2.2. For instance, *iteration* allows for the repetition of a group of activities. *Nesting* means that an activity can be composite (i.e., it contains nested activities). A composite activity is graphically represented through a shaded rectangle under the task rectangle.

As a workflow process is represented by a directed acyclic graph, it has at least one node that has no incoming transitions and at least one node that has no outgoing transitions. These are respectively the *begin* and the *end* node.

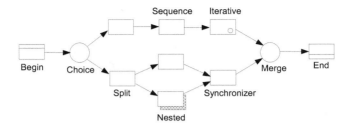

Figure 2.2: A basic graph-based workflow language

This language supports the basic workflow control patterns. The *sequence* pattern is modeled by connecting at most one incoming and one outgoing transition to an activity. The *parallel split* is modeled by connecting two or more outgoing transitions with an activity. The *synchronization* pattern is represented by attaching more than one incoming transitions to an activity. The *exclusive choice* pattern is modeled by attaching two or more transitions to a choice node. At runtime, the workflow selects one of the alternative execution paths for a given instance of the workflow process by activating one of the transitions that originate from the choice/coordinator object. The *simple merge* pattern is represented by attaching two or more incoming transitions to a merge node.

The Business Process Modeling Notation

The Business Process Modeling Notation (BPMN) [144] is an OMG standard for defining business processes. BPMN is a graphical flow-chart based notation that introduces four main categories of modeling elements:

- *Flow objects* are the main elements to define the process behavior. They include activities, events, and gateways. The latter are used to control sequence flows when they converge or diverge within the process.

- *Connecting objects* are used to connect flow objects to other information and to each other. They include sequence flow, message flow, and associations. The latter are used to associate various kinds of information including artifacts with flow objects.

- *Swimlanes* help to partition and organize flow objects. They include pools, which represent the process participants and lanes, which are subpartitions within a pool.

- *Artifacts* provide additional information about the process. They include data objects, text annotations, and groups. BPMN extensibility is based on artifacts, i.e., new artifacts may be introduced by modeling tools.

BPMN can be mapped to executable business process languages such as the Business Process Execution Language (BPEL) to bridge the gap between process modeling and process execution (cf. Section 2.4).

14

2.3 Web Services

Service-Oriented Computing (SOC) [102, 153] is a paradigm for distributed computing, which uses *services* as basic elements in developing software applications. The aim of SOC is to enable a rapid and low-cost composition of services into distributed applications even in open and heterogeneous environments.

Services are self-contained, self-describing, and platform-independent computational entities that can be described, published, discovered, invoked, and composed using standard protocols. A service performs some function that could range from a simple request to a complex business process.

The advent of Service-Oriented Computing has introduced another usage of the Web, which was originally conceived as an environment for publishing documents and information, as an environment for delivering and consuming software services. Web Services [2] manifest the application of the Service-Oriented Computing paradigm to the Web.

The W3C defines a Web Service as a "software system designed to support interoperable machine-to-machine interaction over a network. It has an interface described in a machine-processable format (specifically WSDL). Other systems interact with the Web Service in a manner prescribed by its description (using SOAP messages), typically conveyed using HTTP with an XML serialization in conjunction with other Web-related standards" [93].

The Web Service protocol stack is a set of specifications and standards that cover several aspects in Web Services. This stack, which is shown partly in Figure 2.3, can be divided into *basic* specifications that address the core issues of description, discovery, and interaction and *advanced* specifications that address quality of service and composition issues.

Figure 2.3: The Web Service protocol stack

2.3.1 Basic Web Service specifications

SOAP, WSDL, and UDDI are the basic three Web Service specifications. In the following, each of these specifications is presented shortly.

SOAP: The Web Service Messaging Protocol

SOAP [193] is an XML-based protocol for exchanging structured information in distributed environments. SOAP is the communication protocol for interacting with a Web Service. It works on top of existing transport protocols such as HTTP and SMTP.

A SOAP message has a simple structure consisting of message *headers* (intended for information that is not application-dependent such as quality of service information) and a message *body* (intended for application data). SOAP is generic and extensible as other Web Service specifications were built on top of it by defining new headers, e.g., for security, reliable messaging, etc.

WSDL: The Web Service Description Language

The Web Service Description Language [194] is an XML-based language for describing the functional interface of a Web Service. A WSDL document consists of two parts: an *abstract* description (what the Web Service does) and a *concrete* description (where it is located and how it can be invoked).

The abstract description defines the functional interface of the Web Service in terms of the messages that it sends or receives. The abstract description consists of one or more *port types*, which specify the *operations* of the Web Service and the structure of their input and output *messages*.

The concrete description consists of details on protocol and data marshaling rules for interacting with the Web Service and the physical address where it can be accessed. A *binding* is a mapping of a port type to a transport protocol together with a format for data encoding. A *port* defines the physical address for a binding and a *service* is a collection of related ports.

UDDI: The Web Service Directory

The Universal Description, Discovery and Integration [92] specifications provide a means for publishing and discovering Web Services. UDDI can be considered as the naming and directory service for Web Services.

A UDDI *registry* is an XML-based registry, which contains information about organizations (*business entities*) that provide Web Services (*business services*) and meta-data about those Web Services, such as technical and legal details (*binding templates, technical models*).

The UDDI specification defines several APIs for interacting with a UDDI registry, e.g, the inquiry API and the publishing API. A UDDI registry can also be accessed as a Web Service.

2.3.2 Advanced Web Service specifications

Several important issues are not addressed by the basic protocol stack, such as service composition, security, reliable messaging, transactions, etc. To fill this gap, many so-called WS-* specifications have been proposed on top of the basic

Web Service specifications. The WS-* specifications provide mechanisms for *quality of service* (e.g., WS-Security [138] and WS-ReliableMessaging [45]) and for *service composition* (e.g., BPEL [61]).

WS-* specifications are *composable*: whilst each of them addresses a specific concern and has a value on its own, it can work seamlessly in conjunction with other WS-* specifications. For example, a SOAP message that is secured according to WS-Security can also carry reliable messaging headers as defined by WS-ReliableMessaging. In the following, the WS-* specifications that are relevant to this book will be presented shortly.

Web Service Security

SOAP messages are exposed to several security threats when exchanged between clients and Web Services. The receiver needs to be sure that the message was really sent by the claimed sender, that is was not read or tampered with during transmission, etc.

WS-Security [138] is an OASIS standard, which defines SOAP extensions to implement message integrity, message confidentiality, and single message authentication. WS-Security defines a security header to convey security-related data such as signatures, keys, time stamps, etc. WS-Security supports two kinds of authentication tokens: a *UsernameToken* can be used to carry a user name and password pair and a *BinaryToken* can be used to carry other tokens such as X.509 certificates and Kerberos tickets.

There are other security specifications that build on top of WS-Security and address advanced security issues such as trust [4], secure conversations [90], federation [3], etc.

WS-Trust [4] provide methods for issuing and exchanging security tokens, and for managing and establishing trust relationships. In the trust model of WS-Trust, a client that wants to interact with a given Web Service has to interact with the Security Token Service (STS) of that Web Service. The STS may require its own set of claims in order to subsequently issue a token that the client uses to interact with the Web Service.

WS-SecureConversation [90] builds upon WS-Security and WS-Trust to support the establishment of mutually authenticated security contexts, which can be used to exchange several messages. In WS-Security, each individual message should contain information about the artifacts that were used to secure it. WS-SecureConversation eliminates the overhead of carrying and validating all these security artifacts in each SOAP message.

Web Service Reliable Messaging

Several delivery errors could occur when unreliable communication channels are used, such as message loss, message duplication, and message reordering (i.e., messages that are sent in a certain order are received in a different order).

There are two competing specifications that address reliable messaging in Web Services: WS-ReliableMessaging [45] is a specification by IBM, BEA, Microsoft, and Tibco and WS-Reliability [137] is an OASIS standard.

Both specifications provide similar delivery assurances (exactly-once, at-least-once, at-most-once, and ordered delivery). To enforce these assurances, both specifications define protocols for reliable message delivery and use well-known mechanisms from computer networks such as message acknowledgment and message numbers. A detailed comparison of both specifications can be found in [48, 141].

Web Service Transactions

In several business scenarios, it is important to coordinate multi-party message exchanges between distributed participants, which can be Web Services and their clients. When these message exchanges should achieve a common objective coordination becomes important.

WS-Coordination [65] provides a generic framework for coordinating distributed activities. WS-Coordination is extensible, i.e., new coordination protocols (e.g., for short-running atomic transactions) can be plugged into the framework. WS-Coordination defines three main elements:

- The *coordination context* is a shared context that represents the coordination. It includes a context identifier and the address of the registration service.

- The *activation service* is used by the initiator of the coordination to create a coordination context, which will be propagated to the participants as part of the application messages.

- The *registration service* is used by participants to register for a specific coordination protocol of a given coordination type, e.g., for the completion protocol of atomic transactions [139].

There are two WS-* specifications that leverage WS-Coordination: WS-AtomicTransaction [139], which supports short-running atomic transactions and WS-BusinessActivity [140], which supports long-running compensation-based transactions.

The atomic transaction coordination type comprises three protocols for supporting atomic distributed transactions with the traditional ACID properties: a *completion* protocol to initiate the commitment of a transaction and two *2-Phase-Commit* protocols (*volatile* and *durable*) to decide whether the transaction should be committed or aborted.

The business activity coordination type supports long-running distributed transactions. Unlike atomic transactions, business activities, which model cross-organizational transactions, do not lock resources until the completion of the transaction. These transactions are characterized by relaxed isolation, i.e., intermediary results can be seen by other transactions. If a business activity has to be rolled back, the already completed parts of the transaction must be reversed using appropriate compensation logic.

WS-BusinessActivity defines two coordination types: *AtomicOutcome*, in which the transaction coordinator directs all participants uniformly to either close or compensate their work, and *MixedOutcome*, in which the coordinator can direct some participants to close and some others to compensate.

In addition, WS-BusinessActivity defines two coordination protocols. In the *BusinessAgreementWithParticipantCompletion* protocol, a participant informs the coordinator when it completes his part of the transaction. Then, the coordinator tells the participant to close or compensate. In *BusinessAgreement WithCoordinationCompletion*, the participant waits until the coordinator tells him to complete.

Web Service Policy

Web Services need a means to publish their QoS requirements, capabilities, and preferences to potential clients. For example, a Web Service may need to tell clients that it supports reliable messaging and requires confidentiality through message encryption.

Such policies cannot be expressed in WSDL, which covers only the functional interface of a Web Service. WS-Policy [115] provides a generic model and an extensible XML syntax for describing the policies of a Web Service in a declarative way.

In WS-Policy, a *policy expression* is a collection of one or more *policy assertions* that can be combined using *policy operators*. A policy assertion represents a domain-specific capability, requirement, or preference. Assertion languages such as WS-SecurityPolicy [46] define domain-specific assertions, e.g., for security, reliable messaging, transactions, etc.

The WS-PolicyAttachment [47] specification defines mechanisms for associating policies with subjects such as WSDL documents, UDDI entries, or any other resource. In *internal attachment*, policy annotations are used in an XML document to directly attach policies to subjects that are defined in that document. In *external attachment*, policies are attached to subjects using an external binding from outside the documents where the subjects are defined.

2.3.3 Web Service composition

One of the promises of Service-Oriented Computing is to support a rapid and low-cost composition of services into sophisticated applications. *Web Service composition* provides a means to combine existing Web Services according to some composition pattern in order to solve a complex problem, to achieve a business goal, or to provide a new service in general [2, 62].

Reuse and reducing complexity are the main motivations behind Web Service composition. With the increasing number of available Web Services, reusing existing Web Services becomes more attractive than writing new ones. In some cases, reuse is not optional, e.g., one must use the Web Services of credit card companies to validate credit card numbers. Moreover, it is possible that a complex functionality, which is required by a client, cannot be provided by a single Web Service but by an aggregation of several Web Services.

Web Service composition provides a suitable mechanism for application integration in intra-enterprise (Enterprise Application Integration) and cross-enterprise (Business-to-Business) settings [2, 62]. In addition, it enables a more rapid and efficient integration of distributed and heterogeneous applications than traditional Workflow Management and Enterprise Application Integration technologies [2].

Web Service composition languages

Web Service composition spans two important areas: the *specification* by means of a composition language on the one hand, and the *execution* by means of an appropriate runtime environment on the other hand.

To specify a Web Service composition, one needs to define the control and data flow around a set of Web Service interactions between the parties that are involved in the composition.

Several approaches have been proposed for the specification of Web Service compositions, e.g., by using activity diagrams [172], state charts [20], petri nets [94], process algebras [82, 167], workflow processes [61, 125], etc.

Programming languages such as Java can also be used to implement a Web Service composition. However, programmers would be confronted with many low-level tasks such as converting program data from and to XML, creating SOAP messages and setting their payload, handling faults, assigning messages to different conversations, etc.

Instead of using programming languages, process-oriented Web Service composition languages such as WSFL [125] and BPEL [61] provide high-level programming concepts that allow programmers to focus on the business logic of a Web Service composition and free them from handling low-level concerns. These languages define the Web Service composition using a workflow process.

Orchestration and Choreography

Web Service composition encompasses *orchestration* and *choreography*, which are two different but overlapping concepts corresponding to different viewpoints on a Web Service Composition [73, 155].

Orchestration describes an executable business process that consists of several interactions from the view point of a single participant. An orchestration specifies the ordering of interactions between the party that executes the business process and the other Web Services that participate in the composition. Several process-oriented orchestration languages have been proposed such as BPML [12], WSFL [125], and BPEL [61].

Choreography describes interaction protocols, i.e., the public message exchanges between Web Services from a global view point. Choreography is more collaborative than orchestration. Unlike an orchestration, a choreography tracks only the observable public message exchange and does not reveal internal computations and data transformations; thus choreographies are not executable. Some choreography languages have been proposed such as WSCI [14] and the more recent WS-CDL [196].

2.4 The Business Process Execution Language (BPEL)

The Business Process Execution Language for Web Services (BPEL4WS or BPEL for short) [61] is a process-oriented Web Service composition language, in which the implementation of a composite Web Service is specified using a workflow process. The composition in BPEL is *recursive*, i.e., the result of the composition is also a Web Service.

BPEL 1.0 was proposed in July 2002 by BEA, IBM, and Microsoft as the result of combining two composition languages: IBM's Web Service Flow Language (WSFL) [125] and Microsoft's XLANG [181]. In April 2003, BPEL 1.1 was submitted to OASIS for standardization. The output of the BPEL Technical Committee [136], which was renamed to WS-BPEL 2.0 [13] to better fit into the landscape of the Web Service specifications, has been released for public review in August 2006.

A BPEL workflow process consists of activities for interacting with the Web Services that participate in the composition together with a specification of control and data flow around these interactions.

BPEL supports two kinds of processes: *executable processes*, which define the business logic of a private orchestration and *abstract processes*, which define the public interaction protocol of the composite Web Service. An abstract process can be thought of as a projection of an executable process that omits internal implementation details and keeps only the necessary information on how to interact correctly with the Web Service. For this book, only executable BPEL processes are relevant.

2.4.1 Basic concepts

BPEL is a workflow language, where all participants are Web Services and their clients. In addition, all applications that perform the activities are Web Services. The basic concepts of BPEL are activities, variables, and partners.

Activities

BPEL differentiates *basic* activities and *structured* activities. Basic activities are used, e.g., for interacting with Web Services (e.g., *invoke*) and for manipulating data (e.g., *assign*). Structured activities are composite, i.e., they contain other activities.

The core of a BPEL process are the messaging activities, which define the message exchanges between the different parties in the composition. The *receive* activity blocks the process and waits until a client request is received. The *invoke* activity calls an operation on a partner Web Service. The *reply* activity sends a response to a client of the composite Web Service.

Structured activities such as *sequence* (sequential execution), *flow* (parallel execution), and *switch* (conditional execution) define the execution order of their nested activities. They correspond to the *process algebraic* style of workflow specification, which is derived from process calculi [100, 135].

In the *flow* activity, additional ordering constraints can be expressed by using *links* (i.e., control flow edges connecting a *source* activity with a *target* activity). A *link* specifies that the target activity can only execute after the source activity completes; it may also have a boolean *transition condition* attached to it [118]. *flow* and *link* incorporate the *graph* style of workflow specification in BPEL.

Partners

They represent the parties that a BPEL process interacts with such as the clients and the Web Services that are called by the process. A *partner link* is an instance of a typed connector between two WSDL port types specifying what the BPEL process provides to and what it expects from the partner. A partner link can be considered as a channel for peer-to-peer conversation between the process and the partner [118, 197].

The composition model of BPEL is *type-based*, i.e., Web Services are composed at the port type level and not at the port level. The BPEL process refers only to the abstract WSDL interface of the partners. The binding of partners to concrete Web Services is done by the BPEL runtime according to various binding approaches at design time, deployment time, or runtime [197].

Variables

In BPEL, the workflow data is read from and written to XML typed *variables*. These variables may be read or written by messaging activities or by the data manipulation activity *assign*.

Messaging activities specify input variables and/or output variables. For instance, an *invoke* activity may specify an *input variable* that contains the parameters of the respective Web Service call on a partner and an *output variable* that contains the return data of that call. The *assign* activity is used to move data between variables in an atomic manner.

2.4.2 Advanced concepts

In addition to the basic constructs, BPEL defines constructs for handling faults, compensating already completed activities, matching SOAP messages with process instances, and reacting to external events.

The unit of fault handling and compensation handling in BPEL is the *scope*, which is a structured activity that provides context for fault handling and compensation handling to its nested activities.

Fault handling

BPEL processes have to deal with several kinds of faults (e.g., those resulting from partner invocations or raised as part of the business logic of the process). *Fault handlers* are BPEL constructs that are attached to scopes to catch faults. If a fault occurs during the execution of a scope, the activity of the corresponding fault handler will be executed. If no matching fault handler is found, the fault will be thrown to the parent scope until a matching handler is reached or the process terminates.

Compensation handling

Long-running BPEL processes could not be always completed in a single atomic transaction. Therefore, if a fault occurs at some point during the process execution, it is necessary to reverse the activities that were successfully completed until that point. *Compensation handlers* are BPEL constructs for undoing the effect of successfully completed process activities. Like fault handlers, compensation handlers are defined at the scope level.

A compensation handler, which is associated with a scope *s*, can be called *explicitly* using the *compensate* activity, e.g., from a fault handler of a parent scope of *s*. When a fault occurs in a parent scope of *s* and no fault handler matches that fault, the default fault handler of the parent scope of *s* calls

22

implicitly the compensation handlers of all completed child scopes (including the compensation handler of s) in reverse order of completion.

Correlation sets

As several instances of the same BPEL process may be running concurrently (each of them talking to a different client) a mechanism is needed to correctly route SOAP messages to the respective process instance. BPEL introduces *correlation sets* for that purpose.

The correlation mechanism works as follows: correlation sets are defined as groups of WSDL-typed *properties*, which are named and mapped to parts of the messages that the process sends or receives. Then, correlation sets are attached to messaging activities with a flag indicating whether the activity will initiate the correlation set.

When an incoming SOAP message is received, it can be routed to the corresponding process instance by matching the specific parts of that message with the values of the variables of the running process instances.

Event handling

BPEL introduces *event handlers* to support asynchronous events that take place concurrently to the process execution. Event handlers specify an activity that should be executed when a certain event occurs such as a message that comes in (*message events*) or a timer that goes off (*alarm events*).

2.4.3 BPEL implementations

To execute a Web Service composition, the BPEL process must be deployed on a BPEL workflow engine or *orchestration engine*, which provides the runtime environment for BPEL processes.

The orchestration engine is responsible for managing the process lifecycle and the process instances. This means that the engine creates a new process instance when an incoming SOAP message matches a startable[1] *receive* activity. The engine terminates the process instance once the last activity of the process is completed. The engine is also responsible for binding partners to specific Web Services and executing the process instances according to the process definition.

To date, many BPEL engines are available from both the Open Source community and industry. ActiveBPEL [129], PXE [112], and Bexee [85] are open source engines that are available for free. In addition, several commercial engines are on the market such as IBM WebSphere Process Server [105], Oracle BPEL Process Manager [148], Microsoft BizTalk Server 2006 [134], OpenLink Virtuoso [174], and Cape Clear Orchestrator [54].

When this work started, IBM BPWS4J [63, 106] was the only available BPEL engine. That engine was released shortly after the BPEL 1.0 specification. IBM BPWS4J is especially relevant for this work because the implementation of AO4BPEL was built on top of it.

IBM BPWS4J is packaged as a web application that runs under Tomcat. It has a Web-based user interface, which allows users to deploy, undeploy, and manage BPEL processes. To deploy a process the user has to specify the process

---

[1]A *receive* activity with the *createInstance* attribute set to yes.

definition (.bpel file) and the interfaces of the composite Web Service and its partner Web Services (.wsdl files).

2.5 Aspect-Oriented Programming

Aspect-Oriented Programming (AOP) [121] is a programming paradigm that explicitly addresses the modularization of crosscutting concerns in complex software systems. The hypothesis underlying AOP is that modularity mechanisms so far support the hierarchical decomposition of software according to a single criterion, based for instance on the structure of data (*object-based decomposition*) or on the functionality to be provided (*functional decomposition*).

Crosscutting modularity mechanisms [130] supported by AOP aim at breaking with the *"tyranny of a single decomposition"* [180]. They enable a modular implementation of crosscutting concerns. Several approaches to aspect-oriented software development were presented based on a common modeling framework by Masuhara and Kiczales [130]. These approaches were analyzed and classified into different categories. In this book, when talking about AOP, the *pointcut-advice model* [130] is meant.

AOP introduces a new unit of modularity called *aspect* aimed at modularizing crosscutting concerns in complex systems by means of three key concepts: *join points*, *pointcuts* and *advice*.

Join points are well-defined points in the execution of a program [120]. Which points in the execution of a program are considered as join points is determined by the join point model of an aspect-oriented language. Since AspectJ is an aspect-oriented extension of Java, its join point model defines points in the execution of object-oriented programs such as method calls, constructor calls, field read/write, etc.

In order to modularize crosscuts, a means is needed to identify related join points. Pointcuts, which are predicates on the attributes of join points, can select related method execution points based on the type of their parameters or return values, on matching patterns in the names or modifiers, etc. Similar mechanisms are available to select sets of related setter and getter execution points, sets of constructor calls and executions, exception handlers, etc. Current AOP languages come with predefined pointcut constructs (known as *pointcut designators* in AspectJ).

The common crosscutting functionality at a set of related join points is specified by means of advice. The advice is a piece of code that is executed whenever a join point in the set identified by the respective pointcut is reached. The advice can be executed before, after, or instead of, the join points that are selected by that pointcut. This corresponds to *before*, *after* and *around* advice types in AspectJ.

With around advice, the aspect can integrate the further execution of the intercepted join point in the middle of some other code to be executed around it. In *AspectJ*, the keyword *proceed* is used in the advice as place holder for the join point.

Advice code also has access to the execution context at join points that trigger its execution. In addition to identifying relevant points in the program execution, a pointcut may also declare what part of the join point context is made available to the advice: AspectJ provides dedicated language constructs for exposing the target of a method call, the arguments passed to the call, etc.

An aspect module consists, in general, of several pointcut definitions and advice associated with them. In addition, it may define state and methods, which in turn can be used within the advice code.

```
public aspect Logging
{
  //where ?
  pointcut loggableMethods(Object o): call(* bar (..)) && this(o);

  //when ?
  before(Object o): loggableMethods(o)
  {
    //what ?
    System.out. println ("bar  called  from  object  " + o.toString ());
  }
}
```

Listing 2.1: A logging aspect in AspectJ

Listing 2.1 shows a simple logging aspect in AspectJ. This aspect defines a pointcut, *loggableMethods*, which specifies *where* the logging concern should join the execution of the base functionality. In this example, the interesting join points are the calls (the *call* pointcut designator) to all methods named *bar*, independently of the class they are defined in, their return type (the wildcard "*" is used to abstract over the class/method names and return type), as well as the number and type of the parameters (the symbol ".." serves to abstract over parameters of the call). The object that executes the method call is exposed to the advice using the pointcut designator *this*; it is bound to the object *o*.

The advice specifies *when* and *what* behavior to execute at the selected join points. The advice associated with the pointcut *loggableMethods* prints out a logging message before executing any of the join points that are matched by the pointcut. It also uses the context of the join point by calling the method *toString* on the target of the current method call join point.

The *logging* aspect enables the logging concern to be modularized in a separate module. If the logging functionality is required in other places, one just has to modify the pointcut definition. In a non-AOP object-oriented solution, it would be necessary to go through all locations where logging is required and modify the classes appropriately. With aspects, conversely, a single piece of code needs to be changed, and the logging functionality can be switched on and off without modifying the application code in an invasive way.

Integrating aspects into the execution of the base functionality is called *weaving*. In *static AOP* approaches such as AspectJ, weaving happens at compile time or load time. In *dynamic AOP* approaches [11, 23, 25, 158], aspects can be deployed and undeployed at runtime. Thus, dynamic AOP allows aspects to adapt the behavior of applications to changes in the requirements and runtime environment [99, 169].

2.6 Conclusion

This chapter provides the necessary background knowledge for understanding the work presented in this book. Specifically, a short introduction to Workflow Management, Web Services, and Aspect-Oriented Programming was given.

Workflow management and workflow languages are relevant for this book, which addresses the problems of crosscutting modularity and change modularity in workflow languages in Chapter 3. In that chapter, the simple graph-based language and BPEL will be used as two examples of workflow languages.

The Web Service protocol stack is important not only because BPEL is used as an example of workflow languages, but also for understanding the process container framework that is presented in Chapters 7 and 8. In that framework, AO4BPEL aspects are used to provide support for security, reliable messaging, and transactions to BPEL processes.

Aspect-Oriented Programming is also a key technology in this book, which introduces aspect-oriented workflow languages in Chapter 4 to solve the problems of crosscutting concern modularity and change modularity in current workflow languages. This book will also present AO4BPMN, which is an aspect-oriented language for business process modeling in Chapter 5 and AO4BPEL, which is an aspect-oriented workflow language for Web Service composition in Chapter 6.

CHAPTER 3

Problem Statement

3.1 Introduction

This chapter presents the limitations of current workflow languages with respect to crosscutting concern modularity and change modularity. These limitations will be explained using a travel agency scenario and two workflow languages: a visual graph-based language and the BPEL language for Web Service composition.

The graph-based workflow language illustrates the problems that arise at the activity level when crosscutting concerns are expressed using the constructs of current workflow languages. This language supports only the functional and the behavioral workflow perspectives.

In addition, the BPEL workflow language for Web Service composition is chosen as a representative for state of the art workflow languages. BPEL supports the informational, the organizational, and the operational workflow perspectives. As a result, BPEL shows how the scattering and tangling problems span other workflow constructs beyond activities (the functional perspective) such as variables (the informational perspective) and partners (the organizational and operational perspectives).

In fact, current workflow languages, represented by the visual graph-based language and BPEL, lack means to modularize concerns that cut across process boundaries such as activity execution time measurement, data collection for billing, and security. Consequently, *scattering* and *tangling* problems arise. These problems lead to monolithic and complex workflow schemes that are hard to understand, to maintain, to change, and to reuse.

In addition, current workflow languages and current workflow management systems do not support the expression of workflow changes in separate modules as first-class entities. In static workflow languages, workflow changes are integrated directly into the workflow schema. In adaptive workflow languages, there is also no module for encapsulating the workflow constructs that implement a given workflow change. Dynamic changes are merely supported by low-level operations for adding/deleting activities and transitions, i.e., workflow changes are not expressed at a high abstraction level as first-class entities. Moreover, workflow languages lack a module concept for encapsulating the decision about the activities and processes that are affected by a given change.

The lack of support for change modularity in current workflow languages makes understanding and tracing changes a difficult task, e.g., to understand a workflow change one has to compare the workflow schemes before and after the change has been accommodated. Moreover, it has a negative impact on change management, e.g., to undo some temporary change, one would have to migrate the running workflow instances from one workflow schema to another.

The remainder of this chapter is organized as follows. Section 3.2 introduces a travel agency scenario, which will be used throughout this book. In Section 3.3, the problems of crosscutting concern modularity are illustrated using several examples. Section 3.4 elaborates on change modularity in static and adaptive workflow management systems. Section 3.5 concludes this chapter.

3.2 A Travel Agency Scenario

Consider a travel agency that uses the workflow management technology to automate some of its business processes. For example, when a customer sends a flight request to the travel agency, a flight process is started, which interacts with the information systems of several airline companies to find flights that match the customer needs. A hotel process is used to search for available hotel rooms by interacting with the information systems of several hotels chains. A travel package process is used to compose flight offers and hotel accommodations into full vacation packages.

The workflow processes mentioned above take as input the necessary parameters from the customer search request (e.g., departure city and destination city) and return one or more offers, so that each offer has a unique offer id. If the customer wants to book a given offer, he specifies the offer id and the payment information. This starts another workflow process for booking, which interacts with the airline companies, and/or hotels chains, and a credit card payment company to complete the booking.

In the following, the flight process and travel package process are modeled using a graph-based workflow language. Then, these processes are implemented in BPEL, with the assumption that the airline companies, the hotel chains, and the credit card company expose their services to partners as Web Services.

3.2.1 Workflow graphs for the travel agency scenario

The graph-based workflow language that was presented in Section 2.2.2 of Chapter 2 will be used to illustrate the issues of crosscutting concern modularity in workflow processes graphically. This graph-based language was chosen because it shows well the activity graph, which is the basis for the discussion on crosscutting concerns in Section 3.3. However, the observations that will be made apply also to the other kinds of workflow languages.

In Figure 3.1, the visual graph-based language is used to model the flight process and the travel package process. The flight process, on the left hand side of this figure, starts upon receiving a flight request from a customer. Once such request arrives, two flight search activities interact with airline companies (Berlin Air and Tunis Air) to find flights matching the customer needs. The subsequent activity *make offer* is a composite activity that contains nested activities, e.g., for assigning an offer id to each available flight. The activity *send flight offers* sends the previously generated flight offers to the customer.

The travel package process, shown on the right hand side of Figure 3.1 is quite similar to the flight process. After receiving a client request for a vacation package, this process interacts with Berlin Air to find a flight, and then with the hotel portal *MyHotels* to find an accommodation. In addition to assigning an offer id, the composite activity *make offer* of this process incorporates logic for combining the available flights and the hotel accommodations into full vacation packages. The activity *send package offers* sends the vacation package offers to the customer.

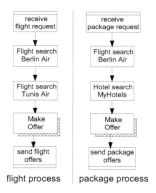

Figure 3.1: Two workflow processes in the travel agency scenario

3.2.2 The travel agency scenario in BPEL

Assuming that the partner companies of the travel agency provide their services using Web Services, the different workflow processes can be implemented with the BPEL language. This workflow-based Web Service composition language allows the travel agency to compose the Web Services of airline companies, hotel chains, and credit card companies. The composition in BPEL is recursive, i.e., the Web Service composition specified by a BPEL process is exposed as a Web Service. That is, the composition specified by the flight process is exposed as a Web Service operation *getFlight*, the composition specified by the travel package process is exposed as a Web Service operation *getTravelPackage*, and the composition specified by the hotel process is exposed as a Web Service operation *getHotel*, as shown in Figure 3.2.

In this figure, the workflow processes are represented by horizontal bars that contain ovals representing the activities. The dashed lines connecting the processes to the Web Services on the right hand side show the Web Services that are invoked from each process. The operations of the composite Web Service of the travel agency are called from a Web application, which is part of the portal of the travel agency.

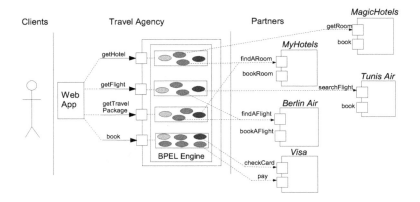

Figure 3.2: The travel agency processes in BPEL

The operation *getTravelPackage* is implemented by the travel package process, which composes the Web Services of Berlin Air and MyHotels. The operation *getFlight* is implemented by the flight process, which composes the Web Services of Berlin Air and Tunis Air. The operation *getHotel* is implemented by the hotel process, which composes the Web Services of the hotel chains My-Hotels and MagicHotels. These operations return one or more offers; each of them contains a description of the flight, the accommodation, or the vacation package in addition to a unique offer id that can be used later for booking.

To book a certain offer, the client calls the Web Service operation *book*, which is also implemented by a BPEL process that composes the hotel and airline partner Web Services of the travel agency and the Visa card payment Web Service. The operation *book* takes two parameters: the offer id (that was previously returned by one of the operations *getFlight*, *getHotel*, or *getTravelPackage*) and the credit card information.

Listing 3.1 shows the travel package process, which implements the operation *getTravelPackage*. This process declares three *partner links* that respectively connect the composition to the client, Berlin Air Web Service, and MyHotels Web Service (lines 3–5). It also declares six variables for holding the client request and response messages, as well as the request and response messages for the invocations of the operations *findAFlight* and *findARoom* on the Web Services of Berlin Air and MyHotels (lines 8–13).

The main activity in this process is the *sequence* activity *packageSequence* (lines 15–49), which contains a *receive* activity that matches the operation *get-TravelPackage* and an *assign* activity for copying data from the variable *clientrequest* to the variables *flightrequest* and *hotelrequest* (lines 19–25).

In addition, the activity *packageSequence* contains two *invoke* activities for calling Berlin Air Web Service (lines 26–28) and MyHotels Web Service (lines 29–31). Moreover, another *assign* activity is used to copy the flight and hotel data from the variables *flightresponse* and *hotelresponse* into the variable *clien-*

```
1  <process name="travelPackage">
2   <partnerLinks>
3    <partnerLink name="client" partnerLinkType="clientPLT" .../>
4    <partnerLink name="flight" partnerLinkType="flightPLT" .../>
5    <partnerLink name="hotel" partnerLinkType="hotelPLT" .../>
6   </partnerLinks>
7   <variables>
8    <variable name="clientrequest" messageType="findPackageRequest"/>
9    <variable name="clientresponse" messageType="findPackageResponse"/>
10   <variable name="flightrequest" messageType="findAFlightRequest"/>
11   <variable name="flightresponse" messageType="findAFlightResponse"/>
12   <variable name="hotelrequest" messageType="findARoomRequest"/>
13   <variable name="hotelresponse" messageType="findARoomIResponse"/>
14  </variables>
15  <sequence name="packageSequence">
16   <receive name="receiveClientRequest" partnerLink="client"
17           portType="travelServicePT" operation="getTravelPackage"
18           variable ="clientrequest" createInstance ="yes"/>
19   <assign>
20    <copy>
21     <from variable=" deptDate">
22     <from variable=" flightrequest" part="DepartOn">
23    </copy>
24    ...
25   </assign>
26   <invoke name="invokeFlightServiceTP"
27           partnerLink="flight" portType="flightPT" operation="findAFlight"
28           inputVariable =" flightrequest" outputVariable="flightresponse" />
29   <invoke name="invokeHotelServiceTP"
30           partnerLink="hotel" portType="HotelPT" operation="findARoom"
31           inputVariable ="hotelrequest" outputVariable="hotelresponse" />
32   <assign>
33    <copy>
34     <from variable="flightresponse" part=" flightDetails " />
35     <to variable ="clientresponse" part=" flightInfo " />
36    </copy>
37    <copy>
38     <from variable="hotelresponse" part="roomDetails" />
39     <to variable ="clientresponse" part="hotelInfo" />
40    </copy>
41    <copy>
42     <from expression="concat(getVariableData(' flightresponse ',' flightnum '),
43                             getVariableData (' hotelresponse ',' id'))" />
44     <to variable ="clientresponse" part="offerid" />
45    </copy>
46   </assign>
47   <reply name="replyToClient" partnerLink="client" portType="travelServicePT"
48          operation="getTravelPackage" variable="clientresponse" />
49  </sequence>
50 </process>
```

Listing 3.1: The travel package process in BPEL

tresponse (lines 32–46). This *assign* activity also creates an offer id for the travel package by concatenating the flight number and the product number returned by the hotel Web Service (lines 41–45). The *reply* activity (lines 47–48) sends the travel package offer to the client.

The specifications of the flight process and the hotel process in BPEL are similar to the travel package process, whereby the flight process invokes the Web Services of Tunis Air and Berlin Air, and the hotel process invokes the Web Services of MyHotels and MagicHotels.

3.3 Crosscutting Concern Modularity

In this section, some examples of crosscutting concerns will be presented in the context of the travel agency scenario. Several limitations are observed when implementing these concerns with the graph-based language and with BPEL.

3.3.1 Case studies

To motivate the need for mechanisms for crosscutting modularity, the implementation of some examples of crosscutting concerns will be studied. Concretely, data collection for billing, measurement of activity execution time, and security will be considered. One could also take other examples of crosscutting concerns for the following discussion.

The implementation of these concerns cuts across several processes and cannot be expressed in a modular way when using the typical constructs of current workflow languages. In conformance with the definition given in [122], the term *modular* means in a *localized* manner and with *well-defined explicit interfaces* to the rest of the composition logic.

Data collection for billing

One assumes that the flight Web Service of Berlin Air is not provided for free. Several pricing models are conceivable. For example, one alternative is to charge only clients who use the service more than 100 times per day. Another alternative pricing model is to charge clients who use the Web Service to search for flights without booking any flights subsequently.

When such pricing policies apply, the travel agency will get a bill from Berlin Air but it has no means to check whether the bill is accurate or not. To verify the bills accuracy, the travel agency decides to count how many times the flight search activity with Berlin Air has been executed from within any workflow process. Thereby, all occurrences of the flight search activity in any process and all instances of these processes must be taken into account.

To implement the data collection for billing functionality, the workflow programmer has to examine all workflow processes of the travel agency. Both the flight process and the travel package process contain a flight search activity, which interacts with Berlin Air. After each occurrence of that activity, the workflow programmer has to add a new activity for incrementing a counter, as shown in Figure 3.3.

To integrate the data collection for billing functionality with the BPEL implementation of the flight process and the travel package process, the workflow programmer has to find all processes that contain an *invoke* activity, which calls the operation *findAflight* on Berlin Air Web Service.

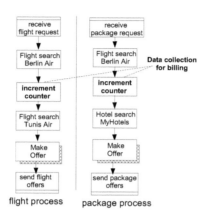

Figure 3.3: Data collection for billing

```
1  <process name="travelPackage" .../>
2    ...
3    <partnerLink name="CounterWS" partnerLinkType="CounterPLT" .../>
4    ...
5    <variable name="increaseRequest" messageType="increaseCounterInput" />
6    ...
7   <sequence name="packageSequence">
8    <receive name="receiveClientRequest" .../>
9    <assign>...</assign>
10   <invoke name="invokeFlightServiceTP" operation="findAFlight" .../>
11   <sequence name="collect billing data">
12    <assign>
13     <copy>
14      <from expression="1" />
15      <to variable="increaseRequest" part="increaseBy" />
16     </copy>
17    </assign>
18    <invoke partnerLink="CounterWS" portType="CounterPT"
19            operation="increaseCounter" inputVariable="increaseRequest" .../>
20   </sequence>
21
22   <invoke name="invokeHotelServiceTP" operation="findARoom" .../>
23    ...
24   <reply name="reply" partnerLink="client" .../>
25  </sequence>
26 </process>
```

Listing 3.2: Collecting billing data in the travel package process

```
1   <process name="flightProcess" .../>
2      ...
3     <partnerLink name="CounterWS" partnerLinkType="CounterPLT" .../>
4      ...
5     <variable name="increaseRequest" messageType="increaseCounterInput" />
6      ...
7    <sequence name="flightSequence">
8    <receive name="receiveClientRequest" .../>
9      ...
10   <invoke name="invokeFlightServiceFP" operation="findAFlight" .../>
11   <sequence name="collect billing data">
12     <assign>
13     <copy>
14      <from expression="1" />
15      <to variable="increaseRequest" part="increaseBy" />
16     </copy>
17    </assign>
18    <invoke partnerLink="CounterWS" portType="CounterPT"
19         operation="increaseCounter" inputVariable="increaseRequest" .../>
20   </sequence>
21
22   <invoke name="invokeTunisair" operation="searchFlight"   .../>
23      ...
24   <reply name="reply" partnerLink="client" .../>
25   </sequence>
26 </process>
```

Listing 3.3: Collecting billing data in the flight process

After each one of these activities, the programmer has to add an *invoke* activity that calls an appropriate Web Service to increment a counter as shown in Listings 3.2 and 3.3 (lines 18–19). Moreover, before each new *invoke* activity, the programmer has to add an *assign* activity that sets the input data of that *invoke* correctly (lines 12–17).

In addition, the workflow programmer has to add appropriate partner links and variables for supporting the data collection for billing concern. In both processes, the programmer adds a *partner link* to the counting Web Service (line 3) and a variable *increaseRequest* (line 5) to held the input parameters of the *invoke* activity that calls *increaseCounter*.

Data collection for billing is crosscutting because it happens at different points in the execution of activities in different workflow processes. The BPEL code, which includes activities, variables, and partners, belonging to that concern is *scattered* across two process modules and cannot be encapsulated in a separate module. It is unclear which partners, variables, and activities pertain to which concern and where the logic for a given concern is executed. Moreover, the BPEL code that implements data collection for billing is *tangled* with the BPEL code that implements other concerns.

Whilst Figure 3.3 shows the scattering and tangling problems at the activity level only, Listings 3.2 and 3.3 show that the scattering and tangling problems span also the variables and the partners that are required for supporting data

34

collection for billing. This is because the graph-based language supports only the functional and behavioral perspectives, whereas BPEL supports also the informational perspective (variables) and the organizational/operational perspectives (partners).

Scattering and tangling result from the lack of a module that encapsulates (i) the logic that belongs to the data collection for billing concern and (ii) the specification of the interface of the latter with the rest of the travel portal logic.

The data collection logic includes:

- the new *sequence* activity (lines 11–20)

- the declaration of partner links (line 3) involved in realizing the collection of data

- the declaration of variables (line 5) involved in realizing the collection of data

- the interface of the data collection concern with the rest of the travel portal, i.e., the specification of the points during the execution of the base workflow processes, where data collection should be triggered

Due to the lack of a module that encapsulates the concern data collection for billing, one has to add the same *sequence* activity to increment the counter after each *invoke* activity that calls Berlin Air Web Service, and the same *partner link* and *variable* definitions to each of the affected processes.

Measurement of activity execution time

In the context of workflow monitoring, organizations that deploy workflows are usually interested in measuring the execution time of certain process activities. If the workflow management system at hand does not provide support for monitoring activity execution time, the workflow programmer must implement this functionality by adding appropriate activities to the workflow process. That is, one activity for starting a timer will be added before the monitored process activity, and one activity for stopping a timer will be added after it. In Figure 3.4, the flight process and the travel package process are extended with activities for measuring the execution time of the flight search activity, which interacts with Berlin Air.

In the case of BPEL workflows, the monitored activity can be a messaging activity or another activity such as *sequence*, *assign*, etc. To measure the execution time of a BPEL activity X, one could set up an auditing Web Service and invoke appropriate operations on it to start (respectively stop) a timer before (respectively after) each occurrence of X.

To measure the execution time of the *invoke* activity that calls Berlin Air Web Service, the workflow programmer modifies the flight process and the travel package process as shown in Listings 3.4 and 3.5.

In both processes, the workflow programmer adds an *invoke* activity (lines 18–19) that calls the operation *startTimer* on the auditing Web Service before each occurrence of the monitored activity. Similarly, the programmer adds an *invoke* activity (lines 29–30) that calls the operation *stopTimer* on the auditing Web Service after each occurrence of the monitored activity.

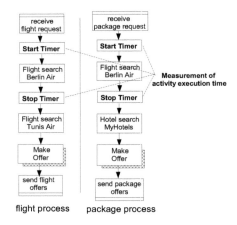

flight process   package process

Figure 3.4: Activity execution time measurement

Both operations *startTimer* and *stopTimer* take a parameter, which identifies the monitored activity. The input data of the *invoke* activities that call these operations is set using appropriate *assign* activities (lines 12–17 and lines 23–28).

In addition to activities, the workflow programmer adds to both processes a *partner link* to the auditing Web Service (line 3) and two *variables* (lines 5–6), which contain the input parameters of the *invoke* activities that call the operations *startTimer* and *stopTimer*.

The measurement of activity execution time is also a crosscutting concern. The scattering and tangling problems in this case are even worse than in the case of data collection for billing because the new activities for measuring activity execution time are required before and after each occurrence of the monitored activity.

Security

Workflow processes have several security requirements such as *confidentiality, integrity, authentication, anonymity,* and *separation of duties* [190]. In [145], three levels of workflow security are presented: *Level 1 security (database-level)* ensures that each activity is performed by an authorized subject, i.e., the subject is granted access to the activity data. *Level 2 security (workflow-level)* ensures that access to that data is granted only during the execution of the respective activity. *Level 3 security (application-level)* focuses on application-specific security requirements.

In the following, workflow-level and application-level security will be considered. Whilst some security requirements can be supported in layers below the workflow level, (e.g., in the database, in the messaging infrastructure, or in the application that implements an activity), workflow-level and application-level security requirements have to be addressed at the workflow process level,

36

```
1   <process name="travelPackage" .../>
2       ...
3       <partnerLink name="AuditingWS" partnerLinkType="AuditingPLT" .../>
4       ...
5       <variable name="startTimerRequest" messageType="startTimerInput"/>
6       <variable name="stopTimerRequest" messageType="stopTimerInput"/>
7       ...
8     <sequence name="packageSequence">
9      <receive name="receiveClientRequest" .../>
10      <assign>...</assign>
11      <sequence name="startTimer Sequence">
12       <assign>
13        <copy>
14         <from expression="'invokeBerlinAirTP'"/>
15         <to variable="startTimerRequest" part="activityName"/>
16        </copy>
17       </assign>
18       <invoke partnerLink="AuditingWS" portType="AuditingPT"
19               operation="startTimer"  inputVariable="startTimerRequest"/>
20      </sequence>
21      <invoke name="invokeFlightServiceTP" operation="findAFlight" .../>
22      <sequence name="stopTimer Sequence">
23       <assign>
24        <copy>
25         <from expression="'invokeBerlinAirTP'"/>
26         <to variable="stopTimerRequest" part="activityName"/>
27        </copy>
28       </assign>
29       <invoke partnerLink="AuditingWS" portType="AuditingPT"
30               operation="stopTimer"  inputVariable="stopTimerRequest"/>
31      </sequence>
32      <invoke name="invokeHotelServiceTP" operation="findARoom" .../>
33       ...
34      <reply name="reply" partnerLink="client" .../>
35     </sequence>
36   </process>
```

Listing 3.4: Execution time measurement in the travel package process

```
1   <process name="flightProcess" .../>
2     ...
3     <partnerLink name="AuditingWS" partnerLinkType="AuditingPLT" .../>
4     ...
5     <variable name="startTimerRequest" messageType="startTimerInput"/>
6     <variable name="stopTimerRequest" messageType="stopTimerInput"/>
7     ...
8    <sequence name="flightSequence">
9    <receive name="receiveClientRequest" .../>
10   <assign>...</assign>
11   <sequence name="startTimer Sequence">
12     <assign>
13      <copy>
14       <from expression="'invokeBerlinAirFP'"/>
15       <to variable="startTimerRequest" part="activityName"/>
16      </copy>
17     </assign>
18     <invoke partnerLink="AuditingWS" portType="AuditingPT"
19            operation="startTimer" inputVariable="startTimerRequest"/>
20   </sequence>
21   <invoke name="invokeFlightServiceFP" operation="findAFlight" .../>
22   <sequence name="stopTimer Sequence">
23     <assign>
24      <copy>
25       <from expression="'invokeBerlinAirFP'"/>
26       <to variable="stopTimerRequest" part="activityName"/>
27      </copy>
28     </assign>
29     <invoke partnerLink="AuditingWS" portType="AuditingPT"
30            operation="stopTimer" inputVariable="stopTimerRequest"/>
31   </sequence>
32   <invoke name="invokeTunisair" operation="searchFlight"   .../>
33     ...
34   <reply name="reply" partnerLink="client" .../>
35   </sequence>
36 </process>
```

Listing 3.5: Execution time measurement in the flight process because they require knowledge about the workflow execution state and the application semantics, which is unavailable in the underlying layers. That is, to support such requirements, programmers have to add security activities to the workflow process.

For example, it might be necessary to ensure the integrity and confidentiality of application data at the workflow level if this feature is not provided by the underlying layers. In the booking process, the travel agency interacts with the credit card company to handle payments. This process contains activities for checking the card data and for charging the card. Assume that these activities are implemented by some applications that are called via CORBA. Then, the credit card company replaces that application by a Web Service that uses WS-Security [138]. If the workflow management system hosting the booking process does not support secure Web Service calls it becomes necessary to add activities to the booking process for securing the credit card data before, and also after the activities for checking the credit card data and for charging the card, because the response of the credit card Web Service may be secured.

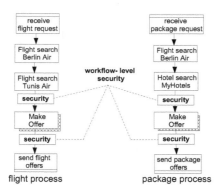

Figure 3.5: Workflow-level security

Another well-known example of workflow-level security requirements is that authorized subjects (e.g., human workflow users) should gain access to the required data only during the activity execution (and not before or after its execution). For example, the workflow participant who sends the flight offers should have access to the data of the offers only during the execution of the activity *send flight offers* and not during the execution of the activity *make offer*.

To enforce this workflow-level requirement, the security component of the workflow management system should authorize the subjects in synchronization with the workflow execution. Several workflow management systems lack mechanisms for such temporal authorization [190]. To support this authorization model in those systems, the workflow designer has to add appropriate activities, which notify the authorization system before and after the execution of some process activities as illustrated in Figure 3.5.

Application-level security requirements are application specific, e.g., *an employee preparing a travel reimbursement claim cannot be the same as the one who issues the reimbursement check* [190]. Another example of application-level security in the context of the travel agency is that the participant performing the activity *make offer* is not allowed to modify the price calculation rules unless he is a manager. To enforce application-specific security requirements, the workflow designer has to add appropriate activities to the workflow process.

Some commercial workflow management systems can be used with add-on tools that provide advanced security support. For example, the *WebSphere MQ Extended Security Edition* is an add-on to the IBM MQ Workflow [104] that supports workflow data protection by signing and/or encrypting messages. With that tool, security activities are added to the workflow process without showing up in the workflow schema. However, even with that tool, workflow-level and application-level security requirements can only be supported by adding security activities explicitly to the workflow process. In fact, there are always cases where adding security activities to the workflow process is required.

Workflow-level security and application-level security are crosscutting concerns. As shown in Figure 3.5, the activities corresponding to these concerns are *scattered* across the flight process and the travel package process, and the resulting workflow processes are *tangled*. These security concerns will not be shown in BPEL code because BPEL does not support human participants. There is however, a recent proposal for such an extension [108].

3.3.2 The need for crosscutting mechanisms

Current workflow languages including BPMN and BPEL do not provide mechanisms for crosscutting modularity. This leads to scattered and tangled workflow schemes: the implementation of a single concern appears in several workflow schemes, and a single workflow schema addresses several concerns. The scattering and tangling span the different workflow perspectives and are not only restricted to activities. They lead to complex and monolithic workflow schemes.

In particular, the implementation of a single concern cannot be changed unless entire workflow schemes are changed in an invasive way. The modification of a crosscutting concern affects in general several locations in different workflow processes, because of the crosscutting structure of such concerns. Consequently, the workflow programmer has to find all locations that are affected by the crosscutting concern and modify them consistently, which is a cumbersome and error-prone undertaking.

Given constructs for modularizing crosscutting concerns, workflow programmers would be in a better position to make design decisions as to what to consider as core composition logic and which crosscutting concerns to separate in well-defined modules. A number of criteria could drive these design decisions: the extent of the crosscutting nature of features, the expected requirements for maintainability and change, etc [123].

The separation of a concern makes it possible to modify the code pertaining to it without changing all the composition (*independent extensibility*) and also to reuse that code in other compositions. In addition, with appropriate composition techniques, modifications of a separated concern can be done dynamically.

The message of this section is not that the crosscutting concerns mentioned above should be separated in any case, but rather that their crosscutting nature motivates the need for new modularization mechanisms in workflow languages. Whether, when, and how to use these mechanisms is a matter of design decisions and proper methodology. But designers should be enabled to capture some concerns in a modularized way if they decide to do so.

One may argue that concerns such as the measurement of activity execution time and security could be addressed in a middleware layer below BPEL. However, if the concern at hand is inherently related to BPEL constructs, it cannot be supported in underlying middleware.

For the measurement of activity execution time, if one considers only *invoke* activities, the response time of a Web Service can be monitored in the SOAP engine. However, if one wants to measure the execution time of a non-messaging activity (e.g., a *flow*), then this information is not accessible to underlying middleware.

Similar arguments apply to workflow-level and application-level security. SOAP message security can be implemented in a middleware layer below BPEL, i.e., incoming and outgoing SOAP messages can be verified/modified in the messaging infrastructure. However, at the SOAP level, relevant information for workflow-level and application-level security (such as the workflow schema, the current execution state, and the assignment of users to activities) is not available. This makes it impossible to support workflow-level security (such as the temporal authorization in sync with activity execution) and application-level security in middleware layers. More details on workflow-level security in BPEL will be given in chapter 7.

In the vein of the seminal papers on the end-to-end argument in system design [168] and on open implementations [88], the decision as to what concerns to capture within the middleware and which ones to capture at the application level is a matter of design considerations. There are always concerns that make more sense to be captured at the application end. For instance, this is why the Enterprise Java Beans component model provides means to express application-level access control within bean implementations, in addition to the security mechanisms provided by any EJB application server.

It is important to give the workflow designers the means to capture crosscutting concerns at the application level in a well-modularized way. The implementation of the middleware can also profit from such crosscutting modularization mechanisms [41, 74, 75, 157, 206].

3.4 Change Modularity

In this section, the issues of change modularity in workflow management systems are addressed. After classifying workflow changes, the need for change in workflow management is motivated. Then, some change scenarios are presented in the context of the travel agency example. After that, the modularity of workflow changes is studied in static workflow management systems such as current BPEL implementations, and adaptive workflow management systems such as ADEPT [162, 163] and WASA [198, 199]. Finally, a discussion will show the necessity and the benefits of a change module concept in workflow management.

Change classification

In the workflow literature [32, 96, 187], workflow changes are classified into *evolutionary* or static changes and *ad-hoc* or dynamic changes.

- *evolutionary changes:* They result from business process re-engineering efforts, new business strategies and collaborations (e.g., acquisition and mergers), new external conditions (e.g., laws and regulations), technical advances, and organizational changes (e.g., new employees, new hierarchy structures). They can be supported by modifying the workflow schema and redeploying the respective workflow process. Evolutionary workflow changes affect the workflow schema, i.e., all workflow instances that are created after an evolutionary change use the modified workflow schema.

- *ad-hoc changes:* They are caused by external events as a result of user involvement (e.g., wrong or incomplete user input), unpredictable events, and erroneous situations (e.g., network failures and mismatches between the real process and the workflow process). As it is impossible to think of all these exceptional situations in advance, workflow management systems should provide support for the dynamic adaptation of running workflow instances. Ad-hoc changes affect individual workflow instances and require ad-hoc deviation of the predefined workflow schema at runtime.

In addition, workflow changes can be classified depending on the workflow perspectives that they affect [96]. That is, there are process-level changes (the functional and behavioral perspectives), organization-level changes (the organizational perspective), data-level changes (the informational perspective), and infrastructure-level changes (the operational perspectives). In general, the effects of a workflow change span more than one perspective.

The need for dynamic workflow changes

With the increasing competition worldwide, the open markets, and the use of distributed computing technologies, the environment of today's organizations has become highly dynamic. In addition, some recent workflow applications such as cross-organizational workflows [161], scientific workflows [133], and clinical workflows [162] are characterized by high flexibility requirements. In such applications, it is unlikely that the workflow processes can be specified once and executed without any change.

When unpredictable events and errors occur, dynamic workflow changes are needed. In such situations, it is not always feasible to stop running workflow instances, especially in the case of long-running processes, which may take several days or weeks for their execution. If one stops a long-running process, one must roll back or compensate all previously performed activities.

For example, the booking workflow process of the travel agency scenario is a long-running process. This process checks the credit card number of the customer and then charges the credit card if it is valid. After that, the booking process issues the necessary travel documents (e.g., flight tickets and hotel vouchers) and sends them using a shipping service. If the booking process is stopped, just before issuing the flight ticket and/or hotel voucher, to accommodate a given change, the resulting state would be inconsistent because the credit card was charged and the flight ticket and the hotel voucher are not issued.

In the context of BPEL workflows, the need for dynamic adaptation is even stronger than in traditional workflows for the following reasons:

- Partner Web Services are provided by external organizations, which are out of the control of the organization that hosts the BPEL process.

- Web Services generally use the unreliable Internet as communication medium, which may lead to more frequent violations of Service Level Agreements (SLA) by the partners. If a partner Web Service performs badly, the BPEL process will also perform badly. In such a case, the organization that hosts the workflow process would probably prefer to make the already running workflow instances use an alternative partner Web Service rather than violate its own SLAs.

- As the Web Service technologies are still maturing (new specifications, standardization, etc.), updates of partner Web Services tend to be frequent, e.g., to support new versions of WS-Security, WS-Reliability, etc. In such cases, the composition has to be adapted appropriately.

- Although interoperability is not a problem in theory, the Web Services provided by different software vendors are not always interoperable [204], because of different interpretations of the specifications, support of different versions of some specification, use of proprietary extensions, etc. Consequently, it may be necessary to replace a partner of the composition by another fully interoperable partner.

- As Web Services are published on the Web, they will allow companies to reach a large number of customers, which should be treated in a differentiated way. This means that these Web Services, which are implemented by BPEL workflows, require to be customized and adapted to the needs of different clients. Expressing each possible customization in the BPEL process using *switch* activities is quite complex and may be impossible and/or undesirable.

3.4.1 Change scenarios

In the following, two examples of workflow changes will be presented in the context of the travel agency scenario. The first one is an evolutionary change and the second is an ad-hoc change.

Adding car rental logic As a result of a new partnership with a car rental company, the travel agency needs to extend the travel package process with some business logic to search for a rental car. In this way, when a customer requests a travel package, he also gets car propositions. This change is an example of evolutionary workflow changes.

It is possible to have variations of this change, so that the car offer is made only to frequent customers, or to the ones who have expressed interest in such offers in their profiles. Another variation could restrict this change to specific destinations, where the car company has subsidiaries. In these two variations, the adaptation should apply to specific workflow instances.

Figure 3.6 shows how the travel package process should be modified. The left hand side of this figure shows the original process. The right hand side shows the new process. The change functionality is implemented by two new activities: an activity *car search* that interacts with the car rental company to find available cars and an activity *update offer* that extends the offers that will be returned to the client with the car proposition.

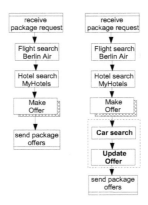

Figure 3.6: Adding car rental logic to the travel package process

Replacement of a bad performing partner The workflow engine that hosts the workflow processes of the travel agency provides some monitoring tools, which can be configured so that an administrator is notified when some activity instance or a process instance runs for a longer time period than a predefined threshold value.

The administrator can test whether the partner Web Services for flight search (i.e., Berlin Air) and hotel search (i.e., MyHotels) are reachable. Assume further that Berlin Air Web Service is temporarily unavailable because of security updates for instance.

If the problem of partner unavailability is not addressed appropriately, several instances of the travel package process and the flight process will raise a fault. This would result in an unacceptable image loss for the travel agency in front of its customers. To fix this situation, the administrator needs appropriate means to dynamically adapt the running instances of the travel package process. Thereby, two possible ad-hoc changes are conceivable.

In the case of workflow processes aggregating similar services from different providers, such as the flight process, the activity that causes the fault should be skipped. That is, the flight process could temporarily use the Web Service of the other partner airline (i.e., Tunis Air).

In the case of workflow processes aggregating different types of services, such as the travel package process, it is necessary to use an alternative partner, which provides the same service as the unavailable one.

In both cases, the change should be applied dynamically in order to fix the already started instances of the travel package process. Such dynamic adaptation is also required for the long-running booking process because the booking operation of Berlin Air Web Service is also temporarily unavailable.

3.4.2 Expressing changes in static workflow management

To study the modularity of change expression in static workflow management BPEL is taken as an example. BPEL and current implementations thereof do not support dynamic changes. The only flexibility feature in BPEL is *dynamic partner binding*, in which a special variant of the *assign* activity is used to map partners to specific Web Services at runtime. Dynamic adaptations such as adding a new partner, adding an activity, modifying the control flow, adding a new variable, and modifying the data flow are not supported.

```
1   <process name="travelPackage" .../>
2      ...
3      <partnerLink name="CarCompany" partnerLinkType="CarPLT" .../>
4      ...
5      <variable name="carRequest" messageType="getCarInput" />
6      <variable name="carResponse" messageType="getCarOutput" />
7
8    <sequence name="packageSequence" >
9    <receive name="receiveClientRequest" .../>
10      ...
11     <invoke name="invokeFlightServiceTP" operation="findAFlight" .../>
12     <invoke name="invokeHotelServiceTP" operation="findARoom" .../>
13      ...
14    <sequence>
15     <assign>
16      <copy>
17       <from variable="clientrequest" part="deptDate" />
18       <to variable="carRequest" part="startDate" />
19      </copy>
20       ...
21     </assign>
22     <invoke partnerLink="CarCompany" portType="CarPT" operation="getCar"
23            inputVariable="carRequest" ouputVariable="carResponse" />
24     <assign>
25      <copy>
26       <from variable="carResponse" part="carInfo" />
27       <to variable="clientresponse" part="optionalinfo" />
28      </copy>
29     </assign>
30    </sequence>
31     <reply name="replyToClient" partnerLink="client"
32    </sequence>
33  </process>
```

Listing 3.6: Adding car rental logic to the travel package process

Adding car rental logic   To add car rental logic to the travel package process, the programmer has to undeploy this process and edit the respective workflow schema. Then, he has to redeploy the modified workflow schema. Listing 3.6

shows the necessary changes to the travel package process for adding car rental functionality.

Listing 3.6 shows that new workflow constructs are needed to integrate this workflow change in the travel package process. These constructs include a new partner link to the car rental Web Service (line 3) and two new variables for holding the input and output data of the car search activity (lines 5–6). To implement the change logic, three activities are needed: an *assign* (lines 15–21) sets the input data of the car search activity, an *invoke* (lines 22–23) implements the car search activity, and another *assign* activity (lines 24–29) copies the output data of the car search activity into the process response variable.

Replacement of a bad performing partner Replacing the bad performing partner Web Service by an alternative one that has a different interface cannot be done dynamically because BPEL and current implementations thereof do not support dynamic changes.

If Tunis Air Web Service and Berlin Air Web Service implement the same WSDL port type, one could use the special variant of the *assign* activity in a fault handler for instance to copy the endpoint reference of Tunis Air Web Service to the flight partner of the travel package process. However, Figure 3.2 shows that the interfaces of these airline Web Services are different as they provide operations that have different names. Consequently, the assignment of endpoint reference will not work in this case.

The replacement of Berlin Air Web Service by Tunis Air Web Service can only be done statically by undeploying the travel package process, editing the respective workflow schema, and redeploying it.

Listing 3.7 shows how the travel package process is modified to support this change. To keep the changes to the workflow schema minimal, the partner link and the variables corresponding to the interactions with Berlin Air Web Service are not removed, because they may be used by other activities of the travel package process (lines 41 and 49). Otherwise, the workflow schema of the travel package process would have to be changed in an even more invasive manner.

In Listing 3.7, the programmer adds a new partner link to the Tunis Air Web Service (line 4) and two new variables for the input and output of the new flight search activity (lines 10–11). Moreover, he replaces the faulty *invoke* activity that calls Berlin Air Web Service by a new *invoke* activity that calls Tunis Air Web Service (lines 24–26). The programmer uses two new *assign* activities: one activity (lines 17–23) to copy the flight request data from the variable *flightrequest* to the input variable *Newflightrequest* of the new *invoke* activity *invokeTunisAirTP*, and another *assign* activity (lines 29–38) to copy the output data of the new *invoke* activity into the variable *flightresponse*, which is used later in the travel package process (lines 41 and 49). The second *assign* is an example of activities for fixing the data flow.

The two change examples show that BPEL lacks a module construct, which encapsulates the workflow constructs that implement a given workflow change. Each change is directly integrated in the workflow schema and it is buried in the process code, i.e., it does not exist as a first-class entity. The change can only be understood implicitly by comparing the original workflow schema before the change with the workflow schema after the change. Consequently, understanding, tracing, and managing workflow changes becomes difficult.

```
1   <process name="travelPackage">
2    <partnerLinks>
3      <partnerLink name="flight" partnerLinkType="flightPLT" .../>
4      <partnerLink name="Newflight" partnerLinkType="TunisairPLT" .../>
5      ...
6    </partnerLinks>
7    <variables>
8     <variable name="flightrequest"  messageType="findAFlightRequest"/>
9     <variable name="flightresponse" messageType="findAFlightResponse"/>
10    <variable name="Newflightrequest" messageType="searchFlightRequest"/>
11    <variable name="Newflightresponse" messageType="searchFlightResponse"/>
12     ...
13    </variables>
14    <sequence name="packageSequence">
15     <receive name="receiveClientRequest" partnerLink="client" .../>
16      ...
17      <assign>
18       ...
19      <copy>
20       <from variable="flightRequest"   part="retDate">
21       <to variable="NewflightRequest" part="returnDate">
22      </copy>
23      </assign>
24      <invoke name="invokeTunisAirTP"
25           partnerLink="newflight" portType="TunisAirPT" operation="searchFlight"
26           inputVariable="Newflightrequest" outputVariable="Newflightresponse"/>
27      <invoke name="invokeHotelServiceTP" partnerLink="hotel" .../>
28      ...
29      <assign>
30       <copy>
31        <from variable="Newflightresponse" part="flightData"/>
32        <to variable="flightresponse" part="flightDetails"/>
33       </copy>
34       <copy>
35        <from variable="Newflightresponse" part="flightNumber"/>
36        <to variable="flightresponse" part="flightnum"/>
37       </copy>
38      </assign>
39      <assign>
40       <copy>
41        <from variable="flightresponse" part="flightDetails"/>
42        <to variable="clientresponse" part="flightInfo"/>
43       </copy>
44       <copy>
45        <from variable="hotelresponse" part="roomDetails"/>
46        <to variable="clientresponse" part="hotelInfo"/>
47       </copy>
48       <copy>
49        <from expression="concat(getVariableData('flightresponse ',' flightnum '),
50                          getVariableData ('hotelresponse ',' id '))"/>
51        <to variable="clientresponse" part="offerid"/>
52       </copy>
53      </assign>
54      <reply name="replyToClient" partnerLink="client" portType="travelServicePT"
55           operation="getTravelPackage" variable="clientresponse" />
56    </sequence>
57   </process>                          47
```

Listing 3.7: Replacing a bad performing partner Web Service

Workflow changes can also be crosscutting, i.e., they can span several workflow processes. For example, one could extend both the travel package process and the flight process with logic for car search. Moreover, one could replace the bad performing partner in both processes. The need for modular change expression is even stronger in the case of crosscutting workflow changes.

3.4.3 Expressing changes in adaptive workflow management

Although flexibility and adaptability are among the main objectives of the workflow technology, most workflow management systems lack support for dynamic change [1, 18, 77]. In order to improve the flexibility of workflows, several research efforts in the area of *adaptive workflow* [29, 95, 162, 187, 198] tried to make workflow management more flexible and adaptable by proposing appropriate models and techniques to support dynamic change.

To study the modularity of change expression in adaptive workflow management, two well-known workflow management systems will be considered: WASA [198] and ADEPT [162]. Both systems provide a set of dynamic change operations, e.g., for adding or deleting activities and edges to/from the activity graph.

In WASA, a special workflow modeling activity can be used to perform change operations. This activity provides an operation for adding a new activity as a child of another. This activity takes as input an activity and two sets of predecessor activity nodes (i.e., the activities that must complete before the new activity starts) and successor activity nodes (i.e., the activities that can only start after the new activity completes).

In ADEPT, a special Java API for dynamic workflow modification is provided. The API method for inserting a new activity into the workflow graph takes similar parameters to those of the WASA operation mentioned above. ADEPT goes a step further than WASA by allowing the specification of a mapping of existing workflow data to the input parameters of the new activity.

Adding car rental logic Assume that the travel package process is implemented using the workflow languages of ADEPT or WASA. To add car rental logic to the travel package process using the approach taken in those management systems, one would have to call the following change operations:

- insert the new participant representing the car rental company

- insert two new variables for the input and output data of the car search activity

- insert a data manipulation activity, which sets the input data of the car search activity

- insert the car search activity

- insert a data manipulation activity, which copies the output data of the car search activity into the process variable, which contains the travel package offers that will be returned to the client

Moreover, the parameters of each activity adding operation should be set correctly to insert the new activities at the right place in the workflow process.

Replacement of a bad performing partner The necessary change operations to replace the bad performing partner service by another service using the approach provided by ADEPT or WASA are listed in the following:

- insert the new participant representing Tunis Air

- insert two new variables for the input and output data of the new flight search activity

- insert the flight search activity that interacts with Tunis Air

- insert a data manipulation activity, which sets the input data of the new flight search activity

- delete the flight search activity that interacts with Berlin Air

- insert a data manipulation activity, which copies the output data of the new flight search activity into the process variable, which contains the offers that will be returned to the client

- insert one or more activities that fix the data flow, i.e., ensure that the process activities that use variables, which should be set by the deleted flight search activity, will still work correctly

3.4.4 The need for change modules

Static workflow management systems such as current BPEL implementations lack mechanisms to express workflow changes in a modular way as first-class entities. Consequently, one can only understand the change implicitly by comparing the original workflow process (e.g., the travel package process shown in Listing 3.1) with the modified one (e.g., the travel package process shown in Listing 3.6), and deriving the change out of this comparison.

In adaptive workflow management systems such as ADEPT and WASA, workflow changes cannot be expressed modularly as first-class entities. They can only be understood by tracing the low-level change operations that were called to integrate them, or by comparing a source workflow schema with a modified one. That is, one has to trace all calls to the change operations to see which operations were called to add new activities and/or control edges, which operations were called to delete existing activities and/or control edges, which operations were called to assign variables to the new activities, which operations were called to assign participants to the new activities, etc.

Workflow management systems lack a module concept for modularizing the decision about where and when a workflow change should be applied in addition to the workflow constructs implementing that change. These constructs include the activities (the functional perspective), the variables (informational perspective), the participants (organizational perspective), and the applications (operational perspective) that implement a workflow change.

As already mentioned, some workflow changes can be crosscutting. In that case, the need for a more modular change expression is even stronger because crosscutting changes are problematic like crosscutting concerns. Without a change module, crosscutting changes would not only be buried in the process code, but also scattered across and tangled in the specifications of several workflow processes.

The availability of a module concept for workflow changes would allow adaptive workflow management systems to support workflow changes at a higher abstraction level than with low-level change operations. Moreover, it allows workflow changes to be supported as first-class entities like workflow processes. This would allow workflow changes to be switched on and off flexibly. In addition, a better modularization of workflow changes would alleviate the problems of change management, e.g., undoing temporary changes can be handled more easily.

In fact, a common solution for undoing temporary changes in adaptive workflow engines [162] consists in using a change history. This solution has been implemented in ADEPT, in which the different versions of a workflow schema are stored together with the changes that lead from one version to another. If there is a module concept for workflow changes, undoing changes becomes much easier. Rather than migrating workflow instances from a source schema to a destination schema as in [31, 162, 198], all what is needed to undo a workflow change is to deactivate the respective change module, i.e., separate at runtime the change module and the workflow process module.

3.5   Conclusion

This chapter identified two limitations in current workflow languages, which lack language constructs for capturing crosscutting concerns and for expressing workflow changes in a modular way. That is, the workflow constructs that belong to a crosscutting concern cannot be encapsulated in a separate module. Moreover, workflow changes cannot be expressed as modular first-class entities

The problems resulting from these limitations were illustrated using a travel agency scenario. In that scenario, the implementation of crosscutting concerns such as data collection for billing and execution time measurement was studied. Moreover, some workflow change examples were presented such as adding car rental logic and replacing a bad performing partner.

Workflow graphs and BPEL were used to illustrate the problems that arise as a result of lacking means for crosscutting concern modularization and change modularization. Workflow graphs illustrated the problems of scattering and tangling in a visual and language-independent manner. BPEL code illustrated these problems and their effects on the different workflow perspectives using a specific XML-based workflow language.

Moreover, this chapter motivated the need for language constructs that encapsulate crosscutting concerns and support a modular expression of workflow changes. It also explained how such constructs would improve the modularity of workflow schemes and increase the flexibility of workflow processes.

Part II

Solution: Concepts and Languages

CHAPTER 4

Aspect-Oriented Workflow Languages

4.1 Introduction

This chapter[1] presents a solution for the problems of crosscutting concern modularity and change modularity in current workflow languages.

In fact, the problems that were presented in Chapter 3 are due to the lack of appropriate decomposition mechanisms and language constructs for capturing concerns that cut across process boundaries and for modularizing workflow changes. To solve these problems, this chapter proposes a concern-based decomposition approach, according to the principle of *separation of concerns*. That is, it allows the workflow code of a given concern to be encapsulated in a separate module. At the level of workflow language, new constructs are introduced to support this decomposition approach.

In the context of programming languages, the problems of crosscutting concern modularity were solved by Aspect-Oriented Programming [121]. This paradigm explicitly addresses the modularity of crosscutting concerns by introducing new programmatic constructs such as aspects, pointcuts, and advice. In many works, aspects have been used to modularize the code of various crosscutting concerns such as logging and profiling [124], resource management [124], persistence [160], security [24, 202], transactions [55, 80], and business rules [69].

So far, aspect-orientation has been mostly used in the context of programming languages. However, aspect-orientation is a general-purpose decomposition and modularization paradigm, which can also be applied in other contexts. In this chapter, concepts from Aspect-Oriented Software Development [56] will be introduced to the domains of workflow modeling and workflow specification to solve the modularity problems that were presented in Chapter 3.

Aspect-oriented workflow languages provide language constructs for crosscutting concern modularity such as aspect, pointcut, and advice. These languages support a concern-based decomposition of workflow specifications: The

---

[1]This chapter is based on the paper *Aspect-Oriented Workflow Languages*, CoopIS 2006 [39].

business logic, as being the main concern, can be specified in a modular way within a workflow process module, whereas crosscutting concerns and workflow changes can be specified in a modular way within workflow aspect modules.

To illustrate the concepts of aspect-oriented workflow languages, an aspect-oriented graph-based language will be used in this chapter. In the next two chapters, concrete aspect-oriented workflow languages for business process modeling and for Web Service composition will be presented as proof-of-concept. That is, this chapter introduces the general concepts of aspect-oriented workflow languages, whereas the next two chapters present concrete aspect-oriented workflow languages for process design and process implementation.

In addition, this chapter will elaborate on the requirements of aspect-oriented workflow languages with respect to join point model and pointcut language, advice language, and composition mechanisms of aspects and processes. These concepts are different from their counterparts in aspect-oriented programming languages because workflow languages, which describe processes, are different from programming languages, which describe computations.

The remainder of this chapter is organized as follows. In Section 4.2, the concern-based decomposition of workflow schemes is proposed as a solution for the problems of crosscutting concern modularity and change modularity in current workflow languages. Section 4.3 introduces an aspect-oriented workflow language that shows the concepts of workflow aspects graphically. Section 4.4 elaborates in more detail on the requirements and concepts of aspect-oriented workflow languages. Section 4.5 surveys some related work and Section 4.6 concludes this chapter.

4.2 Concern-based Decomposition

A workflow schema consists of several constructs that correspond to the different workflow perspectives [175] (cf. Chapter 2). In addition to *activities* (*the functional perspective*), a workflow schema contains constructs that specify the execution order and the control flow dependencies between activities (the *behavioral* perspective), variable declarations and a specification of the data flow between activities (*informational* perspective), declarations of participants that perform the activities (the *organizational* perspective), and declarations of the applications (the *operational* perspective) that support their execution.

So far, workflow languages support a *process-based* decomposition of workflow schemes. In addition, some languages support a *hierarchical* decomposition, i.e., the implementation of an activity can be specified by another workflow subprocess. In both decomposition mechanisms, the parts of the workflow schema that correspond to different workflow perspectives are generally not separated.

To improve the modularity of workflow schemes, MOBILE [113] introduces a *perspective-based decomposition* by expressing the parts of the workflow schema that correspond to the different workflow perspectives separately. In this way, if one needs, e.g., to modify the execution order of two activities, only the part of the schema corresponding to the behavioral perspective has to be changed.

However, the three decomposition mechanisms that were mentioned so far do not appropriately support the modularization of the workflow process code of crosscutting concerns. Even with the perspective-based decomposition, the problems of scattering and tangling arise.

For example, if the data collection for billing concern should be integrated with workflow processes that are specified using MOBILE, the respective workflow constructs would be still scattered across the different workflow schemes. Moreover, the tangling problem remains because the necessary activities for data collection for billing would be intertwined with those belonging to the business logic concern, the necessary variables for data collection for billing would be intertwined with those belonging to the business logic concern, and so on.

To solve the problems of scattering and tangling, a *concern-based decomposition* approach is proposed. In this approach, the workflow constructs that implement a given concern are encapsulated in a separate module.

Two types of modules are provided in this concern-based decomposition. A process module is used for encapsulating the core business logic of the workflow process, which is the main concern. For crosscutting concerns and workflow changes, another type of modules is required, because it is necessary to specify when and where the execution of the respective activities should be triggered during the execution of the workflow process.

Like in Aspect-Oriented Programming [121], this book proposes using aspects as modules for crosscutting concerns in workflow specifications. Moreover, aspects will also be used as change modules.

Workflow languages that support process modules and aspect modules are called aspect-oriented workflow languages. These languages incorporate the concern-based decomposition and break with the *tyranny of the dominant decomposition* [180], which is the process-based decomposition in the case of workflow languages.

Figure 4.1 illustrates the concept of concern-based decomposition using the travel package process and the flight process of the travel agency scenario.

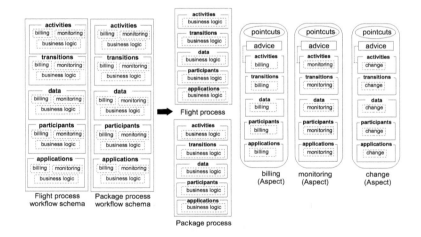

Figure 4.1: Concern-based decomposition of workflow specifications

The left hand side of this figure shows the workflow specification in current workflow languages and illustrates the problems of scattering and tangling and how they span the different workflow perspectives.

The right hand side of this figure shows how workflow specification is done in aspect-oriented workflow languages using aspect modules and process modules. The code of the business logic concern is encapsulated in the process module and the code of each of the concerns data collection for billing and execution time monitoring is encapsulated in an aspect module.

This figure also shows that the workflow specifications of the flight process and the travel package process become simpler and more modular when workflow aspects are used. These specifications are no longer tangled. Moreover, the workflow code of the crosscutting concerns data collection for billing and execution time monitoring is no longer scattered across the workflow schemes of the two workflow processes.

As shown in Figure 4.1, workflow aspects can also be used to express workflow changes as separate first-class entities and to modularize the necessary workflow constructs for their implementation.

4.3   Aspectual Workflow Graphs

Aspectual workflow graphs are a visual means to illustrate the concepts of aspect-oriented workflow languages graphically (i.e., in a form that can be understood even by non-programmers). Aspectual workflow graphs extend the graph-based workflow language that was presented in Chapter 2 with aspect-oriented constructs.

4.3.1   Join points, pointcuts, advice

In aspectual workflow graphs, *join points* are points in the execution of the workflow process corresponding to the execution of activity nodes. A workflow aspect is a set of one or more pointcuts and advice.

The *pointcut* is a construct for selecting *join points*. A pointcut is represented graphically by an oval, which is connected by dashed lines to the activity nodes that it selects. A pointcut selects the points in the execution corresponding to the execution of the graphically selected activities. The pointcut can select activities that are defined in different workflow processes, e.g., the pointcut of the aspect shown in Figure 4.2 selects the flight search activity nodes in the flight process and in the travel package process. This feature, which is called *quantification* [83], is very important for capturing crosscutting concerns.

The *advice* consists of an activity that implements the functionality of a crosscutting concern or a workflow change. Moreover, the advice defines the execution order of that activity with respect to the join point. In addition to the advice types before, after, and around, which are known from AspectJ [120], other execution orders are possible according to the variety of workflow control patterns [188] (cf. Chapter 2).

The advice is represented graphically by a rectangle with rounded corners. The association of advice and pointcut is represented graphically by connecting the advice and the pointcut with a line. The effect of the advice is to replace any join point node captured by the pointcut, by another activity node that may contain the join point node. The advice shown in Figure 4.2 consists of an activity for incrementing a counter. This activity is executed after the selected join points, which are referred to in the advice with the special activity *proceed*.

4.3.2 Composition

To integrate workflow aspects with workflow graphs, an aspect/process composition mechanism is required. In aspectual workflow graphs, the composition of aspects and processes can be conceptually considered as a transformation of the workflow graph, which works as follows.

Each activity node that is matched by a pointcut is replaced by a new composite activity node, which encloses the advice node and may also contain the join point activity node. If the join point activity node is source or target of control flow edges, the composite activity becomes the source or target of those edges. The advice is a self-contained activity, i.e., no transitions are allowed between the advice activity and the other activities of the workflow graphs except the join point activity.

The transitions inside the new composite activity depend on the execution order of the advice and the join point activity. When the advice should be executed before the selected join point, the composite activity has a transition from the advice activity to the join point activity. When the advice should execute after the selected join point, a transition goes from the join point activity to the advice activity. In the around advice, the execution of the join point activity can be skipped or can be integrated in the middle of other activities by using the special activity node *proceed*. This node is a place holder for the join point activity node.

4.3.3 Examples

In the following, aspectual workflow graphs are used to illustrate how workflow aspects allow the modularization of the crosscutting concerns and the workflow changes that were presented in Chapter 3.

Data collection for billing

The left hand side of Figure 4.2 shows the workflow graphs of the flight process and the travel package process. In addition, it shows a workflow aspect, which modularizes the data collection for billing concern in these processes.

The pointcut of this aspect selects the flight search activities in both processes. The advice of this aspect contains an activity for incrementing a counter. This activity is executed after the join point, which is referred to by the *proceed* activity. This advice executes after the join point activity (after advice).

The logical effect of composing this aspect with the workflow graphs of the travel package process and the flight process is shown on the right hand side of Figure 4.2. The graph transformation that is shown in this figure can be performed either logically or physically.

Activity execution time measurement

Figure 4.3 shows an aspect, which modularizes the execution time measurement concern. The pointcut of this aspect selects the flight search activities in the

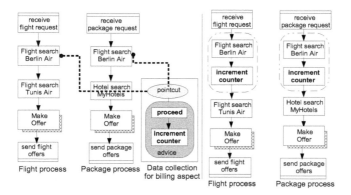

Figure 4.2: Data collection for billing as an aspect

flight process and in the travel package process. The execution time of these activities should be measured.

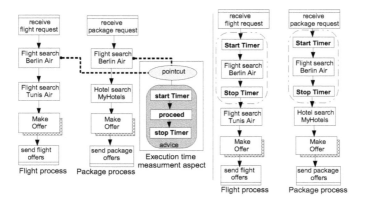

Figure 4.3: Activity execution time measurement as an aspect

The advice of this aspect contains an activity for starting a timer, which is executed before the join point as well as an activity for stopping a timer, which is executed after the join point. The logical effect of composing this aspect with the workflow graphs of the flight process and travel package process is shown on the right hand side of Figure 4.3.

Workflow-level security

The level-2 authorization concern can be modularized using an aspect, which works in a similar way to the execution time measurement aspect. The pointcut of the security aspect selects the activities for whose data the users should gain access only during the execution of the activity.

Like the execution time monitoring aspect, the security aspect uses an around advice, which calls the authorization system before and after the execution of each activity that is selected by the pointcut. The execution of the join point activities is integrated between the two calls to the authorization system by using the *proceed* activity. This aspect will not be shown because it is very similar to the execution time measurement aspect.

A workflow change: adding car rental logic

The workflow aspects presented so far modularize crosscutting concerns. Aspects can also be used for expressing workflow changes in a modular way.

In Figure 4.4, an aspect adds car rental logic to the travel package process and to the flight process. The pointcut of this aspect selects the activities *send package offers* and *send flight offers*.

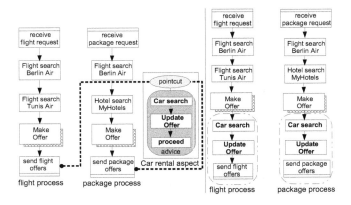

Figure 4.4: A change aspect for adding car rental logic

The advice activity of this aspect is a composite activity that encloses a car search activity and another activity that extends the current offers of the workflow process with a car rental proposition.

The effect of composing this change aspect with the workflow graphs of the flight process and the travel package process is to add the advice activity before the activities *send flight offers* and *send package offers*, as shown on the right hand side of Figure 4.4.

This figure might wrongly suggest that aspects and processes are composed statically at design-time. This work advocates dynamic composition mechanisms, which enable workflow aspects such as the car rental aspect to modify workflow processes at runtime, and thus make them more adaptable. How such a dynamic composition mechanism can be embedded in the workflow engine is elaborated in more details in Section 4.4.5.

4.3.4 Discussion

The examples of workflow aspects presented so far improve the modularity of the workflow schemes of the flight process and the travel package process.

All activities that belong to a crosscutting concern or a workflow change are encapsulated in workflow aspects. They are no longer scattered across the different workflow schemes. The base workflow processes focus only on the business logic concern and are not tangled.

The decision about where to integrate the advice activities during the execution of the workflow process is also localized in the pointcut, which can be easily extended to select other activities without modifying the processes[2]. Moreover, with workflow aspects, any changes to the crosscutting functionality can be done in a non-invasive way by modifying the advice only, and not several workflow processes as it is the case without workflow aspects (cf. Chapter 3).

In addition, workflow aspects allow a modular expression of workflow changes as first-class entities. With aspects, workflow changes are expressed at the same abstraction level as workflow processes. Consequently, they can be understood and managed more easily. Moreover, they can be switched on and off flexibly as needed.

Aspectual workflow graphs support only the functional and behavioral workflow perspectives. Consequently, they illustrate only how the activities are modularized in a better way by using workflow aspects. In addition to the modularization of activities, workflow aspects also modularize the workflow constructs that correspond to the informational perspective (e.g., variables), the organizational perspective (e.g., participant declarations), and the operational perspective (e.g., application declarations). This will be shown in the next chapter with the AO4BPEL workflow language, which supports the informational and the operational/organizational perspectives in addition to the functional and behavioral perspectives. That is, workflow aspects modularize all workflow constructs that implement a given workflow change in addition to the decision on where and when a workflow change should be applied.

4.4 Aspect-Oriented Workflow Languages

Like any other aspect-oriented language, aspect-oriented workflow languages have a join point model, a pointcut language, and an advice language. However, these concepts are different from their counterparts in aspect-oriented programming languages.

In the following, the requirements of aspect-oriented workflow languages with respect to join point models, pointcut languages, and advice languages will be presented. Moreover, two different approaches for the composition of workflow aspects and workflow processes will be discussed.

---

[2]This property is called *obliviousness* [83].

4.4.1 Join point model

The *join point model* defines the set of points in the execution, which can be captured by the pointcut of an aspect-oriented language. As the advice and the base application are defined separately, join points provide a means to specify when the advice should join the execution of the base application.

In aspect-oriented programming languages, join point models allow to select points in the execution of an object-oriented program such as method calls, field accesses, constructor calls, exception throwing, etc.

In aspect-oriented workflow languages, the activity-based join point model is the most intuitive one. In such a model, join points correspond to the execution of activities. Thereby, two kinds of join points can be differentiated: *activity join points* (or *process-level join points*) and *internal join points* (or *interpretation-level join points*). The former are coarse-grained points capturing the start or the completion of activity execution, whereas the latter are more fine-grained capturing internal points during the execution of an activity. Internal join points are needed when the granularity level of the activity is not sufficient to support some crosscutting concern. In aspectual workflow graphs, only activity join points are supported.

Besides the activity-based join point model, it is useful that the join point model exposes other points in the workflow execution such as the creation or termination of a workflow process instance, the assignment of a participant to an activity, the reading or writing of some workflow data, the invocation of an external application that executes an activity, etc.

4.4.2 Pointcuts

The pointcut language provides means to select a set of related join points. For example, the pointcut language of AspectJ provides a set of *pointcut designators* such as *call* (for selecting method call join points), *execution* (for selecting method execution join points), *get* and *set* (for selecting read/write field access).

To express crosscutting structures, the pointcut languages of aspect-oriented workflow languages should support *quantification* [83, 123], i.e., the ability to select join points spanning different workflow processes. For example, it should be possible to select all occurrences of some activity that is reused in several workflow processes such as the flight search activity, which is used in the flight process and in the travel package process.

The pointcut language of aspectual workflow graphs supports only the functional perspective, which is the minimal requirement to pointcut languages for workflows. A powerful pointcut language should provide means for a *perspective-oriented selection* of join points.

Beyond the functional perspective, it makes sense to select all join points where some activity a is executed after another activity b (behavioral perspective), where some participant executes any activity (organizational perspective), where a given workflow variable is read or modified (informational perspective), where an external application is called (operational perspective), etc.

Although such higher-level *perspective-oriented pointcuts* can be mapped to activity-oriented pointcuts, supporting the different workflow perspectives directly brings several benefits.

First, it allows the expression of the crosscutting structure of some concerns in a more natural and easy way. For instance, the join points where *data persistence* is needed could be selected in a more direct way when the pointcut language supports the informational perspective. This would allow programmers to express pointcuts such as *select all join points where a variable var is modified*, or *select all join points where the performer is not a manager*.

Second, perspective-oriented pointcuts are robust. For instance, assume that a data manipulation activity is added to a workflow process and that the new activity modifies the workflow variable *var*. If a persistence aspect uses an activity-oriented pointcut, where activities are referenced by name, the existing pointcut will not match the new activity. If that aspect uses a data-oriented pointcut, the new activity will be matched because the pointcut references only the variable *var* and not the activities that modify it.

Sometimes, a combination of several perspective-oriented pointcut designators allows for a more direct expression of crosscutting structures. For instance, in the case of security aspects, join points where security advice should be executed can be expressed more easily with a pointcut language that supports the organizational perspective (which user performs the activity) and the operational perspective (which application is invoked for that and whether it is local or remote).

The pointcut language could operate on a graphical representation of the workflow processes like in aspectual workflow graphs (*visual pointcuts*), or on a text-based workflow schema like in XML-based workflow languages such as BPEL or XPDL. Visual pointcuts can be defined easily by business analysts, who model workflow processes using graphical tools. Visual pointcuts can be transformed to pointcuts that operate on a text-based workflow schema. For instance, in the case of BPEL, one could extend a graphical BPEL editor with some functionality to define pointcuts visually and generate some XPath-based pointcuts out of them.

4.4.3 Advice

The advice language defines the crosscutting functionality that needs to be executed at the set of join points that are captured by a pointcut. The advice of a workflow aspect can be applied either to all instances of the workflow process (*process-level deployment*) or to some workflow instances only (*instance-level deployment*). These two deployment strategies allow workflow aspects to support *evolutionary* and *ad-hoc workflow* changes. The pointcut language should provide constructs to specify the advice deployment strategy.

In aspect-oriented programming languages, the advice language is generally the same as the base programming language. For example, the advice language of AspectJ is Java. In aspect-oriented workflow languages, the advice language should be the same as the base workflow language [27, 35] to avoid any paradigm mismatches for the workflow designers. There are some proposals for using some programming language as advice language [59] in a similar way to BPELJ [19], which allows adding Java code snippets to BPEL processes.

Proposals such as [19, 59] break the *two-level programming paradigm* [127], which is a key principle in workflow management denoting the separation between *activity specification* and *activity implementation*. These proposals mix the process flow logic and the activity implementation. In addition, they break the portability of workflow processes (e.g., BPEL processes will no longer run on any BPEL engine) and are also very dependent on the workflow engine (e.g., BPEL processes with BPELJ code will not run on a BPEL engine that is implemented in C++).

Moreover, when the workflow language is used as advice language it is important to think about the effects of aspects on the base workflow processes because the advice add new activities to the workflow processes. Designers of aspect-oriented workflow languages should consider and study how the advice affects and interferes with constructs of the base workflow language such as fault handling and compensation handling constructs.

Aspect-oriented programming languages support three types of advice: *before*, *after*, and *around*. These advice execute respectively before, after, or instead of the join points that are selected by the pointcut. The advice in workflow aspects also need to specify the execution order of the advice activity with respect to the join point activity. This order can be specified using workflow control patterns [188] such as *sequence, parallel split*, and *synchronization*.

The *sequence* pattern covers the advice types before and after, which are known from aspect-oriented programming languages. It is also possible to integrate the join point activity in the middle of the advice activity, which is similar to the around advice in aspect-oriented programming languages. In addition, it is possible to define a *parallel advice*, which executes the advice activity concurrently to the join point activity, and a *synchronization advice*, which ensures that the advice activity and the join point activity wait for each other before the workflow execution proceeds.

In aspect-oriented workflow languages, the advice language may extend the base workflow language with special constructs such as the *proceed* activity, which acts as a place holder for the join point activity. Moreover, the advice language must provide *context collection* constructs that allow the advice activity to access the context of the current join point activity. For example, a persistence advice needs to access the input and output variables of the join point activity before saving them to the database. Advice languages without context collection constructs are not very useful.

The join point context includes the input and output variables of the join point activity, the participant assignment information, and the application assignment information. In addition, that context may also provide access to the data, the participants, and the applications that are declared in the parent process of the join point activity.

The advice language should provide context collection constructs that allow a generic access to the join point context. Genericity is important because a pointcut could select many activities and may be different types of activities. Therefore, the advice cannot for instance refer to the input variable of an activity join point by name.

In addition to context collection, the advice language should also provide *reflective constructs* to access meta-data about the current join point activity (e.g., activity name, activity type) and its parent workflow process (after the composition). For example, a logging advice, which logs invocations of some partner, needs to access the name of the current join point activity to produce a useful log entry.

It is also necessary to provide constructs for specifying advice precedence to avoid incorrect behaviors. For instance, the data collection for billing aspect must execute after the execution time measurement advice. Otherwise, the measured execution time of the flight search activity would include the execution time of the activity *increment counter*.

4.4.4 Aspects

The examples presented in Section 4.3.3 show only the activities that implement a crosscutting concern or a workflow change and the control-flow edges between them because aspectual workflow graphs support only the functional and behavioral perspectives. However, the activities that implement a crosscutting concern or a workflow change need their input and output data to be defined and set appropriately. They may also require new workflow participants and external applications for their execution.

A workflow aspect is a module that encapsulates all workflow constructs (i.e., the activities, the transitions, the variables, the participant declarations, and the application declarations) that implement a crosscutting concern or a workflow change.

Aspects in workflow languages do not replace aspects in programming languages. They are rather complementary. That is, in certain scenarios one may need workflow aspects at the workflow level (programming in the large [68]) and programming aspects at the activity implementation level (for programming in the small [68]). For example, workflow aspects can be used to implement process-level security, whereas AspectJ aspects can be used in the Java-based implementation of a partner Web Service to secure SOAP messages.

When writing workflow aspects, the programmer has to care about the effects of the aspect on the different workflow perspectives. In particular, the advice may have to fix the data flow of the workflow process. For example, an around advice may skip some activity that sets a workflow variable, which is used later in the workflow process. In such a case, the programmer is responsible for fixing the data flow.

In addition to modularizing crosscutting concerns, workflow aspects can also be used for expressing workflow changes as first-class entities in a modular way. The pointcut selects the activities that are affected by the change and the advice defines the change logic. As in the case of crosscutting concerns, the aspect provides a module concept that encapsulates all workflow constructs that implement the change.

The use of workflow aspects for expressing changes brings several benefits. First, workflow changes can be switched on/off flexibly, i.e., certain variations such as switching pricing policies on and off can be accommodated easily without editing workflow schemes. Second, some variations can be applied more selectively to specific instances. Third, undoing temporary changes is no longer a problem. Rather than migrating workflow instances from a source schema to a destination schema as done in [31, 162], one must just undeploy the change aspects. Fourth, with appropriate composition mechanisms, workflow aspects can be used to dynamically adapt workflow processes.

4.4.5 Aspect/Process composition

A mechanism is required for the integration of workflow aspects with workflow processes. In aspect-oriented programming languages, this mechanism is called *weaving*. The composition of aspects and processes is performed at compile time in *static weaving* approaches and at runtime in *dynamic weaving* approaches. Similarly, in aspect-oriented workflow languages, the composition of workflow aspects and workflow processes can be performed statically (i.e., before deploying the process) or dynamically (i.e., at workflow execution time). Moreover, the composition can be done physically or logically, which results in two composition approaches:

Process transformation

In this approach, the composition tool merges the workflow aspects with the workflow processes (physical transformation). This tool performs the reverse work of what is shown in Figure. 4.1. It takes a workflow process and a set of workflow aspects as input and generates a new workflow process as output. This approach is implemented in the composition mechanism of the recent aspect-oriented workflow language *Padus* [27].

The process transformation approach supports static composition. It is similar to the static weaving approach of AspectJ [98], in which the weaver transforms the byte code of Java classes to integrate aspects. The output classes of the AspectJ weaver have ordinary Java byte code and can be therefore interpreted by any Java interpreter.

One advantage of static process transformation is that the output workflow schema, which is generated by the process transformation tool is an ordinary schema without any aspect-oriented extensions. That is, the output workflow schema can be deployed on any workflow engine that supports the base workflow language.

Moreover, with static process transformation one would have two versions of the workflow schema: one before the composition and one after the composition. When workflow aspects are used for capturing non-functional concerns, the version before the composition allows to understand the business process by abstracting away from technical details, whereas the version after the composition can be used to exactly understand and predict the workflow process that will be executed, which is necessary for workflow auditing, workflow log mining, and workflow debugging.

However, the process transformation approach has several limitations. First, the composition cannot be done at runtime unless the workflow engine provides appropriate APIs for modifying the runtime representation of a workflow process, which is generally not the case. If such APIs are provided, the aspect-oriented workflow language would no longer be independent of the engine. Second, the process transformation approach cannot support pointcuts that depend on runtime data and instance-based aspect deployment, unless complex checks are added to the workflow process. Third, it is not possible in the process transformation approach to deploy/undeploy aspects at runtime. Fourth, aspect-orientation is supported at the workflow specification level in this approach but not at the workflow execution level, i.e., workflow aspects do not exist as first-class runtime entities inside the workflow engine.

Aspect-aware workflow engine

In this approach, the workflow engine is modified to check for aspects before and after executing each activity. These checks are built at appropriate points in the activity lifecycle. If a pointcut matches the execution of some activity, the corresponding advice will be executed. This approach was adopted for the implementation of the AO4BPEL language, which will be presented in the next chapter.

Unlike the process transformation approach, the workflow process is not transformed physically. Only the interpretation of the engine is modified (logical transformation).

This approach supports easily the dynamic composition of aspects and processes, which improves the flexibility and adaptability of workflow-based applications. It allows to deploy and undeploy aspects that change running workflow instances. These aspects can be switched on and off flexibly without editing the workflow schema or starting another static process transformation and redeploying the process (as in the previous approach). This is especially important for long-running processes where it is unfeasible to stop a workflow instance, edit the schema, and redeploy the process, because in such a case one would have to undo the previously completed work of the interrupted workflow instance and ensure that no inconsistency occurs. Moreover, the dynamic adaptation is necessary when unpredicted events such as faults happen.

In the aspect-aware engine approach, aspects are supported as first-class entities (like processes) even at runtime. This approach allows several aspect management functionalities to be provided by the aspect-aware engine, rather than requiring users to implement them manually in the workflow process. For example, pointcuts that depend on runtime data and instance-based aspect deployment can be supported without adding complex hook activities to the workflow process to evaluate runtime conditions, as it is the case in the process transformation approach. The latter requires adding hook activities to the workflow process, which raises the complexity of the workflow schema and makes it difficult to understand.

One may also argue that the aspect-aware engine approach makes the aspect-oriented workflow language dependent on a particular workflow engine. However, this work proposes to have standard workflow engines built with native support for workflow aspects according to the aspect-aware engine approach. This means that standard BPEL engines should provide native support for aspect-oriented constructs. The benefits of such aspect-aware workflow engines will be shown in the next chapters.

Tasks of the composition mechanism

Independently of the composition approach, the composition mechanism has to tackle several common tasks such as *pointcut matching* and *resolution of special constructs*.

First, the composition mechanism has to decide whether an activity of the workflow process is matched by some pointcut (*pointcut matching*). Once a pointcut matches a process activity, the composition mechanism has to integrate the execution of the respective advice activity as explained in Section 4.3. The resulting execution order should be the same as if the join point activity is replaced by a composite activity that may contain the join point activity. The ordering constraints of advice activity and join point activity depend on the advice type.

Second, the composition mechanism must enable the execution of the advice activities by the workflow engine as any other process activities. That is, aspect-local declarations for data, participants, and applications should be added to those declared by the workflow processes that are affected by the aspect (i.e., the processes to which the advice activity will be added). Moreover, the composition mechanism has to resolve all special constructs that are used in the advice, such as context collection constructs, reflection constructs, and the *proceed* activity.

For example, assume that a generic context collection construct is used in an after advice to access the input variable of the join point activity. Moreover, the pointcut that is associated with this advice matches three activities. In such a scenario, the composition mechanism will insert the advice activity after three different activities. At each join point, the composition mechanism should replace the generic context collection construct by the name of the respective input variable.

4.5 Related Work

This section presents some works that propose using aspects in the context of workflow management. None of these works uses aspects at the level of workflow languages.

In a position paper [16], Bachmendo and Unland propose an aspect-based approach for the dynamic evolution of workflow instances. In that approach, AspectJ aspects are woven with the object-oriented implementation of a workflow management system to support several kinds of control flow adaptations (e.g., insertion of a new activity to the process or replacement of an activity by another) and resource adaptations (i.e., the dynamic assignment of resources to activities). In that work, Aspect-Oriented Programming is used at the workflow implementation level and not at the workflow specification level.

Another paper [170] proposes the decomposition of a workflow specification into several aspect specifications, respectively an aspect for each workflow perspective. The vision of that paper is to have the different perspectives merged by an appropriate weaver, but that work does not explain whether and how such a weaver can be implemented. In aspect-oriented workflow languages, workflow aspects, which specify the different concerns rather than the different perspectives, are composed with the workflow process. This chapter presented two approaches for composing aspects and processes.

In [184], Odgers and Thompson propose an aspect-oriented process engineering approach, which combines Business Process Management and Aspect-Oriented Programming to enable more flexible business processes. In that approach, the definition of a business process consists of a *generic process pattern* and several *process aspects*. The latter are activities that can be included in order to customize the process execution by a particular resource. In that work, processes are specified in Java and process aspects are implemented in AspectJ.

The papers mentioned so far do not introduce any aspect-oriented constructs (such as pointcuts, join points, advice) to workflow languages. They just use aspect-oriented programming languages at the workflow implementation level.

In contrast, aspect-oriented workflow languages provide the workflow designer with aspect-oriented language constructs that support the modularization of crosscutting concerns and workflow changes.

Currently, there are three proposals for aspect-oriented workflow languages. The first one is AO4BPEL [34, 35, 40], which will be presented in the next chapter. The other two proposals [27, 59] are also extensions to the Web Service composition language BPEL. A detailed comparison of the languages presented in [59] and [27] with AO4BPEL will be given in the next chapter.

4.6 Conclusion

This chapter introduced aspect-oriented workflow languages as a solution for the problems of crosscutting concern modularity and change modularity in current workflow languages.

Aspect-oriented workflow languages enable a concern-based decomposition of workflow specifications and introduce workflow aspects as language means for crosscutting concern modularization and workflow change modularization.

Moreover, this chapter presented aspectual workflow graphs, which illustrate the concepts of aspect-oriented workflow languages in a visual and generic manner. In addition, this chapter defined several requirements on the join point models, the pointcut languages, the advice languages, and the composition mechanisms of aspects and processes in aspect-oriented workflow languages.

To show the feasibility of the concepts that were presented in this chapter, the next two chapters will introduce two aspect-oriented workflow languages covering process design and process implementation. Chapter 5 will present AO4BPMN, which is an aspect-oriented extension to the Business Process Modeling Notation (BPMN) and Chapter 6 will present AO4BPEL, which is an aspect-oriented extension to the Business Process Execution Language (BPEL).

CHAPTER 5

AO4BPMN: an Aspect-Oriented Business Process Modeling Language

---

5.1 Introduction

This chapter presents AO4BPMN, which is an aspect-oriented notation for business process modeling. AO4BPMN extends OMG's Business Process Modeling Notation (BPMN) [144] with many of the concepts of aspect-oriented workflow languages that were introduced in Chapter 4.

This chapter will define the join point model and pointcut language of AO4BPMN as well as the advice language. Moreover, it will discuss the composition approaches that were presented in Chapter 4 with respect to their feasibility in the AO4BPMN context. It will also show examples of AO4BPMN aspects that modularize the crosscutting concerns and workflow changes that were discussed in Chapter 3. Unlike aspectual workflow graphs, which is a simple graph-based tool for explaining the basics of aspect-oriented workflow languages, AO4BPMN is based on a widely accepted OMG standard for business process modeling.

The remainder of this chapter is organized as follows. Section 5.2 introduces AO4BPMN and its concepts. Section 5.3 gives some examples of AO4BPMN aspects for illustration. Section 5.4 presents some related works and Section 5.5 concludes this chapter.

5.2 Overview of AO4BPMN

The aspect-oriented concepts of AO4BPMN were designed according to BPMN 1.0 extensibility, which is based on artifacts. Artifacts are process modeling elements that are not directly related to the sequence or message flow in a BPMN process. They can be linked to existing BPMN flow objects (i.e, activities, events, or gateways) through associations. BPMN 1.0 defines three types of artifacts: data objects, text annotations, and groups. Other types of artifacts can be introduced by BPMN modelers to add non-standard elements in order to satisfy a certain need such as the requirements of some vertical domain. In this chapter, artifacts are used to define some of the aspect-oriented constructs introduced by AO4BPMN.

In the following, the AO4BPMN language is presented at the meta-model level. Then, two concrete syntax alternatives are proposed. The first one is a light-weight visual syntax that uses existing artifacts and BPMN elements to represent the aspect-oriented constructs and thus it is directly supported by BPMN tools. The second one is a heavy-weight visual syntax that introduces new graphical elements for representing the aspect-oriented constructs and thus it is not supported by BPMN tools. The advantage of this syntax over the first one is that the aspect-oriented constructs, which are conceptually different from the standard BPMN constructs, are also represented in a different way.

5.2.1 Join point model and pointcut language

Join points are points in the business process model where logic implementing a crosscutting concern can be integrated. In AO4BPMN, activities and events are the only allowed join points (gateways are not join points).

A pointcut is a means for selecting join points. According to the BPMN extensibility guidelines, a pointcuts is defined as a new artifact that optionally has a query property.

In the light-weight visual syntax of AO4BPMN, pointcuts are represented as data objects that have an associated annotation with the text *Pointcut*. The queries are stored in the document property of the data object. In the heavy-weight syntax, a pointcut is represented by an oval as in aspectual workflow graphs. For defining the pointcut language of AO4BPMN three alternatives were considered:

- **Explicit Pointcut to Join Points Associations** The first alternative consists in using a simple visual pointcut language by connecting the pointcut to the join points via BPMN associations. This alternative is the one taken in aspectual workflow graphs. The problem with this approach is that the processes and aspects should be always displayed in the same view in order to connect them.

- **A Query-based Pointcut Language** This alternative consists in using a textual query language as pointcut language. For that purpose, one could use existing model query languages such as OCL [142] or QVT [143], which allow to select the activity or event elements based on their types, their attributes, their associations to data objects, their connections via sequence flow to other flow objects, etc. The problem with this approach is that BPMN users generally do not have knowledge of model query languages. To address that problem one may define a simple query language in which activities are selected for example by specifying their names, the names of their parent lane/pool, and the name of their parent process.

- **Annotating the Join Points** The third alternative consists in adding BPMN text annotations to the join points and defining the pointcut as a simple annotation-based query. That is, one could for instance add a text annotation with the text *monitoring* to all activities for which the execution time should be measured. Then, the pointcut will simply select all activities that have an associated text annotation with the value *monitoring*. Although this alternative would relax the *obliviousness* [83] property of AOP it seems appropriate for BPMN users.

5.2.2 Advice

The advice language of AO4BPMN is BPMN, i.e., the advice contains standard BPMN modeling elements. At the visual syntax level, the advice is represented as a BPMN sub-process that has an attached text annotation with the text *Advice*. An advice is associated with a pointcut using BPMN associations.

In the advice, a special activity named *Proceed* is used to integrate the join point in the middle of the advice and to indicate the order of the advice activity with respect to the join points. The decision of always using a *proceed* inside the advice avoids the need for creating a new meta-model element for the advice in AO4BPMN. Otherwise, one would need an advice element that consists of the advice activity and an advice type property indicating when the crosscutting logic executes with respect to the join points. The advice is self-contained, which means that no sequence or message flows are allowed between the advice and the other activities of the business process except the join point.

The advice language of AO4BPMN provides context collection constructs, which allow the advice to access the input and output data objects of the join points that are selected by the pointcut. This is done by using the data object artifacts *ThisJPInData* and *ThisJPOutData*, which refer to the input (resp. output) data object of the join point. If the join point has more than one input/output data object then an integer index needs to be specified. Moreover, the advice language of AO4BPMN provides the special data object *ThisJPData*, which is a context collection data object providing reflective information about the join point such as type and name.

5.2.3 Aspects

At the meta-model level aspects are elements that modularize the process logic that belongs to a certain crosscutting concern. They consist of one or more pointcuts and associated advice. They may define their own state with data objects.

In the light-weight visual syntax aspects are represented by means of a BPMN pool that has an associated text annotation with the text *Aspect*. Pools are normally used to represent the process participants. The reason for using a pool to represent an aspect is that a crosscutting concern such as execution time measurement or process monitoring can to some extent be seen as a technical participant in the process. In the heavy-weight visual syntax aspects are represented as pools that have rounded corners.

5.2.4 Aspect/Process composition

The composition of aspects with processes can be explained as in aspectual workflow graphs (cf. Section 4.3.2 in Chapter 4). The composition mechanism of AO4BPMN replaces the matched join points by a sub-process that contains the join point activity or event in addition to activities implementing the cross-cutting concern. If the join point activity is source or target of sequence or message flows, the sub-process becomes the source or target of those flows.

In the following, the feasibility of the two composition approaches proposed in Section 4.4.5 of Chapter 4 is discussed in the context of AO4BPMN.

- **Process transformation:** In this approach a tool composes the process and aspects models into new process models. In the case of BPMN this approach can be implemented using model transformation techniques. For instance, one could realize the composition mechanism as a two-phase model transformation: in the first phase *pointcut matching* is performed, i.e., the join point activities and events selected by the pointcut are matched and annotated; in the second phase *advice composition* is performed, i.e., the advice activity is inserted in the process model at the selected join points and according to the advice semantics. If the annotation-based pointcut mechanism is chosen the composition transformation would consist only of the advice composition transformation.

  The advice composition transformation has also to update the sequence and message flow that starts from or targets the join points as defined by the composition semantics. Moreover, it has to resolve the special constructs such as data collection constructs (e.g., by adding appropriate associations) and the *proceed* activity.

  The process transformation approach results in standard BPMN models that can be viewed and manipulated by existing tools. Moreover, with this approach, one would have various versions of the business process at different levels of abstraction (e.g., one would have the base process, which is appropriate for business users, in addition to the base process plus execution time measurement, which is appropriate for process monitoring experts, etc.). This is helpful for understanding the processes and also supports multiple-views with varying abstraction levels for different user groups.

- **Aspect-aware engine:** BPMN is a modeling notation and consequently it is not directly executable by a workflow engine. For this reason, the aspect-aware engine approach is not applicable for composing AO4BPMN aspects and BPMN processes. However, one could generate executable AO4BPEL aspects from the AO4BPMN aspects and BPEL processes from the BPMN processes. Then, the generated aspects and processes could be deployed on the AO4BPEL engine, which is an aspect-aware workflow engine (cf. Chapter 6).

5.3 Examples

Figure 5.1 shows the BPMN process models of the travel package process and the flight process, which were introduced in Chapter 3. Next, the aspects that were shown in Chapter 4 using aspectual workflow graphs will be modeled using AO4BPMN.

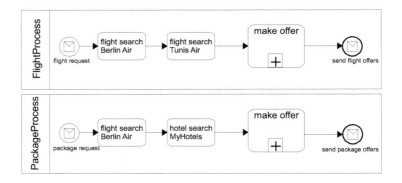

Figure 5.1: The travel agency processes in BPMN

5.3.1 Crosscutting concern modularization

The first aspect modularizes the concern data collection for billing and the second one modularizes the concern measurement of activity execution time.

Data collection for billing

Figure 5.2 shows an AO4BPMN aspect that modularizes the data collection for billing concern. The pointcut of this aspect selects the flight search activities that interact with Berlin Air with an appropriate query. The advice, which is associated with this pointcut, contains an activity for increasing the counter, which executes after the join point activity represented by the *proceed* activity. Thus, this advice corresponds to an after advice. This aspect also defines a data object that holds the input data of the activity *increase counter*.

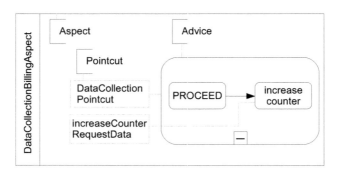

Figure 5.2: The data collection for billing aspect in AO4BPMN

72

Execution time measurement aspect

Figure 5.3 shows an aspect that modularizes the activity execution time measurement concern.

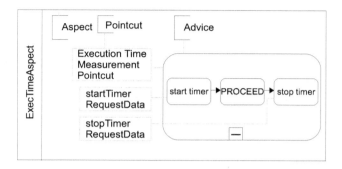

Figure 5.3: The execution time measurement aspect in AO4BPMN

The pointcut of this aspect selects the flight search activities that interact with Berlin Air. The advice associated with that pointcut integrates the monitored activities using the *proceed* activity between two activities respectively for starting and stopping a timer. Thus, it corresponds to an around advice. This aspect declares two data objects for holding the input data of the activities *start timer* and *stop timer*.

5.3.2 Workflow change modularization

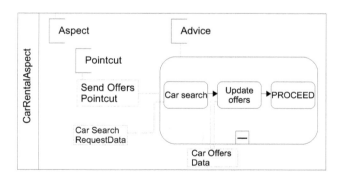

Figure 5.4: The car rental aspect in AO4BPMN

Figure 5.4 shows an AO4BPMN aspect that adds car rental logic to the travel package process and to the flight process. The pointcut of this aspect selects the activities *send flight offers* in the flight process and the activity *send package offers* in the travel package process. This pointcut is associated with an advice that comprises an activity that searches for a rental car and an activity *update offers*, which updates the input data of the offer sending activities (represented by the *proceed* activity) with the output data of the activity *car search*. This advice corresponds to a before advice. This aspect declares two data objects for holding the input and output data of the activity *car search*.

5.4   Related Work

Aspect-Oriented Modeling is a related research area to AO4BPMN. A survey on existing approaches in that field is given in [44]. However, it is important to note that most works on Aspect-Oriented Modeling target object-oriented models and especially structural models.

The most related work to AO4BPMN is that of Barros and Gomes [17]. That work proposes aspect-oriented extensions to UML activity diagrams by introducing horizontal decomposition (as opposed to the vertical decomposition i.e., the hierarchical decomposition). The authors define a UML profile specifying three types of activity nodes where horizontal decomposition can happen: interface nodes, activity nodes and subtraction nodes. Addition nodes are activity nodes that are added to an activity diagram during horizontal composition whereas subtraction nodes are deleted from an activity diagram during that step. An interface node represents a join point at which an advice (i.e., a horizontally decomposed activity diagram) can be integrated into another activity diagram.

5.5   Conclusion

This chapter presented AO4BPMN, which is aspect-oriented business process modeling language that extends BPMN with aspect-oriented constructs according to the BPMN extensibility guidelines. AO4BPMN incorporates several of the concepts of aspect-oriented workflow languages, which were introduced in Chapter 4. This chapter has also shown through examples how AO4BPMN allows a better modularization of crosscutting concerns and workflow changes in business process models.

After introducing the AO4BPMN language for aspect-oriented business process modeling, the next chapter will present AO4BPEL, which an aspect-oriented workflow language supporting the definition of executable Web Service processes. With both languages, which span process design and process implementation, one has the necessary means for an aspect-oriented workflow management approach supporting crosscutting concerns from the modeling phase to the execution phase.

CHAPTER 6

AO4BPEL: an Aspect-Oriented Workflow Language for Web Service Composition

---

6.1 Introduction

This chapter[1] presents AO4BPEL, which is an aspect-oriented workflow language for Web Service composition. The design and implementation of this language can be considered as a proof-of-concept for aspect-oriented workflow languages.

AO4BPEL incorporates many of the concepts that were presented in Chapter 4. Its join point model supports both activity join points and internal join points. Its pointcut language is based on XPath. The advice language of AO4BPEL is BPEL, whereby some special constructs can be used, e.g., for context collection. This chapter will also define the effects of AO4BPEL advice on advanced BPEL concepts such as fault handling, compensation handling, and message correlation.

To illustrate things, this chapter will present several examples of AO4BPEL aspects, which modularize the crosscutting concerns and workflow changes that were introduced in Chapter 3. At the process modeling level, these aspects were shown in Chapter 4 using aspectual workflow graphs and in Chapter 5 using AO4BPMN. The current chapter will show these aspects at the process execution level. AO4BPEL aspects span all workflow perspectives as they modularize the activities (the functional perspective), the variables (the informational perspective), and partners (the organizational/operational perspective) that implement a given crosscutting concern or a workflow change.

In addition, this chapter will present the AO4BPEL engine, which was implemented on top of BPWS4J [106]. The AO4BPEL engine is an aspect-aware engine that supports the dynamic composition of aspects and processes.

---

[1]This chapter is based on the papers *Aspect-Oriented Web Service Composition with AO4BPEL*, ECOWS 2004 [35] and *AO4BPEL: An Aspect-Oriented Extension to BPEL*, World Wide Web Journal 2007 [40].

The remainder of this chapter is organized as follows. Section 6.2 introduces the main concepts of the AO4BPEL language and explains the effects of advice on fault handling, compensation handling, and correlation. Section 6.3 presents examples of AO4BPEL aspects. Section 6.4 describes the implementation of the AO4BPEL engine. Section 6.5 reports on related work and Section 6.6 concludes this chapter.

6.2   Overview of AO4BPEL

AO4BPEL is an aspect-oriented extension to BPEL that supports the definition of workflow aspects for BPEL processes.

AO4BPEL aspects are XML documents, in which the *aspect* element is the top level element. An aspect defines one or more pointcuts (the *pointcut* element) and advice (the *advice* element).

The content of the *pointcut* element is an XPath [52] expression that selects a set of activities. The content of the *advice* element is a BPEL activity that implements a crosscutting concern or a workflow change. A pointcut and advice can be associated by nesting the respective *pointcut* and *advice* elements in a *pointcutandadvice* element.

Like a BPEL process, an AO4BPEL aspect can define *partner links*, *variables*, *fault handlers*, *compensation handlers*, and *correlation sets*. These constructs have the same syntax as in BPEL.

6.2.1   Join point model and pointcut language

Join point model

AO4BPEL supports two kinds of join points: *activity join points*, which correspond to the execution of BPEL activities, and *internal join points*, which correspond to internal points during the interpretation of messaging activities.

Internal join points capture well-defined points at the interpretation level rather than at the process level. The interpretation of a messaging activity is broken into several internal join points, which capture for instance the point where the outgoing SOAP message of an *invoke* activity will be sent out.

Internal join points allow the aspect to express statements such as *"before a SOAP message is sent out in the course of interpreting a messaging activity, get that message and do this and that"*. In this example, the internal join point is the point in the execution where a SOAP message of a messaging activity has been generated and it is about to be sent out.

Internal join points are especially relevant for capturing middleware concerns such as security [37] and reliable messaging [42]. More details on the usage of these join points for providing middleware support to BPEL processes will be given in Chapter 7.

A query-based pointcut language

In aspect-oriented programming languages such as AspectJ, pointcuts are defined by means of *pointcut designators*, which are predicates on join points. AspectJ provides a set of predefined pointcut designators such as *call*, which selects method call join points.

The pointcut language of AspectJ has three limitations: a) it does not provide a general-purpose mechanism to relate different join points, b) it is not extensible, i.e., the user cannot define further pointcut designators, and c) it does not support *semantic pointcuts* [91, 119], i.e., it specifies *how* the interesting join points are implemented rather than *what* these join points are [76].

Query-based pointcut languages [76] solve these limitations by using query languages such as XQuery [195]. First, such languages allow a more precise specification of the pointcuts because the semantics of query languages are generally clear. Second, they enable open pointcut languages, where users can define their own pointcut designators. Third, they support more semantic pointcuts by specifying what the interesting join points are rather than how these join points are implemented [76].

AO4BPEL also uses a query-based pointcut language. As BPEL process definitions are XML documents, XPath [52] is a natural choice as pointcut language. AO4BPEL does not come with predefined pointcut designators, i.e., each XPath expression that selects BPEL activities is a valid pointcut.

The pointcuts can use the attributes of BPEL activities as predicates to choose relevant join points. For example, to refer to all invocations of the operation *findAFlight*, the pointcut can use the attribute *operation* of the *invoke* activity as shown below:

```
<pointcut>
//invoke[@operation="findAFlight"]
</pointcut>
```

This pointcut selects the *invoke* activities that have their *operation* attribute set to *findAFlight* in any BPEL process. This example shows that the pointcut language of AO4BPEL supports the selection of activities across different processes. Thus, this pointcut language provides sufficient support for *quantification*. To restrict the selection of join points to a given process, e.g., to the travel package process, one can use the following pointcut:

```
<pointcut>
/process[@name="travelPackage"]//invoke[@operation="findAFlight"]
</pointcut>
```

It is also possible to define composite pointcuts by using the set operators of XPath such as the union operator and the intersection operator.

Cross-layer pointcuts

The pointcuts that result from combining process-level and interpretation-level pointcut designators intercept points in the execution of two different layers. Therefore, they are called *cross-layer pointcuts*.

In AO4BPEL, the *pointcut* element has a *type* attribute, which specifies whether the pointcut selects activity join points (the default) or internal join points. In addition, it has a *designator* attribute, which specifies the pointcut designator.

For capturing internal join points, AO4BPEL introduces two pointcut designators: *soapmessagein* and *soapmessageout*. These pointcut designators are used together with pointcut designators that select messaging activities.

The *soapmessagein* pointcut designator works in conjunction with the activities *invoke* and *receive*. When used with *invoke*, it captures the join points where a SOAP message has been received by the engine as a response for an *invoke*. When used with *receive*, *soapmessagein* captures the join points where a SOAP message that matches a *receive* activity is received by the BPEL engine.

The *soapmessageout* pointcut designator works in conjunction with *invoke* and *reply*. When used with *reply*, it captures the join points where the engine has generated the SOAP response message corresponding to that *reply* and will send it. When used with *invoke*, *soapmessageout* captures the join points where the engine has generated the SOAP request message corresponding to that *invoke* and will send it.

The pointcut shown below selects the internal join points, where the SOAP request message of the *invoke* activity, which calls the operation *findAFlight*, has been generated and is about to be sent out.

```
<pointcut type="internal" designator="soapmessageout">
//invoke[@operation="findAFlight"]
</pointcut>
```

Perspective-oriented pointcuts

The pointcut language described so far is *activity-oriented*. It covers only the functional and the behavioral workflow perspectives. Beyond these two perspectives, AO4BPEL supports perspective-oriented pointcuts such as *variable-oriented* pointcuts (the informational perspective) and *partner-oriented* pointcuts (the operational and organizational perspectives).

A variable-oriented pointcut selects all activities that read or write a given process variable. In such pointcuts, the *name* attribute, which should be set to the name of the variable, is required and the *access* attribute is optional. For example, the following pointcut selects all activities that write the variable *clientresponse*.

```
<pointcut>
// variable [@name="clientreponse" and @access="write"]
</pointcut>
```

A partner-oriented pointcut selects all interactions with a given partner. Thereby, one could specify whether data is sent to or received from that partner. In such pointcuts, the *name* attribute is required and the *pattern* attribute is optional. For example, the following pointcut selects all activities, in which the process interacts with the partner *flightService* and sends data to that partner.

```
<pointcut>
//partner[@name="flightService" and @pattern="send"]
</pointcut>
```

The support for variable-oriented and partner-oriented pointcuts allows to specify the crosscutting structure of some concerns in a more natural and direct way. The variable-oriented pointcuts are better suited for data-related concerns such as persistence, whereas the partner-oriented pointcuts are better suited for concerns such as authorization and auditing.

Process-level and instance-level aspect deployment

AO4BPEL supports both *process-level* and *instance-level* aspect deployment. With process-level aspect deployment, which is the default case, the advice applies to all instances of a workflow process. With instance-level aspect deployment, the advice applies only to some workflow instances. The pointcut specifies whether the associated advice should be applied at the instance level by using the optional *condition* attribute of the *pointcut* element.

The support for instance-level deployment in AO4BPEL is especially useful when aspect activation depends on runtime data such as the value of some process variable. For example, in an extended version of the travel agency scenario, one could activate a different pricing aspect for each process instance according to the pricing strategy selected by the customer. Thereby, some discounts may be given depending on the customer identifier.

Instance-level aspect deployment is also needed when a car rental aspect should extend the travel package process with car rental propositions for some destinations only. Below is a pointcut that selects the *reply* activities in the workflow instances of the travel package process, in which the destination city is Tunis.

```
<pointcut condition="getVariableData(' clientrequest ',' destination ') == 'Tunis'">
//process[@name="travelPackage"]//reply[@operation="getTravelPackage"]
</pointcut>
```

6.2.2 Advice

The advice language of AO4BPEL is BPEL, i.e., the content of the *advice* element is a BPEL activity. However, some special constructs can be used in the advice, e.g., for context collection and reflection.

The *advice* element has an attribute *type*, which specifies whether the advice is a *before*, *after*, or *around* advice. These advice types are executed respectively before, after, or instead of the join point activities that are selected by the associated pointcut. In addition, AO4BPEL supports the advice types *before soapmessageout*, *after soapmessagein*, *around soapmessagein*, and *around soapmessageout*. These advice types are used only in conjunction with cross-layer pointcuts. They are executed respectively before, after, or instead of the internal join points that are selected by the associated pointcuts.

The advice can also define fault handlers, compensation handlers, and correlation sets. The handlers are added to the *scope* activity that encloses the advice activity. If the advice activity is not a *scope* activity, the composition mechanism of AO4BPEL embeds it automatically into a *scope* activity. More details on fault handlers, compensation handlers, and correlation sets will be given at the end of this section.

Context collection and reflection

In most cases, the advice activity needs to access the variables that are used by the current join point activity or to get reflective information about the current join point activity and/or its parent process. To support these requirements, AO4BPEL provides special variables for *context collection* and for *reflection*.

Since a pointcut may select different activities that may have different types, the context collection constructs should be generic. For example, consider a logging aspect that logs the id and the price of all flight and travel package offers that are sent to clients. The pointcut of this aspect selects the *reply* activities of the flight process and the travel package process. The logging advice cannot access the variable of the join point activity by specifying its name because the two variables have different names.

To collect the data context of the join point activity, AO4BPEL provides the special variables *ThisJPInVariable* and *ThisJPOutVariable*, which refer to the input and output variables of the join point activity. *ThisJPInVariable* is an alias to the input variable of an *invoke* activity, or to the variable of a *receive* activity. *ThisJPOutVariable* is an alias to the output variable of an *invoke* activity, or to the variable of a *reply* activity.

The following snippet shows an excerpt of the logging advice mentioned above. With the variable *ThisJPOutVariable*, the advice accesses the part *offerid* of the two *reply* join points in a generic way.

```
<copy>
<from variable="ThisJPOutVariable" part="offerid" />
<to variable ="logVar" part="id" />
</copy>
```

The individual parts of the variables *ThisJPInVariable* and *ThisJPOutVariable* can be accessed by name as shown in this snippet. They can also be accessed in a more generic way by using the reserved part names *firstpart*, *lastpart*, and *partN* (where N is the index of the part).

To get reflective information about the join point, AO4BPEL provides the special variable *ThisJPActivity*, which contains information about the current join point activity such as process name, activity name, activity type, partner link, port type, and operation name. The last three parts of this variable are only set if the join point activity is *invoke*, *reply*, or *receive*.

Assume that the logging advice should be extended to log the name of the *reply* activity that sent the flight or travel package offer to the client. This can be done by using the variable *ThisJPActivity* as shown in the following code snippet.

```
<copy>
<from variable="ThisJPActivity" part="name" />
<to variable ="logVar" part="activityName" />
</copy>
```

To access the parent process of the join point activity, the advice can use the special context collection construct *ThisProcess(x)*, whereby x is the name of a variable or a partner link that is defined in the parent process of the advice. The following code excerpt shows how the advice invokes an operation on the partner *ppartner* of the parent process.

```
<invoke name="invokeProcessPartner" partnerLink="ThisProcess(ppartner)" .../>
```

For the advice types that are associated with cross-layer pointcuts, AO4BPEL provides two special variables *soapmessage* and *newsoapmessage*. These variables allow the programmer to access and interact with the SOAP messaging layer.

The variable *soapmessage* is used to expose the SOAP message as part of the context of an internal join point that is captured by the pointcut designators *soapmessagein* and *soapmessageout*. For example, consider an encryption advice of the type *after soapmessageout*, which encrypts the SOAP message of an *invoke* activity using a security service. This advice can use the variable *soapmessage* to access the SOAP request message of the *invoke* activity and pass it subsequently to the security service.

The variable *newsoapmessage* is used in two ways. In conjunction with the advice types *before soapmessageout* and *after soapmessagein*, this variable allows the advice to override the SOAP message of the current join point activity by a modified SOAP message. For example, the encryption advice can use that variable to override the request message of the *invoke* activity by the encrypted message after calling the security service.

In conjunction with around advice that do not contain a *proceed* activity, the variable *newsoapmessage* is used to pass the response message of a synchronous *invoke* activity to the process if needed. For example, consider a reliable messaging advice, which sends the SOAP message of an *invoke* activity with the exactly-once assurance using a reliable messaging service. This service has to send the SOAP message on behalf of the process to ensure the required assurance. Consequently, this service will receive the response message of that *invoke* activity and not the process. In such a case, the variable *newsoapmessage* can be used by the advice to pass the response message of the *invoke* activity back to the process.

Advice execution order

Several advice can be executed at the same join point if their pointcuts select the same join point activity. When these advice have different types, the AO4BPEL implementation executes them in the following order: *before → around → before soapmessageout → around soapmessageout → around soapmessagein → after soapmessagein → after*.

In this order, advice that should be triggered before and instead of activity join points are executed first. Then, advice that should be triggered at internal join points during the execution of messaging activities are executed. Finally, the after advice that should be triggered after activity termination.

When these advice have the same type, there can be ambiguity with regard to the execution order. To avoid such ambiguities, the *order* attribute of the *advice* element can be used to define the advice priority. The allowed values of this attribute are integers (whereby low numbers mean high priority) and the reserved keywords *first* and *last*.

For example, consider two after advice for logging and encryption. To ensure that the encryption advice is executed before the logging advice, the programmer can set the attribute *order* of the encryption advice to 1 and the attribute *order* of the logging advice to 2.

Advice and faults

Fault handlers are BPEL constructs for handling the different faults that may occur during the execution of the process activities. After composing the aspects with the processes, faults may occur during the execution of the advice activity, which could affect the parent process. For example, consider the data collection for billing advice, which calls an operation on a counting Web Service to increment a counter after each invocation of some partner Web Service. If the invocation of the counting Web Service fails the fault may be thrown to the parent process of the join point activity.

However, as the aspect is an add-on to existing processes, it must take care of the potential faults that may occur within the advice. That is, faults should not propagate from the aspect to the process.

To enforce this requirement, the composition mechanism embeds each advice in a *scope* activity that defines an empty *catchall* fault handler. The purpose of the *scope* and the default *catchall* fault handler is to absorb any faults. Thus, if the aspect does not define appropriate fault handlers for the faults that may be thrown during the execution of the advice, the *catchall* fault handler absorbs the fault and the process continues its execution normally. In this way, faults never propagate from the advice to the process.

When a fault occurs inside the advice activity and the default *catchall* fault handler is executed, the outgoing links of the advice are fired normally because the advice scope handles the fault. As a result, the *scope* ends normally and the values of its outgoing links are evaluated as usual. In particular, links leaving from the enclosing *flow* are fired normally.

Advice and compensation

Long-running BPEL processes may not complete in a single atomic transaction. Consequently, if a fault occurs during the execution of such a process, it becomes necessary to reverse the effects of the activities that were completed.

For example, the booking process of the travel agency is such a long-running process. First, the booking process checks the credit card number. Then, it charges the credit card if the number is valid. After that, it issues the necessary travel documents and sends them to the customer using a shipping service. If the activity that issues the travel documents fails, the resulting state would be inconsistent unless the charging of the credit card is reversed.

Compensation handlers are BPEL constructs for undoing previously completed activities. Compensation handlers are associated with a scope. They are either called implicitly by the default fault handler, which calls the compensation handlers of child scopes in reverse order of completion, or explicitly by using the *compensate* activity.

For example, the programmer can embed each of the booking process activities that may need to be reversed in a *scope* and define an appropriate compensation handler to undo that activity. The parent activity of the booking process should also be embedded in a *scope*. If the activity that issues the travel documents throws a fault, the default fault handler of the parent scope will call the compensation handler of all so far completed activities in reverse order of completion, i.e., the compensation handler of the activity that charges the credit card will be called.

In AO4BPEL, the composition mechanism inserts the advice activity into the enclosing scope of the current join point. If some child activities of that scope should be compensated for some reason (e.g., in a fault situation), it may also be necessary to undo the advice activity. For example, consider a notification aspect, which defines a pointcut for selecting the activity that charges the credit card of the customer, and an after advice for sending an e-mail to the customer about the success of the payment. If the activity that charges the credit card needs to be compensated, e.g., because the activity that issues the travel documents has failed, the advice of the notification aspect should be also compensated by sending another e-mail to the customer.

If the advice defines a compensation handler, then this handler should be called by the AO4BPEL implementation in the same way as the compensation handlers of the child scopes of the parent scope of the advice activity. That is, if the notification advice defines a compensation handler (e.g., that sends another e-mail to the customer to tell him that the booking could not be completed and that his credit card will be credited), then this handler should be called by the AO4BPEL implementation.

In the current implementation of AO4BPEL, this requirement is enforced as follows: when the advice is composed with the process, the composition mechanism gets a reference to the parent scope of the advice and adds the compensation handler of the advice (if it exists) to the list of compensation handlers that is managed by that parent scope. When the advice is unwoven, its compensation handler is removed from that list. In this way, the compensation handler is called correctly and the advice can be compensated as defined by the BPEL specification.

Advice and correlation sets

Consider two different instances of the travel package process: one instance searches for a vacation package in Tunis and another searches for a vacation package in Frankfurt. As each instance calls the hotel Web Service to find an accommodation two SOAP messages will be received by the BPEL engine.

These messages need to be routed correctly to the respective workflow instance, i.e., the SOAP message with a hotel offer in Tunis should be delivered to the workflow instance that looks for a vacation package in Tunis and not to the other workflow instance.

Correlation sets are BPEL constructs for routing a SOAP message to the respective process instance. This is done by matching parts of the message with parts of the process variables. In the travel package process, the destination city can be used in a correlation set. In this way, when the BPEL engine receives two response messages from the hotel Web Service, it compares the name of the destination city in these messages with the value of the part *destination* of the process variable *clientrequest* in both instances. Then, the BPEL engine routes the messages accordingly.

The problem of message routing exists also when aspects are used. In fact, when the advice calls a partner Web Service via an *invoke* activity and the response message comes in, the engine must identify the aspect instance that made the invocation.

For example, consider a change aspect that adds functionality to search for a rental car to the travel package process. Assume further that this aspect applies to the two instances of the travel package process mentioned above. As the advice of this change aspect calls the car rental Web Service, the AO4BPEL engine will receive two response messages: one with a car proposition in Tunis and the other with a car proposition in Frankfurt. Each of these messages should be routed to the respective advice instance.

However, at runtime, the advice does not have an identity of its own because it is triggered during the execution of several processes that are selected by the pointcut. Consequently, even if the car rental aspect defines its own correlation sets, the engine would have a problem in correlating the messages with the two aspect instances.

This problem is solved as follows: the correlation sets that are defined by the aspect are added by the composition mechanism of AO4BPEL to the parent processes, in which the advice is integrated. For instance, when the response messages of the car rental Web Service are received, the engine uses the correlation sets that were added to the travel package process to route these messages. In this way, the engine can route the messages correctly.

Advice restrictions

Aspects are only meant to modify the implementation of a composite Web Service (the BPEL process) and not its interface (the WSDL). Therefore, using the messaging activities *receive*, *pick*, *reply*, and event handlers for message events in the advice should be only allowed when these BPEL constructs do not require any change to the WSDL of the composite Web Service.

For example, the messaging activity *receive* requires a matching operation in the WSDL file of the composite Web Service. If the advice uses that activity it is necessary to modify the WSDL interface of the composite Web Service, unless the matching operation is already present.

6.2.3 Aspect/Process composition

In the case of pointcuts selecting activity join points, the composition of aspects with processes can be explained as a process transformation. In this transformation, which was illustrated in Chapter 4 using aspectual workflow graphs, the composition mechanism inserts the advice activity into the parent activity of the current join point. This explanation holds only when the pointcut of the aspect captures activity join points and not internal join points.

The logical effect of this process transformation is to replace the join point activities with a *flow* activity that may contain the join point activity. If the join point activity is the source or target of some *links*, the *flow* becomes the source or target of these links.

In the case of before advice, the composition mechanism adds a *link* that goes from the advice activity to the join point activity. In the case of after advice, the composition mechanism adds a *link* that goes from the join point activity to the advice activity.

In the case of around advice, the join point activity can be integrated in the middle of the advice execution using the special activity *proceed*, which is a place holder for the join point activity.

For the advice types *before soapmessageout*, *after soapmessagein*, *around soapmessageout*, and *around soapmessagein*, the advice activity is executed at internal join points during the execution of the messaging activity according to the semantics of the pointcut designator.

The composition of AO4BPEL aspects with BPEL processes can be done either with the process transformation approach (physical transformation), or with the aspect-aware engine approach (logical transformation), as explained in Chapter 4. However, the process transformation approach works only for aspects whose pointcuts select activity join points, because internal join points are concepts at the interpretation level that have no counterpart at the process level.

The current implementation of AO4BPEL is based on the aspect aware engine approach, which allows the dynamic composition of aspects and processes and supports internal join points. More details on the implementation of the AO4BPEL engine will be given in Section 6.4.

6.3   Examples

In this section, some examples of AO4BPEL aspects will be presented. These aspects were shown in Chapter 4 using aspectual workflow graphs.

6.3.1   Crosscutting concern modularization

The first aspect modularizes the concern data collection for billing and the second aspect modularizes the concern measurement of activity execution time.

```
 1  <aspect name="Counting">
 2   <partnerLinks>
 3    <partnerLink name="CounterWS" partnerLinkType="CounterPLT"
 4                        myRole="caller"   partnerRole="counter" />
 5   </partnerLinks>
 6   <variables>
 7    <variable name="increaseRequest" messageType="increaseCounterInput" />
 8   </variables>
 9   <pointcutandadvice>
10    <pointcut name="Berlin Air Invocations">
11     //invoke[@operation="findAFlight"]
12    </pointcut>
13    <advice type="after">
14     <sequence>
15      <assign>
16       <copy>
17        <from expression="1" />
18        <to variable="increaseRequest" part="increaseBy" />
19       </copy>
20      </assign>
21      <invoke partnerLink="CounterWS" portType="CounterPT"
22            operation="increaseCounter" inputVariable="increaseRequest" />
23     </sequence>
24    </advice>
25   </pointcutandadvice>
26  </aspect>
```

Listing 6.1: The data collection for billing aspect

Data collection for billing

Listing 6.1 shows the AO4BPEL aspect that modularizes the data collection for billing concern. This aspect declares a partner link (lines 3–4) to a counter Web Service *CounterWS*, which provides the operation *increaseCounter* for incrementing a counter. This operation takes an integer parameter that will be added to the total number of invocations. This aspect declares also a variable (line 7) for holding this input parameter.

The pointcut of this aspect (lines 10–12) selects all *invoke* activities that call the operation *findAFlight* on Berlin Air Web Service in any process. An after advice (lines 13–24) is associated with the pointcut of this aspect. This advice uses a *sequence* activity for defining the advice logic. The *sequence* activity has a nested *assign* activity (lines 15–20) to set the variable *increaseRequest*, and an *invoke* activity (lines 21–22) to call the operation *increaseCounter* on the counter Web Service.

```
1   <aspect name=" PerformanceMonitor" >
2    <partnerLinks>
3     <partnerLink name=" AuditingWS" partnerLinkType=" AuditingPLT"
4                  myRole=" caller"  partnerRole=" measurer" />
5    </partnerLinks>
6    <variables >
7     <variable   name=" startTimerRequest" messageType=" startTimerInput" />
8     <variable   name=" stopTimerRequest" messageType=" stopTimerInput" />
9    </variables >
10   <pointcutandadvice>
11    <pointcut name=" monitored activities" >
12       //invoke[@operation=" findAFlight"]
13    </pointcut>
14    <advice type=" around" >
15     <sequence>
16      <assign>
17       <copy>
18        <from variable=" ThisJPActivity" part=" name" />
19        <to variable=" startTimerRequest" part=" activityName" />
20       </copy>
21       <copy>
22        <from variable=" ThisJPActivity" part=" name" />
23        <to variable=" stopTimerRequest" part=" activityName" />
24       </copy>
25      </assign>
26      <invoke partnerLink=" AuditingWS" portType=" AuditingPT"
27            operation=" startTimer"   inputVariable =" startTimerRequest" />
28      <proceed/>
29      <assign>...</assign>
30      <invoke partnerLink=" AuditingWS" portType=" AuditingPT"
31            operation=" stopTimer"  inputVariable =" stopTimerRequest" />
32     </sequence>
33    </advice>
34   </pointcutandadvice>
35  </aspect>
```

Listing 6.2: The execution time measurement aspect

Listing 6.2 shows the AO4BPEL aspect, which modularizes the activity execution time measurement concern.

This aspect declares the auditing Web Service as partner (lines 3–4). It also declares two variables (lines 7–8) for holding the input parameters of the calls to the operations *startTimer* and *stopTimer* on that partner.

The pointcut of this aspect (lines 11–13) selects all *invoke* activities that call the operation *findAFlight* on Berlin Air Web Service. This pointcut can be easily extended to monitor the execution time of other activities by using the XPath union operator.

This aspect uses an around advice, which calls the operations *startTimer* (lines 26–27) and *stopTimer* (line 30–31) on the auditing Web Service, respectively before and after executing the join point activity. The *proceed* activity (line 28) allows the advice to integrate the execution of the join point activity.

The operations *startTimer* and *stopTimer* take an input parameter that identifies the monitored activity. This parameter is set by an *assign* activity (lines 16–25) to the name of the current join point activity, which is accessed by using the reflective AO4BPEL variable *ThisJPActivity* (lines 18 and 22).

6.3.2 Workflow change modularization

In Chapter 3, two examples of workflow changes were presented. The first change is about adding car rental logic to the travel package process and to the flight process. The second change is about replacing a bad performing partner Web Service by another. These workflow changes will be modularized using AO4BPEL aspects.

Adding car rental logic

The aspect *AddCarRental*, shown in Listing 6.3, declares a partner link to the car rental Web Service (lines 3–4) and two variables (lines 7–8) for holding the input and output parameters of the operation *getCar* that is called on that Web Service (lines 24–25).

The pointcut of this aspect (lines 11–14) selects the *reply* activities in the flight process and the travel package process. This pointcut is associated with a before advice (lines 15–33) that comprises a *sequence* activity, which implements the car rental logic.

This *sequence* activity contains an *assign* activity (lines 17–23) for setting the input parameters of the operation *getCar*. These input parameters are taken from the client request that was passed to the parent process by using the context collection construct *ThisProcess(clientrequest)* (line 19).

After invoking *getCar* on the car rental Web Service (lines 24–25), the advice uses an *assign* activity (lines 26–31) to add the car proposition to the return data of the flight process and to the travel package process.

The return data of these processes is stored in the variables of the *reply* activities that are selected by the pointcut. These variables are accessed from the advice by using the context collection variable *ThisJPOutVariable* (line 29).

```
1   <aspect name="AddCarRental">
2     <partnerLinks>
3       <partnerLink name="CarCompany" partnerLinkType="CarPLT"
4                    myRole="caller" partnerRole="carWS" />
5     </partnerLinks>
6     <variables>
7       <variable name="getCarRequest" messageType="getCarInput" />
8       <variable name="getCarResponse" messageType="getCarOutput" />
9     </variables>
10    <pointcutandadvice>
11      <pointcut name="about to reply">
12      //process[@name="travelProcess"]//reply[@operation ="getTravelPackage"] |
13      //process[@name="flightProcess"]//reply[@operation="getFlight"]
14      </pointcut>
15      <advice type= "before">
16        <sequence>
17          <assign>
18          <copy>
19           <from variable="ThisProcess(clientrequest)" part="deptDate" />
20           <to variable ="getCarRequest" part="startDate" />
21          </copy>
22           ...
23          </assign>
24          <invoke partnerLink="CarPortal" portType="CarPT" operation="getCar"
25               inputVariable ="getCarRequest" ouputVariable="getCarResponse" />
26          <assign>
27          <copy>
28           <from variable="getCarResponse" part="carinfo" />
29           <to variable ="ThisJPOutVariable" part="optionalinfo" />
30          </copy>
31          </assign>
32        </sequence>
33      </advice>
34    </pointcutandadvice>
35  </aspect>
```

Listing 6.3: The car rental aspect

Replacing a bad performing partner

Listing 6.4 shows an aspect, which replaces all calls to the operation *findAFlight* on Berlin Air Web Service by calls to the operation *searchFlight* on Tunis Air Web Service.

The pointcut of this aspect (lines 11–13) selects the *invoke* activities that call the operation *findAFlight* on Berlin Air Web Service.

The around advice of this aspect (lines 14–37) replaces each *invoke* activity that is selected by the pointcut by an *invoke* activity (lines 23–25) that calls the operation *searchFlight* on Tunis Air Web Service. In addition, the advice of this aspect uses two *assign* activities. The first *assign* (lines 16–22) sets the input variable of the new *invoke* activity. Thereby, the input variable of the join point is accessed using the context collection variable *ThisJPInVariable* (line 19). The

88

second *assign* (lines 26–35) fixes the data flow in the modified workflow process by setting the necessary parts of the output variable of the replaced join point activity. The output variable of the join point activity is accessed using the AO4BPEL context collection variable *ThisJPOutVariable* (lines 29 and 33).

```
1   <aspect name="ReplacePartner">
2    <partnerLinks>
3     <partnerLink name="newFlight" partnerLinkType="TunisAirPLT"
4                  myRole="caller" partnerRole="flightprovider"/>
5    </partnerLinks>
6    <variables>
7     <variable name="newflightRequest" messageType="searchFlightRequest"/>
8     <variable name="newflightResponse" messageType="searchFlightResponse"/>
9    </variables>
10   <pointcutandadvice>
11      <pointcut name="Berlin Air Invocations">
12      //invoke[@operation="findAFlight"]
13      </pointcut>
14      <advice type="around">
15        <sequence>
16        <assign>
17          ...
18        <copy>
19         <from variable="ThisJPInVariable" part="retDate">
20         <to variable="newflightRequest" part="returnDate">
21        </copy>
22        </assign>
23        <invoke name="invokeTunisAirTP" partnerLink="newflight"
24         portType="TunisAirPT" operation="searchFlight"
25         inputVariable="newflightrequest" outputVariable="newflightresponse"/>
26        <assign>
27         <copy>
28          <from variable="newflightresponse" part="flightData"/>
29          <to variable="ThisJPOutVariable" part="flightDetails"/>
30         </copy>
31         <copy>
32          <from variable="newflightresponse" part="flightNumber"/>
33          <to variable="ThisJPOutVariable" part="flightnum"/>
34         </copy>
35        </assign>
36        </sequence>
37      </advice>
38    </pointcutandadvice>
39  </aspect>
```

Listing 6.4: The partner replacement aspect

6.3.3 Discussion

To better see the advantages of AO4BPEL over other solutions with respect to modularization of crosscutting concerns, recall the travel package process and the flight process that were presented in Listings 3.2 and 3.3 in Chapter 3.

In order to keep track of the invocations of Berlin Air Web Service without AOP, the programmer had to add the same activity (i.e., the advice activity of the data collection for billing aspect) as well as the corresponding partner link and variable to the flight process and to the travel package process. Similarly, to measure the execution time of some process activities, the programmer had to insert activities before and after each occurrence of the monitored activities, in addition to the respective partner link and variables.

The data collection for billing aspect and the execution time measurement aspect shown above modularize the workflow constructs (partners, variables, and activities) that pertain to these crosscutting concerns and separate them from the business logic of the travel package process and the flight process.

The collection of billing data/measurement of activity execution time functionality is no longer intertwined with the process code of other concerns. The logic for collecting data/measuring execution time is now explicit, and so is the decision as to where and when to collect which data/measure activity execution time during the execution of the BPEL processes. Moreover, the workflow process specifications of the travel package process and the flight process are no longer tangled.

In addition, one could define aspects with different implementations of a certain concern and weave the appropriate ones according to the context. Also, the concerns that are modularized in the form of aspects can be plugged in and out as needed.

To better see the advantages of AO4BPEL with respect to workflow change modularization, recall the two versions of the travel package processes that were presented in Listings 3.6 and 3.7 in Chapter 3.

The aspects *AddCarRental* and *ReplacePartner* show how AO4BPEL supports the modular expression of workflow changes. All workflow constructs (partners, variables, and activities) that implement some workflow change are encapsulated in an aspect module.

Expressing changes modularly with aspects makes them easy to understand. The pointcut of the aspect specifies when and where the change should be applied during the execution of the workflow processes. In addition, as the AO4BPEL engine is based on the aspect-aware engine approach, it supports change aspects as first-class runtime entities. Thus, change management becomes simpler. For instance, to undo a temporary change, one just has to undeploy the corresponding aspect.

The dynamic composition mechanism of the AO4BPEL engine solves the problem of dynamic change in BPEL. That is, ad-hoc workflow changes such as the replacement of a partner service can be accommodated at runtime. Thus, AO4BPEL improves the flexibility of BPEL processes significantly.

6.4 Implementation

A prototype implementation[2] of AO4BPEL was developed on top of IBM's
orchestration engine BPWS4J [106], the only engine that was available when
this work started.

The implementation is based on the aspect-aware engine approach, i.e., the
interpreter of the BPWS4J engine was extended with additional checks for aspects at well-defined points in the execution of process activities. The aspect-
aware engine approach was chosen because it supports easily the dynamic composition of aspects and processes and also because it supports internal join
points (cf. Chapter 4).

6.4.1 Architecture of the AO4BPEL engine

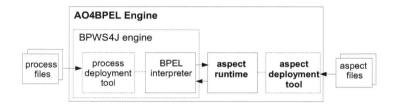

Figure 6.1: Architecture of the AO4BPEL engine

The architecture of the AO4BPEL engine is shown at a high level in Figure 6.1. The BPWS4J engine is extended with two components: the *aspect
deployment tool* and the *aspect runtime*.

The aspect deployment tool is the user interface to the AO4BPEL implementation. This tool allows the deployment/undeployment of aspects and also the
listing of all currently deployed aspects. It is implemented as a Web application
based on Java Server Pages [66], in a similar way to the process deployment tool
of BPWS4J.

The process deployment tool of BPWS4J was extended with *aspect visual-
ization* support, so that it shows the aspects that affect each deployed process.
This feature allows AO4BPEL users to better understand and predict the behavior that results after the composition of aspects and processes.

The aspect runtime component is responsible for managing and executing
the aspects. This component builds a wrapper around the BPEL interpreter. It
intercepts the execution of each process activity at well-defined points and checks
whether there is an aspect with a pointcut that matches the current activity. If
such an aspect is found, the respective advice activity will be executed according
to the advice type.

---

[2]This implementation was presented in a formal demonstration at AOSD 2006 [38].

6.4.2 Composition mechanism

The composition mechanism of AO4BPEL has three major tasks. First, it extends the activity lifecycle of the BPEL engine with dynamic checks for aspects. Second, it decides at all these checks whether there is a pointcut that matches the current activity. Third, if a matching pointcut is found, the composition mechanism ensures the execution of the respective advice.

Modification of the activity lifecycle

The activity lifecycle denotes the different states in which an activity can be during its execution. The BPWS4J engine follows an *activate-enable-run-complete* lifecycle [63] as shown in Figure 6.2.

In this lifecycle, an activity starts running (the *running* state) once two things happen: The activity receives control from its enclosing activity (the *activate* state) and its incoming links fire positively so that the join condition evaluates to true. When a fault occurs, the activity enters the *disabled* state and can be revived later. To support loops, an activity that is in the *completed* state can be revived.

Figure 6.2 shows the points in the activity lifecycle where dynamic checks for aspects are integrated. These checks depend on the advice types. For the advice types before and around, checks are performed when the activity goes from the state *enabled* to the state *running*. For the after advice, checks are performed when the activity exits the state *complete*.

Figure 6.2 also shows the internal points during the execution of messaging activities where additional checks are integrated. These checks affect not only the BPEL engine but also the underlying SOAP engine.

Checks for the advice types *before soapmessageout* and *around soapmessageout* are done after the generation of the outgoing SOAP message of the current messaging activity. Checks for the advice types *after soapmessagein* and *around soapmessagein* are done after receiving an incoming SOAP message that matches the current messaging activity.

For the composition mechanism of AO4BPEL, the process meta model constructs of BPEL such as join conditions, transition conditions, and links are irrelevant because the composition mechanism is embedded in the orchestration engine itself, as opposed to composition mechanisms that are based on the process transformation approach such as the work presented in [27]. What matters for the composition mechanism of AO4BPEL is that an activity, which is matched by a pointcut, is currently being executed.

Pointcut matching

At all points where checks for aspects are performed, the composition mechanism has to decide whether there is a pointcut (and an associated advice) that matches the current activity. The pointcut matching process in the AO4BPEL engine consists of three steps.

In the first step, variable-oriented and partner-oriented pointcuts are transformed into activity-oriented pointcuts. This step is necessary because the pointcuts should match points in the execution of activities (and not partners or variables).

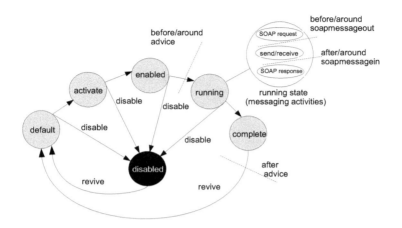

Figure 6.2: Advice weaving and the activity lifecycle

After that, the pointcut matcher proceeds with the second step and checks whether one of the activity-oriented pointcut expressions matches the current activity. Thereby, two implementation approaches are possible.

In the first approach, pointcut matching can be implemented by evaluating the XPath pointcut expressions for each activity that is executed by the BPEL engine. That is, the pointcut matcher retrieves all pointcut expressions that are defined in the deployed aspects, and evaluates each of them against the XML process document, in which the current activity is defined. Then, the pointcut matcher compares the element name and the attributes of each matching XML node with the type and attributes of the current activity. This approach requires costly XPath evaluations of all pointcut expressions for each BPEL activity.

In the second approach, which is implemented by the AO4BPEL engine, a fast match pass is used to improve performance. In this approach, pointcut matching is done in two phases *2a* and *2b*.

In the phase *2a*, the pointcut matcher evaluates pointcut expressions only when a new process or aspect is deployed or undeployed. This evaluation, which uses Xalan-J [6], operates on the XML process documents and returns a set of matching XML nodes for each pointcut expression. These nodes are comparable with the *join point shadows* in the AspectJ implementation [98]. For each pointcut, the meta-data of the returned activity nodes (e.g., activity type, activity name, attribute names and their values) is stored in some internal data structure.

In the phase *2b*, the pointcut matcher compares the metadata of the current activity with the meta-data stored in the internal data structure without performing any costly XPath evaluations.

If the pointcut is a *dynamic pointcut*, i.e., it specifies an instance selection condition, the pointcut matcher performs the third step of the pointcut matching process and evaluates that condition against the current process instance.

This step is comparable with the dynamic tests (*residues*) in the AspectJ implementation [98]. If the pointcut does not specify an instance selection condition, this third step is skipped.

Advice execution

In case a pointcut match is found for the current activity, the aspect runtime has to execute the respective advice activity. If the current join point activity is matched by more than one pointcut, the aspect runtime has to determine the order in which the advice should be executed.

If the advice have different types, the aspect runtime executes them in the order defined in Section 6.2.2. If the advice have the same type, the aspect runtime executes them depending on the values of the *order* attributes of the respective advice elements. If no order is defined, the aspect runtime executes them according to their order of deployment: the first deployed aspect will be executed first and so on.

Since the advice activity is a BPEL activity, the aspect runtime can delegate the execution of that activity to the BPEL interpreter. Thereby, two steps are necessary before the BPEL interpreter can execute the advice activity.

First, special AO4BPEL constructs need to be resolved. If the advice uses context collection variables such as *ThisJPInVariable*, this construct should be replaced by the name of the input variable of the join point activity. If the advice uses some parts of the reflective variable *ThisJPActivity*, these parts should be set to the corresponding reflective information of the join point activity.

For example, recall the logging aspect that was mentioned in Section 6.2.2. The pointcut of this aspect selects two *reply* activities in the flight process and in the travel package process. The advice of this aspect uses the reflective variable *ThisJPActivity* to log the name of the join point activity.

```
<copy>
<from variable="ThisJPActivity" part="name" />
<to variable ="logVar" part="activityName" />
</copy>
```

In this example, the aspect runtime should set the parts of the variable *ThisJPActivity* differently depending on the current join point activity. That is the part *name* will be set once to the name of the *reply* activity of the travel package process and once to the name of the *reply* activity of the flight process.

The resolution of context collection constructs and reflective constructs is implemented as follows: whenever the advice uses a context collection or reflection construct, the aspect runtime collects the context data of the current join point (meta-data of the activity and its parent process, the input and output variables used by the activity, etc). Then, the aspect runtime uses the collected data to resolve the special constructs.

Second, aspect-local declarations for partners and variables are added to the parent process of the current join point activity. In this way, the advice activities that use the variables and partners that are defined in the process can be executed by the BPEL engine as if they were activities of the process.

After these two steps, the aspect runtime delegates the execution of the advice activity to the BPEL interpreter and coordinates that execution with the process execution as follows.

- If the advice is a before (resp. before soapmessageout) or after advice (resp. after soapmessageout), the process execution is suspended until the advice activity completes. After that, the process proceeds with the suspended activity.

- If the advice type is around (resp. around soapmessageout) and the advice does not use the *proceed* activity, the process execution is suspended until the advice activity completes. After that, the join point activity skips the *running* state to avoid executing the join point activity and goes to the *complete* state.

- If the advice type is around (or around soapmessageout) and the advice uses the *proceed* activity, the process execution is suspended until the completion of the child activities of the advice that are defined before the *proceed* activity. Then, the join point activity executes. After that, the child activities of the advice that are defined after the *proceed* activity execute.

6.4.3   Performance

In the following, some performance measurements of the AO4BPEL engine are presented. These measurements confirm two claims. First, the additional overhead for aspect checks is negligible when compared with the process execution time. Second, the dynamic composition based on the aspect-aware engine approach compares well to the static composition based on the process transformation approach.

Tests	Engine	Number of invokes		
		2	4	6
T1: No checks for aspects	BPWS4J	367ms	657ms	951ms
T2: Checks without deploying an aspect	AO4BPEL	373ms	672ms	971ms
Overhead for aspect checks		1.6%	2.2%	2.05%
T3: Advice embedded in the process	BPWS4J	525ms	842ms	1111ms
T4: Advice defined in an aspect	AO4BPEL	535ms	863ms	1135ms
Aspect machinery incl. checks		1.9%	2.4%	2.11%
Aspect machinery without checks		0.3%	0.2%	0.06%

Table 6.1: Performance measurements for the AO4BPEL engine

Overhead of the additional checks for aspects

Additional checks are needed during the execution of process activities to test whether these activities are matched by the pointcut of some aspect. Clearly, these checks induce some performance overhead. However, this overhead is negligible when compared with the execution time of a messaging activity such as *invoke*, which carries out a costly interaction with a partner over the network.

There are no standard benchmarks for BPEL. To measure the additional overhead for aspects checks, two tests were done with three variants of the travel package process (respectively with two, four, and six *invoke* activities). The partner Web Services were deployed on the Internet. In each test, the travel package process was called 50 times and the average time elapsed between the creation of the process instance (as a result of a request message matching the *receive* activity) and the termination of that instance was measured in milliseconds.

In the test T1, the three variants of the travel package process were deployed on the original BPWS4J engine (without aspect support). In the test T2, these variants were deployed on the AO4BPEL engine (with additional checks for aspects), without deploying any aspects. The results of these two tests are shown in the upper part of Table 6.1.

The overhead caused by the additional checks for aspects is the difference between the process execution time in the test T2 and the process execution time in the test T1. The measurements for these two tests confirm that this overhead is negligible (around 2%) compared with the cost of interactions with partner Web Services.

Overhead of aspect machinery

The dynamic composition of aspects and processes has several benefits such as improving the adaptability of BPEL processes, providing more flexibility to switch aspects on and off as needed, allowing an easier support of pointcuts that depend on runtime data such as perspective-oriented and instance-based pointcuts.

In addition to these benefits, the runtime overhead induced by the aspect-aware engine approach is small and acceptable, when compared with the process transformation approach. To confirm this claim, the runtime overhead of the aspect machinery in the AO4BPEL engine was measured by means of two further tests.

In the test T3, which simulates static composition by the process transformation approach, the data collection for billing functionality (i.e., the partner link, the variable, and the necessary activities to call the counting Web Service) was directly integrated into the three variants of the travel package process. Then, the resulting three process variants were deployed on the BPWS4J engine.

In the test T4, the data collection for billing functionality was defined in a separate aspect that was deployed on the AO4BPEL engine. This aspect was composed together with the three variants of the travel package process.

In both tests, the travel package process was called 50 times and the average process execution time was measured as in the tests T1 and T2. The results of the tests T3 and T4 are shown in the lower part of Table 6.1.

The runtime overhead caused by the aspect machinery is the difference between the process execution time in the test T4 and the process execution time in the test T3. The measurements confirm that the runtime overhead induced by the aspect machinery is small (less than 0.3%) compared with the cost of interactions with partners. Moreover, this overhead decreases (from 0.3% to 0.06%) when the process contains more messaging activities.

6.5　Related Work

This section starts by comparing AO4BPEL and AspectJ. Then, two other aspect-oriented extensions to BPEL are compared with AO4BPEL. After that, some works on AOP in the context of Web Services and some research efforts on adaptability in BPEL are presented.

6.5.1　AO4BPEL and AspectJ

AspectJ [120] is the most known and the most mature aspect-oriented programming language to date. Like AspectJ, AO4BPEL has a *join point model*, a *pointcut language*, and an *advice language*. Unlike the join point model of AspectJ, which defines points in the execution of object-oriented Java programs such as method calls and field reading/writing, the join point model of AO4BPEL selects points in the execution of BPEL processes corresponding to the execution of process activities.

In addition, the join point model of AO4BPEL supports internal join points, which span the process level and the messaging level. This kind of join points is specific to workflow languages, which incorporate a *two-level programming paradigm* [127] (i.e., they separate the *activity specification* in the one level and the *activity implementation* in the other level). There is no counterpart for internal join points in AspectJ.

Similarly to the pointcut language of AspectJ, which provides pointcut designators to select, e.g., method calls and field reading/writing, the pointcut language of AO4BPEL provides activity-oriented pointcuts. However, AspectJ comes with a predefined set of pointcut designators, whereas AO4BPEL uses XPath as pointcut language, which provides a calculus for building pointcuts as needed. Moreover, AO4BPEL supports cross-layer pointcuts (corresponding to the two-level programming paradigm) and perspective-oriented pointcuts (corresponding to the workflow perspectives). These pointcuts do not have counterparts in AspectJ.

The advice language of AspectJ is Java, whereas the advice language of AO4BPEL is BPEL. Like AspectJ, AO4BPEL defines the advice types before, after, and around. In addition, AO4BPEL defines further advice types such as *before soapmessageout* and *after soapmessagein*.

6.5.2　Other aspect-oriented extensions to BPEL

In the following, two recent aspect-oriented extensions to BPEL [59, 27] will be presented and compared with AO4BPEL.

In a position paper [58], Courbis and Finkelstein present a BPEL-specific aspect language, which uses XPath as pointcut language and Java as advice language. That work proposes using aspects to implement an extensible, configurable, and adaptable BPEL engine, i.e., to extend and modify the engine's behavior, to select and replace Web Services, and to modularize crosscutting concerns in the engine implementation such as profiling and debugging. The first work on AO4BPEL [34] was presented at the same conference as the proposal in [58].

In [59], Courbis and Finkelstein present their aspect-oriented extension to BPEL, which uses XPath as pointcut language and BPEL as advice language, like AO4BPEL. The purpose of that extension as stated by the authors is to hot-fix and adapt workflows dynamically by transforming the abstract syntax tree representation of the BPEL process at runtime, e.g., by adding or removing activities to/from the process.

The work presented in [59] does not address the issues of crosscutting concern modularity and change modularity. The language introduced in that paper is more *interceptor-based* than aspect-oriented because the pointcut expressions cannot span several processes. That is, if a crosscutting concern spans three processes, three aspects are needed (respectively one for each process). Changes and adaptations that span more than one BPEL process are not supported.

In [27], the most recent aspect-oriented workflow language is presented. That language is called *Padus*. It has a logic-based pointcut language and it uses BPEL as advice language. Pointcuts in Padus are written as constraints on the type and properties of the allowed join points. Moreover, pointcut matching is done by a Prolog engine.

Padus supports the modularization of crosscutting concerns, but it does not address the problem of change modularization. This is probably due to the static composition mechanism of Padus. Unlike AO4BPEL, which supports dynamic composition, the implementation of Padus follows the static process transformation approach. Consequently, Padus aspects cannot be used for dynamic adaptation.

The aspect-oriented extensions that are presented in [27, 59] support only activity join points. The concept of internal join points does not exist in those proposals, which is a major limitation. That is, these extensions are not suitable for non-functional concerns such as security, reliable messaging, and transactions. These concerns require support for defining cross-layer pointcuts because Web Service middleware is based on WS-* specifications such as WS-Security [138] and WS-ReliableMessaging [45], which define SOAP message extensions.

The pointcut languages of the works presented in [27, 59] do not support the selection of cross-layer pointcuts and instance-based pointcuts. Moreover, these pointcut languages lack support for perspective-oriented pointcuts such as the data-oriented or participant-oriented pointcuts. Unlike AO4BPEL and the extension presented in [59], which use XPath as pointcut language, Padus comes with a predefined set of pointcut designators, such as *invoking* and *replying*. Consequently, it is not possible to define new pointcut designators in Padus.

Moreover, the advice language presented in [59] does not provide any context collection or reflection constructs. Padus provides some context collection constructs. However, these constructs are not generic. That is, the advice in Padus must reference the variables that are used by the join point activity by their names to access the join point context. Consequently, the pointcut of a Padus aspect can select only one activity or occurrences of the same activity whenever the join point context is needed.

Besides, the works presented in [27, 59] propose an aspect-oriented extension to BPEL without addressing the relationship between aspects, which add new activities to the workflow processes, and fault handling, compensation handling, and message correlation. In both proposals, the behavior of the system when a fault occurs during the execution of the advice is unclear. Moreover, important issues such as compensating the effects of the advice activity and routing the messages that go to the advice are not addressed.

6.5.3 Work on AOP and Web Services

In the following, some works on Aspect-Oriented Programming in the context of Web Services are presented.

WSML [189] is a client-side Web Service management layer that realizes dynamic selection and integration of Web Services. It is implemented using the aspect-oriented programming language JAsCo [177], which is an extension to Java. WSML offers management functionalities such as service selection and service redirection but it does not support Web Service composition, unlike AO4BPEL.

The Contextual Aspect-Sensitive Services platform (CASS) [57] is a distributed aspect platform, which targets the encapsulation of specific crosscutting concerns in service-oriented environments such as coordination, activity lifecycle management, and context propagation. The pointcut and advice languages of CASS are geared toward low-level message processing. The pointcut language allows to define message patterns for the messages that should be intercepted. The advice language allows to transform, to synchronize, to forward the intercepted messages, etc. The advice operate at the level of the SOAP engine. Unlike AO4BPEL, CASS does not introduce any aspect-oriented constructs to the workflow process level.

In [151], Ortiz et al. use AspectJ aspects to modularize and add non-functional properties to Java-based Web Services. In another work [150], Ortiz and Leymann use WS-Policy [115] to describe the requirements of Web Services in a declarative way. They mention the idea of generating AspectJ aspects to enforce the policies without presenting an implementation. The use of aspects in these two proposals allows for a more modular and reusable implementation of the Java based Web Service. However, Web Service compositions that are implemented in BPEL are not supported in these two works.

6.5.4 Work on flexibility in BPEL

AO4BPEL supports the dynamic composition of aspects and processes, which increases the flexibility and adaptability of BPEL processes. There are some other works on flexibility in BPEL.

In [117], Karastoyanova et al. introduce BPEL extensions to increase the flexibility of BPEL processes. The *find and bind* extension allows the explicit selection at runtime of the Web Services that participate in a BPEL process instance, e.g., based on some dynamic service selection policies. The *evaluate* extension to the *invoke* activity enables port types to be modified at runtime. These extensions are supported by a special BPEL engine.

In [79], Ezenwoye and Sadjadi introduce the TRAP/BPEL framework, which adds autonomic behavior to existing BPEL processes. In that framework, a tool generates an adapt-ready version of the BPEL process, which uses a *generic proxy* for all interactions between the process and its partners. The proxy allows the dynamic selection of partner Web Services at runtime. TRAP/BPEL does not require any extensions to the BPEL language or to the BPEL engine.

In [78], Erradi et al. present a policy-based middleware, called Manageable and Adaptive Service Compositions (MASC). This middleware supports the dynamic self-adaptation of Web Service compositions. According to a set of Quality of Service policies that define non-functional requirements such as

SLAs, security, and persistence, MASC adapts the Web Service composition by controlling and guiding the selection of partner Web Services, intercepting and modifying SOAP messages, etc.

6.6 Conclusion

This chapter presented AO4BPEL and its implementation, which can be considered as a proof-of-concept for aspect-oriented workflow languages.

The AO4BPEL language incorporates many of the concepts of aspect-oriented workflow languages that were presented in Chapter 4. In addition to presenting the join point model, the pointcut language, and the advice language of AO4BPEL, this chapter explained the relationship of AO4BPEL aspects to advanced BPEL concepts such as fault handling and compensation handling.

Several examples illustrated how AO4BPEL aspects support the modularization of crosscutting concerns and workflow changes by encapsulating all activities, variables, and partners that implement them in separate modules.

This chapter also described the implementation of the AO4BPEL engine, which extends the BPWS4J engine according to the aspect-aware engine approach. Since the AO4BPEL engine supports dynamic composition, AO4BPEL aspects provide a suitable vehicle for adapting BPEL processes at runtime.

After introducing the AO4BPEL language in this chapter, the next chapters will present two applications of AO4BPEL. In the first application [37, 41, 42], AO4BPEL aspects are used to implement a process container that provides support for security, reliable messaging, and transactions to BPEL processes. In the second application [36], AO4BPEL aspects are used to implement business rules in BPEL processes in a separate and modular way.

Part III

Applications

CHAPTER 7

A Process Container Framework for Middleware Support in
BPEL Processes

7.1 Introduction

Three years ago, IBM and Microsoft published a joint white paper on secure, reliable, and transacted Web Services [81]. That paper explained how the non-functional properties of Web Services can be supported by composing appropriate WS-* specifications such as WS-Security [138], WS-ReliableMessaging [45], and WS-AtomicTransaction [139]. However, it did not address the specific case of composite Web Services such as those implemented in BPEL, which is addressed in this chapter[1].

In fact, BPEL processes have several non-functional requirements. For example, a BPEL programmer may need to specify that a certain *invoke* activity should be executed with confidentiality support (i.e., the corresponding SOAP message should be encrypted) or that a *sequence* activity should be executed as an atomic transaction. Supporting the non-functional requirements is essential to enable Web Service based *production workflows* [128] with BPEL. These are workflows that define not only the functional logic, but also the non-functional properties that are needed to integrate distributed and heterogeneous applications [179].

When implementing a Web Service in BPEL, the programmer looks at the Web Service from an internal implementation perspective, i.e., he sees the process definition (the BPEL file) and not only the interface definition (the WSDL file). WS-* specifications such as WS-Security look at the Web Service from an external perspective and do not make any assumptions about its implementation. They consider the Web Service as a black-box that consumes and generates SOAP messages as defined in its WSDL interface.

---

[1]Parts of this chapter were published in the paper *Reliable, Secure, and Transacted Web Service Compositions with AO4BPEL*, ECOWS 2006 [41].

The increased visibility that BPEL programmers have from their internal implementation perspective gives rise to several non-functional requirements, which are not addressed by WS-* specifications. These new requirements are called *process-level requirements*, as opposed to *messaging-level requirements*.

Messaging-level requirements correspond to messaging activities, e.g., sending the message of a *reply* activity with exactly-once semantics. They can be supported to a large extent by using implementations of WS-* specifications. The enforcement of these non-functional requirements can be done outside and independently of the BPEL engine. Such an approach does not work for process-level requirements, which require knowledge about the process structure, BPEL semantics, and the process execution state.

This chapter illustrates the non-functional requirements of BPEL processes with respect to security, reliable messaging, and transactions using a banking scenario. Then, it presents a survey on the support for these requirements in several current BPEL implementations. In this survey, two aspects are considered: the *specification* and the *enforcement* of non-functional requirements.

The survey reveals that only a few recent BPEL engines [54, 60, 174] provide support for the expression and enforcement of messaging-level requirements. Process-level requirements such as interacting with a partner using a secure conversation and multi-party ordered message delivery are not supported in all currently available commercial and Open Source BPEL engines.

To solve the problem of the lacking support for non-functional requirements in current BPEL engines, a container-based framework is proposed. This framework is inspired by enterprise component models such as Enterprise Java Beans (EJB) [67]. In this framework, the non-functional requirements are specified declaratively using an XML-based *deployment descriptor* and they are enforced by a *process container*, which intercepts the execution of the process activities at well-defined points and plugs in calls to dedicated *middleware services*.

The remainder of this chapter is organized as follows. In Section 7.2, the non-functional requirements of BPEL processes w.r.t. security, reliable messaging, and transactions are illustrated using a bank transfer scenario. Section 7.3 studies the support for these non-functional requirements in some current BPEL engines. Section 7.4 presents the process container framework. Section 7.5 concludes this chapter.

7.2 Non-functional requirements in BPEL processes

This section introduces an online banking scenario, which shows the non-functional requirements of BPEL processes w.r.t. security, reliable messaging, and transactions in a more realistic way than the travel agency scenario.

In the banking scenario, a customer needs to perform a transfer of money. He first accesses the Web site of his bank (called mybank) and logs in to the online banking application before proceeding with a bank transfer. After the authorization step, the customer fills in the necessary data for the transfer, which includes the account number of the receiver, the code of the receiver's bank, and the amount of the transfer. When the customer confirms the transfer, a request is sent and queued at mybank's Web server, which later calls the operation *transfer* on a Web Service that runs on a back-end server to complete the transfer. The operations *login* and *transfer* are implemented by the BPEL process shown in Listing 7.1. To log in the customer, this process invokes an authorization Web Service (lines 4 and 26–28). To carry out a transfer, this process invokes the Web Service of the customer's bank subsidiary (lines 5 and 44–46) and the Web Service of the receiver's bank (lines 6 and 47–49).

7.2.1 Classification

BPEL processes such as the transfer process have several non-functional require-ments, which can differentiated into *messaging-level requirements* (at the SOAP level) and *process-level requirements* (at the BPEL level).

Messaging-level requirements are associated with messaging activities, which have corresponding operations and messages in the WSDL interface definition. Given appropriate means to specify messaging-level requirements, one could use implementations of WS-* specifications to enforce them. Thereby, the enforce-ment of these requirements can be done fully outside the BPEL engine, e.g., by using message interceptors in the SOAP engine.

Process-level requirements are associated with non-messaging activities such as the structured activities *sequence* and *flow*. The latter do not show up in the WSDL interface and cannot be directly associated with SOAP messages. To enforce process-level requirements, it is necessary to have knowledge about the process structure, BPEL semantics, and the process execution state. Con-sequently, process-level requirements cannot be enforced at the messaging layer independently of the process layer; they rather require the coordination of both layers.

In the following, the non-functional requirements of BPEL processes with respect to security, reliable messaging, and transactions will be presented using the classification schema proposed so far. The point that the following discussion intends to make is that security for BPEL is more than SOAP message security [37], reliable messaging for BPEL is more than reliable SOAP messaging [42], and transactions for BPEL [179] are also more than Web Service transactions.

7.2.2 Security requirements

In 2002, IBM and Microsoft stated in a joint security white paper [107] that "security has been a key factor that was holding companies back from adopting Web Services". In 2006, the Web Services landscape has changed especially after the emergence of several specifications for Web Service security such as WS-Security [138], WS-Trust [4], and WS-SecureConversation [90]. Whilst these specifications address the general case of Web Services, they do not consider the specific case of Web Service compositions implemented in BPEL.

In fact, BPEL processes such as the bank transfer process have several secu-rity requirements that range from messaging-level requirements such as message confidentiality and message integrity to process-level requirements such as se-cure conversations and federation.

Messaging-level requirements

The messaging-level security requirements are driven by various security threats that arise when the BPEL process interacts with its partners [37]. For example, the BPEL programmer may need to specify the following requirements on the

```
1  <process name="BankTransfer">
2    <partnerLinks>
3      <partnerLink name="customer"       partnerLinkType="customerSLT"/>
4      <partnerLink name="authorization"  partnerLinkType="authorizationSLT"/>
5      <partnerLink name="subsidiary"     partnerLinkType="subSLT"/>
6      <partnerLink name="receiverbank"   partnerLinkType="tobankSLT"/>
7    </partnerLinks>
8    <variables>
9      <variable name="loginrequest"        messageType="loginIn"/>
10     <variable name="loginresponse"       messageType="loginOut"/>
11     <variable name="checkloginrequest"  messageType="checkloginIn"/>
12     <variable name="checkloginresponse" messageType="checkloginOut"/>
13     <variable name="transferrequest"     messageType="transferIn"/>
14     <variable name="transferresponse"    messageType="transferOut"/>
15     <variable name="creditrequest"       messageType="creditIn"/>
16     <variable name="creditresponse"      messageType="creditOut"/>
17     <variable name="debitrequest"        messageType="debitIn"/>
18     <variable name="debitresponse"       messageType="debitOut"/>
19   </variables>
20   <sequence name="MainSequence">
21     <sequence name="LoginSequence">
22     <receive name="receiveLogin" partner="customer"
23        portType="transferServicePT" operation="login"
24        variable ="loginrequest"  createInstance = "yes"/>
25     <assign> ... </assign>
26     <invoke name="invokeChekLogin" partner="authorization"
27        portType="authorizationPT" operation="checkLoginData"
28        inputVariable ="checkloginrequest"  outputVariable ="checkloginresponse"/>
29     <switch>
30      <case condition="getVariableData('checkloginresponse ',' success')=  false">
31       <assign>...</assign>
32       <reply partner ="customer" portType="transferServicePT"
33             operation="login"  variable ="loginresponse"/>
34       <terminate/>
35      </case>
36     </switch>
37     </sequence>
38     <sequence name="TransferSequence">
39     <receive name="receiveTransfer" partner="customer"
40        portType="transferServicePT" operation="transfer"
41        variable ="clientrequest"  createInstance = "no"/>
42     <assign> ... </assign>
43     <sequence name="debit_credit">
44     <invoke name="invokeDebit" partner="subsidiary"
45            portType="subsidiaryBankService" operation="debit"
46            inputVariable ="debitrequest"  outputVariable ="debitresponse"/>
47     <invoke name="invokeCredit" partner="tobank"
48            portType="toBankService" operation="credit"
49            inputVariable ="creditrequest"  outputVariable ="creditresponse"/>
50     </sequence>
51     <assign>
52       ...
53     </assign>
54     <reply partner ="customer" portType="transferServicePT"
55            operation="transfer"  variable ="clientresponse"/>
56     </sequence>
57    </sequence>                  105
58  </process>
```

Listing 7.1: A bank transfer process in BPEL

SOAP messages of the *invoke* activities (lines 44–49) that call the operations *credit* and *debit* in the bank transfer process:

- **Integrity**: SOAP messages should not be tampered with on their way to the partners.

- **Confidentiality**: SOAP messages with sensitive data such as account information should not be seen by other parties.

- **Authentication**: SOAP messages that are exchanged between the banking process and its partners should carry appropriate credentials to prove the sender's identity.

- **Non-repudiation**: A client that invokes an operation on a BPEL process such as the *transfer* process cannot deny having done so or claim that someone else misused his identity.

- **Replay attacks**: A request message that was captured by a malicious third party and then resent later should be recognized as such.

Given appropriate means to express the messaging-level security requirements mentioned above, these requirements can be enforced by using an implementation of WS-Security [138]. This specification provides mechanisms for signing and encrypting SOAP messages, adding authentication tokens and time stamps to messages, etc.

Process-level requirements

Several process-level requirements arise when addressing advanced security issues that go beyond SOAP message security such as secure conversations, federation, and trust. Unlike WSDL, which does not provide any construct for grouping messages or operations, structured BPEL activities such as *sequence* and *flow* can enclose messaging activities and provide a context for their execution. Some structured activities may have secure conversation requirements as it is the case in the banking scenario.

In fact, the process shown in Listing 7.1 integrates *mybank* with exactly one partner bank (let us say bank *A*). Similar BPEL processes are needed to integrate *mybank* with other banks (banks *B*, *C*, etc) in order to perform transfers that involve those partners. Assume that such processes exist and that each of them provides an operation *transferToX*, whereby X is the name of the partner bank (e.g, *transferToA* and *transferToB*). Further, assume that the Web Service of *myBank* collects the transfer requests and sorts them according to the receiver's bank. Then, it calls the operation *transferToX* for all transfers that involve a given partner bank *X*. This functionality can be implemented using a BPEL process *router*, which uses different *while* activities to invoke the operation *transferToX* multiple times for each partner bank *X*. In this scenario, there are several interactions between the *router* process and the Web Service of each partner bank.

When using WS-Security to secure these interactions, each message must contain all security artifacts that are used to secure it. From a performance point of view, the single message security model of WS-Security is inefficient when many messages are exchanged between two parties because it results in high overheads for message processing (i.e., for securing or verifying the message) and for message transmission (because the message gets larger).

In scenarios like the one mentioned above, it is better to set up a security context at the beginning of a session of interactions with a given partner (so-called *conversation*) and then use that context for securing the subsequent interactions with that partner.

The WS-SecureConversation specification [90] defines how a security context can be established between two parties. In addition, it specifies how this context can be used, e.g., to sign or to encrypt SOAP messages. If the Web Services of mybank's partners support WS-SecureConversation, the overhead for message processing and for message transmission can be reduced significantly, which improves the overall performance of the BPEL process.

The secure conversation requirements are process-level requirements that apply to structured activities that contain nested messaging activities. The component that enforces these process-level requirements needs to know when the execution of the structured activity starts. At this point, that component should establish a security context. Then, the enforcement component should use the created context to secure each messaging activity that is nested in the structured activity. When the execution of the structured activity completes, the security context should be destroyed.

7.2.3 Reliable messaging requirements

The execution of a messaging activity results in exchanging one or more SOAP messages with a partner Web Service. When these messages are sent via unreliable channels several risks could arise on the transport path, such as message loss, message duplication, and message reordering.

In the following, the reliable messaging requirements of the messaging activities *invoke*, *reply*, and *receive* are studied. Moreover, several combinations of messaging activities and structured activities are considered.

Messaging-level requirements

Messaging activities may require a particular delivery assurance such as *exactly-once*, *at-most-once*, and *at-least-once*. Without support for these assurances, the SOAP messages corresponding to messaging activities may be lost or delivered multiple times to the partner.

For example, in the bank transfer scenario, it is not acceptable that the SOAP messages corresponding to the *invoke* activities that call the operations *credit* or *debit* get lost. If the response message of the *invoke* activity that calls the operation *credit* is lost, the process will block waiting for it and the transfer will not be completed. Even if the process terminates after some time because of a timeout for instance, one would have to undo the effect of the previously completed *invoke* that called the operation *debit*. In addition, it is not acceptable that the request message of these *invoke* activities is received more than once by the partner because in such a case, the corresponding operation (*credit* or *debit*) will be called more than once.

WS-ReliableMessaging (WS-RM for short) [45] and WS-Reliability [137] are the currently available specifications for reliable messaging in the context of

Web Services. Both specifications provide the delivery assurances *at-least-once*, *at-most-once*, *exactly-once*, and *in-order*.

Given appropriate means to express reliable messaging requirements, the messaging-level requirements mentioned so far can be enforced by using an implementation of WS-RM or WS-Reliability. In this chapter, WS-RM will be used to support reliable messaging in BPEL because WS-RM is less complex than WS-Reliability [48]. Moreover, WS-RM can be composed with other Web Service specifications such as WS-Addressing and WS-Policy.

Process-level requirements

Structured BPEL activities such as *sequence*, *flow*, and *while* define the execution order of their nested messaging activities. The SOAP messages of these nested messaging activities should be delivered to the respective partners in the same order as defined in the process.

The two *invoke* activities that call the operations *debit* and *credit* in the transfer process (lines 44 and 47) are nested in a *sequence* activity (lines 43–50). As both activities define synchronous request-response interactions, there is no reordering risk, i.e., the second *invoke* (line 47) will be executed only after the first *invoke* (line 44) completes. The latter completes only after getting a response message from the partner *subsidiary*, i.e., that partner must have already received the corresponding request message.

The process-level requirement of ordered message delivery makes sense for one-way interactions via the messaging activities *receive*, *reply*, and *invoke* as explained in the following.

For example, consider the two *receive* activities in the bank transfer process. The first *receive* is for the *login* operation (lines 22–24) and the second is for the *transfer* operation (lines 39–41). In lack of an assurance about the ordered delivery of SOAP messages from the client to the transfer process it is possible that the client sends the messages for calling the operations *login* and *transfer* in the correct order but for some reason the second message is received at the process side before the first message. In such a case, the process will not be executed properly because the second SOAP message does not match the *receive* activity for the *login* operation. Moreover, since the *receive* for the operation *transfer* is not yet active, it will not consume the second SOAP message, which will be probably discarded by the BPEL engine. When the message corresponding to the first *receive* finally arrives, the *receive* for the operation *login* executes but the *receive* for the operation *transfer* will block waiting indefinitely. Consequently, the client would not get any response from the process although it has called the operations *login* and *transfer* in the correct order.

The requirement of ordered message delivery applies also to *reply* activities. For instance, consider two *reply* activities that interact with two different partners Pa and Pb and that are nested inside a *sequence*. In certain scenarios, the SOAP message of the first activity should be received by Pa before the SOAP message of the second activity is received by Pb.

Ordered message delivery is also important for one-way *invoke* activities that are nested in a structured activity. Such *invoke* activities are used for one-way interactions and for asynchronous invocations (i.e., the request message is sent by an *invoke* and the response message is received by a *receive*). One-way *invoke* activities are not blocking, i.e, they just send out the message and complete. Like for *receive* and *reply*, message reordering should also be avoided when one-way *invoke* activities are nested inside a structured activity.

The *ordered message delivery* requirement is a process-level requirement, which is associated with structured activities that contain nested messaging activities. The order of message delivery to the different partners should be the same as the order of activity execution (which is defined in the BPEL process). Two cases can be distinguished: either all messaging activities interact with the same partner or they interact with different partners.

WS-Reliability and WS-RM support ordered message delivery only in the first case, i.e., when the messaging activities talk to the same partner (reliable messaging between two endpoints). The in-order assurance provided by these specifications guarantees that calls to the operations of the same Web Service are delivered in the correct order. Both specifications do not support multi-party reliable messaging [42], which is required when the messaging activities talk to different partners (reliable messaging between more than two end points).

7.2.4 Transaction requirements

There are two kinds of transactions in the context of Web Services: *atomic transactions* [139], which are short-running distributed transactions with the traditional ACID properties, and *business activities* [140], which are long-running compensation-based transactions with relaxed isolation.

When studying the transactional requirements of BPEL activities two cases can be differentiated. In the first case, the BPEL process is the initiator of the transaction, i.e., the process side controls the start and the commitment of the transaction, which contains at least an invocation of a partner Web Service. In the second case, the composite Web Service that is implemented by the BPEL process is a participant in a transaction that is controlled by another party. The following discussion will focus on the first case because the second case is not specific to the Web Services that are implemented in BPEL.

Messaging-level requirements

Messaging activities may have transactional requirements. For example, it may be necessary for the execution of an *invoke* or a *reply* to create a new atomic transaction or to use an existing transaction. Given appropriate means to express transactional requirements of messaging activities, these requirements can be enforced by using an implementation of WS-AtomicTransaction [139] or WS-BusinessActivity [140].

Process-level requirements

Structured activities are more interesting with respect to transactions than individual messaging activities because structured activities provide means to group their child activities into a logical unit of work. Defining a structured activity as transactional means that the transaction starts when the activity starts and terminates when the activity completes. All messaging activities that are nested in the structured activity participate with the transaction.

Moreover, it should be possible to flexibly define whether the transaction associated with the structured activity is an atomic transaction or a business activity. This depends on the application requirements and the deployment setting of the process and the partner Web Services. For example, the *sequence* activity *debit_credit* of the bank transfer process should be executed as an atomic transaction to ensure strict isolation. This activity requires that either both *invoke* activities succeed or none of them. If one *invoke* is executed successfully and the other *invoke* fails, the resulting state would be inconsistent. To avoid such inconsistency, the transaction associated with the *sequence* activity *debit_credit* must be rolled back in case of a fault.

In BPEL, there is no support for atomic transactions and only a local support for long-running transactions through the use of compensation handlers. A compensation handler can be added to a named *scope* activity. This handler can be invoked explicitly from a fault handler or from another compensation handler using the *compensate* activity to reverse the already completed activities that should be undone. The default fault handler of a *scope* calls implicitly the compensation handlers of all nested *scopes* in the reverse order of completion.

The compensation handling mechanism of BPEL does not replace the long-running transactions provided by WS-BusinessActivity [140]. Business activities are a more powerful concept for several reasons. First, with WS-BusinessActivity it is possible to model more complex transactions. Second, implementing the compensation logic in BPEL is the task of the BPEL programmer, whereas in WS-BusinessActivity, each Web Service just knows how to compensate once it receives the *compensate* message from the coordinator. Third, all participants of a transaction are predefined in BPEL, whereas the list of participants in WS-BA is dynamic as participants can join and leave the transaction flexibly.

In the context of transactional activities, it is important that the process and the partner Web Services decide together on the outcome of the transaction (*external coordination*), and not only the process (*internal coordination*). Currently, BPEL supports only the internal coordination of long-running transactions through the use of compensation handlers.

Internal coordination, in which the BPEL process decides locally on the outcome of the transaction, is not sufficient for reliable distributed transactions because a fault may occur inside a partner Web Service without being signaled to the BPEL process. This problem can be solved by using external coordination, in which all partners agree on the outcome of the transaction. WS-AtomicTransaction [139] and WS-BusinessActivity [140] can be used to support external coordination in BPEL.

7.3 Support for Non-functional Requirements in Current Engines

The problem of non-functional requirements in BPEL encompasses the *specification* and the *enforcement* of those requirements.

On the one hand, BPEL 1.1 and WS-BPEL 2.0 do not provide any constructs for supporting non-functional requirements. Both focus only on the functional specification of a Web Service composition and do not provide any means for specifying non-functional requirements. This is not a limitation of BPEL, which leaves out non-functional issues for several good reasons such as language simplicity and separation of concerns.

On the other hand, it is widely assumed that non-functional requirements are deployment issues that should be addressed by the BPEL engine somehow. This section will show however that current BPEL engines support only messaging-level requirements.

First, this section will survey the support for security, reliable messaging, and transactions in several current BPEL engines. Then, it will group these engines into three approaches to non-functional requirements and it will discuss the limitations of each.

7.3.1 Survey

When this work started at the beginning of 2004, there was no support for non-functional requirements in the BPEL engines available at that time. Three years later, the author conducted a survey of non-functional requirements support in more than 17 BPEL engines. The inspected implementations are provided by the research community, the Open Source community, and industry. The results of this survey are presented in Tables 7.1, 7.2, and 7.3.

BPEL Engine	Support for Security
Active BPEL 2.0	None, but messaging-level requirements can be supported with custom handlers
Cape Clear Orchestrator	Messaging-level requirements using WS-Security
Bexee - BPEL Execution Engine	None, but supporting messaging-level requirements possible through Axis handlers
Intalio BPMS	Messaging-level requirements with WS-Security
IBM BPWS4J 2.1	None
IBM Research Colombo	Messaging-level requirements using policy attachment and WS-Security
IBM WebSphere Process Server 6.0	Messaging-level requirements using WebSphere ESB (WS-Security)
Microsoft Biztalk	Messaging-level requirements using send & receive pipelines (WS-Security)
OpenLink Virtuoso Universal Server 3.0	Messaging-level requirements using WS-Security and WS-Trust
OpenStorm Service Orchestrator	Messaging-level requirements using WS-Security and IBM MQ Series
Oracle BPEL Process Manager 10.1	Messaging-level requirements using WS-Security
ParaSoft BPEL Maestro	None
SeeBeyond ICAN Suite	Messaging-level requirements using WS-Security

Table 7.1: Security support in current BPEL engines

BPEL Engine	Support for RM
Active BPEL 2.0	None, planned for next release
Cape Clear Orchestrator 6.5	*exactly-once* at the partner link level using WS-RM
Bexee - BPEL Execution Engine	None
Intalio BPMS	Messaging-level requirements using WS-RM
IBM BPWS4J 2.1	None
IBM Research Colombo	Messaging-level requirements using policy attachment and WS-RM
IBM WebSphere Process Server 6.0	*exactly-once* using JMS
Microsoft Biztalk	Messaging-level requirements using a proprietary protocol
OpenLink Virtuoso Universal Server 3.0	*exactly-once* and *in-order* at the level of partner links using WS-RM
OpenStorm Service Orchestrator	Not documented
Oracle BPEL Process Manager 10.1	None
ParaSoft BPEL Maestro	Support for *exactly-once* using JMS
SeeBeyond ICAN Suite	Not documented

Table 7.2: Reliable messaging support in current BPEL engines

BPEL Engine	Support for Transactions
Active BPEL 2.0	None
Cape Clear Orchestrator 6.5	None
Bexee - BPEL Execution Engine	None
Intalio BPMS	Messaging-level requirements using WS-AT
IBM BPWS4J 2.1	None
IBM Research Colombo	Messaging-level requirements using policy attachment and WS-AT
IBM WebSphere Process Server 6.0	Transactional *scope* activities using language extensions
Microsoft Biztalk	Transactional *scope* activities
OpenLink Virtuoso Universal Server 3.0	Not documented
OpenStorm Service Orchestrator	Not documented
Oracle BPEL Process Manager 10.1	None
ParaSoft BPEL Maestro	Messaging-level requirements using WS-AT and WS-BA
SeeBeyond ICAN Suite	Not documented

Table 7.3: Transaction support in current BPEL engines

In addition to the engines shown in these tables, other engines were examined such as Agila BPEL [5], Digite Enterprise BPM [72], Lombardi Teamworks [173], and SEEBURGER Business Integration Server [171]. However, the support for security, reliable messaging, and transactions is these engines was and is still undocumented.

The survey shows that only some BPEL engines support the messaging-level non-functional requirements. Moreover, none of these implementations support secure conversations and multi-party ordered message delivery. Transactional structured activities are supported only in IBM WebSphere Process Server and Microsoft Biztalk Server.

7.3.2 Classification

The BPEL engines that support messaging-level non-functional requirements can be grouped according to three different approaches to requirements specification: using policies, using partner links, and using language extensions.

Using policies

BPEL engines such as Colombo [60] and Oracle BPEL Process Manager [148] use policies to define the non-functional properties of Web Service interactions.

Colombo Colombo [60] is a light-weight platform for developing, deploying, and executing service-oriented applications. It was developed at IBM Research. Colombo supports transactional, reliable, and secure Web Service interactions. It uses WS-Policy [115] to specify the non-functional properties of messaging activities declaratively.

The unit of development and deployment in Colombo is called *servicelet*. In the case of a BPEL process, the servicelet contains the BPEL file, the WSDL file of the composite Web Service, and the WSDL files of the partner Web Services. In addition, the servicelet may contain policy files that are defined in WS-Policy.

In Colombo, the requirements of messaging activities are expressed indirectly by attaching WS-Policy policies to the partner WSDL file, which is packaged into the servicelet jar file. Policies are attached to the WSDL using the internal attachment mechanism of WS-PolicyAttachment [47], i.e., the attribute *wsp:policyRef* is used as extensibility attribute in WSDL elements such as *operation* and *binding*. For instance, to express that the *invoke* activity that calls the operation *credit* requires confidentiality support, one could attach a security policy to the operation *debit* that is defined in the WSDL of the partner *subsidiary*.

When a servicelet is deployed, the policy manager component of Colombo interprets the policies and sets up a handler chain for each incoming or outgoing message to enforce them. This chain may contain WS-* based handlers for security, reliable messaging, transactions, and persistence.

Oracle BPEL Process Manager To secure Web Service interactions, Oracle provides a tool called Oracle Web Service Manager (WSM) [146]. The WSM platform consists of three components: the policy manager, the message interceptors, and the monitor.

The *policy manager* is a graphical browser-based tool that allows administrators to define security policies for a Web Service. These policies will be linked together into a *policy pipeline* that is attached to one or more Web Services. Unlike Colombo, the security policies of the WSM are not based on WS-Policy.

The *interceptors* are components that intercept messages and enforce the security policies. The *policy manager* sends periodically updates of the policy pipelines to the interceptors.

When the interceptors enforce policies on messages, they collect statistical information that is sent to the *monitor*, which is a Web-based tool for monitoring service availability, service level agreements, etc.

Oracle BPEL Process Manager [148] is Oracle's implementation of BPEL. When used with Oracle Web Service Manager, Oracle BPEL Process Manager provides authentication, encryption, and signature support for both outbound security (i.e., invoking secure partner Web Services) and inbound security (securing BPEL processes) [149]. Moreover, Oracle BPEL Process Manager allows processes to access and manipulate the headers of SOAP messages, which is necessary for authorization.

```
<assign>
 <copy>
   <from>
    <EndpointReference
    xmlns="http://schemas.xmlsoap.org/ws/2003/03/addressing">
    <Address>http://securehost/myService</Address>
      <ReferenceProperties>
       <wsOptions>
        <addressing version="http://schemas.xmlsoap.org..."/>
        <delivery>
         <in type="ExactlyOnce" />
         <out type="InOrder" />
        </delivery>
       </wsOptions>
      </ReferenceProperties>
    </EndpointReference>
   </from>
   <to partnerLink= "mypartner"/>
 </copy>
</assign>
```

Listing 7.2: Configuring a partner link in Virtuoso

Using partner links

In BPEL implementations such as OpenLink Virtuoso [174] and Cape Clear Orchestrator [54], messaging-level requirements are expressed at the level of partner links.

OpenLink Virtuoso OpenLink Virtuoso Universal Server [174] is a BPEL engine that allows the deployer to configure various properties of a partner link such as reliable messaging and security. For example, one could specify that all interactions with some partner should be executed with the exactly-once assurance or that calls to some other partner must be encrypted or signed.

OpenLink Virtuoso allows to define the reliable messaging properties of some partner directly in the BPEL process code using the *WSOptions* element as part of an endpoint reference assignment. Listing 7.2 shows an *assign* activity, which sets the endpoint of the partner *mypartner*. The *delivery* element specifies the reliable messaging requirements for interactions with that partner. To enforce the non-functional properties of partner links, Virtuoso uses implementations of WS-Security and WS-RM.

Cape Clear Cape Clear Orchestrator [54] allows users to select partner links and graphically configure their security and reliable messaging properties. To enforce the non-functional properties of partner links, Cape Clear relies on the Cape Clear Enterprise Service Bus [53].

The aim of an Enterprise Service Bus (ESB) is to integrate the applications and data of some enterprise. The ESB provides native support for all relevant XML and Web Service standards. That is, the messages sent via the ESB can be secured according to WS-Security or be sent in a reliable way as specified in WS-RM. Moreover, the ESB provides extended message transformation and routing capabilities in addition to a variety of adapters for integrating legacy applications.

Several other BPEL engines use an underlying ESB to enforce the non-functional requirements of Web Service interactions. For example, the Web-Sphere Process Server [105] relies on the WebSphere Enterprise Server Bus [103] to support reliable and secure partner interactions according to WS-Security and WS-RM.

Using language extensions

A third approach to the specification of non-functional requirements in BPEL processes is based on language extensions. In the following, two BPEL extensions for transaction support are presented.

Choreology defined several BPEL extensions for supporting business transactions in a proposal to the WS-BPEL standardization committee [84]. In that proposal, a new element *businessTransaction* is used to create or terminate transactions, BPEL variables are used to hold coordination contexts and participant identifiers, and messaging activities are extended with two attributes *businessTransactionContext* and *businessTransactionParticipant* for the propagation of business transactions.

The *WebSphere Integration Developer* allows the process modeler to graphically specify the transactional properties of the messaging activities such as *commit before, commit after, participate, require own*, etc. The process definition of such transactional processes contains several proprietary extensions having the prefix *wpc*, as shown in Listing 7.3. The *transactionBehavior* attribute defines the transactional behavior of the *invoke* activity. The WebSphere Process Server interprets these proprietary extensions and enforces the messaging-level transactional requirements accordingly.

```
<process xmlns:bpws="http://schemas.xmlsoap.org/ws/2004/03/business−process/"
  xmlns:wpc="http://www.ibm.com/xmlns/prod/websphere/business−process/">
  ...
 <sequence name="HiddenSequence" wpc:id="1073741827">
  <receive createInstance ="yes" name="Receive" operation="op1"
    partnerLink="TransferProcess" portType="TransferPT" >
   <wpc:output>
    <wpc:parameter name="input1" variable="Input1"/>
   </wpc:output>
  </receive>
  <invoke inputVariable ="debitRequest" name="Debit" operation="debit"
    outputVariable="debitReturn" partnerLink="subsidiaryBank"
    portType="CommerzBankWS" wpc:transactionalBehavior="participates"/>
  <invoke inputVariable ="creditRequest" name="Credit" operation="credit"
    outputVariable="creditReturn" partnerLink="toBank"
    portType="DeutscheBankWS" wpc:transactionalBehavior="participates"/>
    <wpc:adminTask name="tel:TransferProcessTask1"/>
  </invoke>
  <reply operation="op1" partnerLink="TransferProcess" portType="TransferPT">
   <wpc:input>
    <wpc:parameter name="output1" variable="Input1"/>
   </wpc:input>
  </reply>
  </sequence>
</process>
```

Listing 7.3: A BPEL process with transactional extensions

7.3.3 Discussion

In the following, the shortcomings of the three approaches that were mentioned above are discussed with respect to requirement specification and requirement enforcement.

With respect to requirement specification, the BPEL implementations that were presented support to a large extent the expression of messaging-level requirements but they do that in a non-intuitive way.

Approaches that use policies such as Colombo and Oracle Web Service Manager do not allow to define the non-functional requirements directly on the BPEL activities. Instead, one has to define the requirements on the WSDL of partner Web Services in Colombo or on the partner Web Service in Oracle Web Service Manager. In addition, WSDL-based approaches such as Colombo do not allow to differentiate two messaging activities with the same partner link, port type, and operation attributes.

This problem of granularity also exists in approaches that use partner links to express non-functional requirements. That is, messaging activities that interact with the same partner cannot have different properties. A more straight-forward and fine-grained mechanism to express the non-functional requirements of BPEL activities is needed.

Approaches that introduce BPEL extensions to specify non-functional requirements break the portability of BPEL. In fact, process specifications that contain proprietary extensions become dependent on a specific BPEL engine and cannot be interpreted by other BPEL engines. In addition, as said earlier, extending BPEL with new constructs increases the language complexity and it is also against the principle of separation of concerns. For this reason, the proposal of Choreology [84] was rejected by the WS-BPEL technical committee.

In the context of requirement specification, it is important to separate the specification of the non-functional requirements from the process definition. By doing so, the same BPEL process can be deployed several times on different engines with different requirements. For example, in one deployment the BPEL process could use partner Web Services that run inside the organization. In such a case, security might not be an issue. In another deployment the same process can use external partner Web Services. In that case, it becomes necessary to address the security requirements of the process as part of the process deployment configuration.

With respect to enforcement, all BPEL implementations enforce the non-functional requirements of the process activities outside the process interpreter. They intercept the SOAP messages and modify or verify them by using some implementations of WS-* specifications (provided by a message handler, by a policy handler, or by an Enterprise Service Bus). That is, the enforcement of non-functional requirements is completely decoupled from the process interpreter in all BPEL implementations. Consequently, these implementations cannot enforce process-level requirements. To enforce such requirements, a tighter integration and coordination between the process execution and the WS-* based handlers is needed.

7.4   Overview of the Framework

BPEL allows building composite Web Services by gluing together other Web Services in a similar way to Component-Based Software Development [178], which allows building applications by assembling software components. Inspired by this analogy, the approach taken by enterprise component models such as Enterprise Java Beans (EJB) [67] and Corba Component Model (CCM) [89] for the specification and enforcement of non-functional properties was studied.

Enterprise component models introduce a *deployment descriptor* to specify declaratively the non-functional properties of the application and a *container* to enforce those properties. The container is the runtime environment of the component-based application. The client never interacts directly with the native component implementation, but rather via the container, which calls infrastructural services to enforce the non-functional requirements of the application. The container concept allows component developers to focus on the business logic and takes over technical concerns such as security and persistence.

Enterprise component models introduce different roles in software development: the *component provider* implements software components using some programming language, the *application assembler* composes applications from components that may originate from other companies (off-the-shelf), the *application deployer* sets up a component-based application in a given runtime environment and configures its non-functional properties.

In analogy to enterprise component models, this chapter introduces a container framework to support the non-functional requirements of BPEL processes.

This framework has three main components as shown in Figure 7.1: the *deployment descriptor*, the *process container*, and the *middleware services*. These components will be explained in the following subsections.

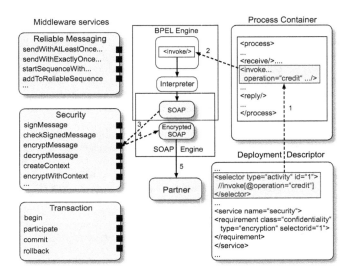

Figure 7.1: The process container framework

Figure 7.1 illustrates how the process container uses the middleware services to enforce the non-functional requirements of the process activities. In that figure, the container of the transfer process intercepts the execution of the *invoke* activity that calls the operation *credit* as specified in the deployment descriptor (arrow 1). Then, the container suspends that *invoke* activity (arrow 2) and calls the security service. The latter takes the SOAP message corresponding to the *invoke* activity in input (arrow 3), encrypts that message, and returns the encrypted message to the container (arrow 4). After that, the container resumes the suspended *invoke* activity, which sends the encrypted message instead of the original one (arrow 5).

The container framework introduces different roles in the development of Web Service compositions: the *programmer* implements a Web Service, the *composer* writes a BPEL process that composes existing Web Services, the *deployer* configures the non-functional properties of the BPEL process depending on the hosting engine, the process requirements, and the partner Web Services.

The components of the process container framework can be grouped based on whether they address the specification or the enforcement of the non-functional requirements in BPEL. The framework user need only to know about the components that are necessary for requirement specification.

118

7.4.1 Requirement specification

From the user perspective, the framework takes an XML-based deployment descriptor as input in addition to the BPEL process definition. The BPEL process defines the *functional logic* of the composition, whereas the deployment descriptor defines the *non-functional requirements* of the process activities in a declarative way.

The deployment descriptor specifies non-functional requirements such as which messaging activities need guaranteed delivery assurances, which activities are transactional, etc. In addition, the deployment descriptor specifies the parameters that are needed to enforce the non-functional requirements. For instance, if confidentiality support is required for some *invoke* activity, the deployment descriptor should specify the parameters that will be used by the container to encrypt and decrypt the messages corresponding to that activity.

For illustration, Listing 7.4 shows a deployment descriptor for the bank transfer process that was presented in Section 7.2.

The deployment descriptor consists mainly of activity *selectors* and *requirements* that are grouped according to the non-functional concern they belong to. The activity selectors are XPath expressions that identify a set of activities, which will be associated with some non-functional requirements. In Listing 7.4, the deployment descriptor defines three selectors (lines 2–12). The first two select the *invoke* activities that call the operations *credit* and *debit*. The third one selects the *sequence* activity *debit_credit*.

The deployment descriptor also contains one or more *service* elements, which group the requirements that belong to a specific middleware service. For example, the deployment descriptor shown in Listing 7.4 defines requirements on the middleware services for reliable messaging, security, and transaction.

Each requirement is specified using a *requirement* element. The necessary parameters for enforcing requirements are specified using the *parameter* element. The type of a requirement is uniquely defined by combining the values of the attributes *class* and *type* of the *requirement* element. For example, the requirement *req1* (lines 26–37) is an encryption requirement, which also specifies the necessary parameters such as encryption algorithm, transport key id, etc (lines 28–36). The attribute *selectorid* of the *requirement* element allows to associate the requirement with a selector, e.g., the requirement *req1* is associated to the selector that has the id 1 (defined in lines 6–8).

To make the framework more user-friendly, a graphical user interface tool has been developed. This tool allows the automatic generation of the deployment descriptor without writing the XML code manually. This tool can also load existing deployment descriptor files and allows the user to modify them and save them. The deployment descriptor graphical tool provides three views: one for defining selectors as shown in Figure 7.2, one for defining requirements as shown in Figure 7.3, and one for associating requirements with selectors.

```
 1  <bpel−dd>
 2   <selectors>
 3    <selector id="0" name="credit" type="activity">
 4    //invoke[@operation="credit"]
 5    </selector>
 6    <selector id="1" name="debit" type="activity">
 7    //invoke[@operation="debit"]
 8    </selector>
 9    <selector id="2" name="debit_credit" type="compoundActivity">
10    //sequence[@name="debit_credit"]
11    </selector>
12   </selectors>
13   <services>
14    <service name="reliablemessaging">
15     <requirements>
16      <requirement name="req0" class="semantics"
17                   type="exactlyOnce" selectorid="1"/>
18      <requirement name="req0" class="semantics"
19                   type="exactlyOnce" selectorid="0"/>
20     </requirements>
21    </service>
22    <service name="security">
23     <requirements>
24      <requirement name="req2" class="confidentiality"
25                   type="decryption" selectorid="1"/>
26      <requirement name="req1" class="confidentiality"
27                   type="encryption" selectorid="1">
28        <parameters>
29         <parameter name="symmetricEncAlgorithm">
30          xmlenc#tripledes−cbc</parameter>
31         <parameter name="keyEnc">
32          http://www.w3.org/2001/04/xmlenc#rsa−1_5</parameter>
33         <parameter name="transportKeyId">
34          16c73ab6−b892−458f−abf5−2f875f74882e</parameter>
35         <parameter name="keyIdentifierType">−1</parameter>
36        </parameters>
37      </requirement>
38     </requirements>
39    </service>
40    <service name="transaction">
41     <requirements>
42      <requirement name="req3" class="atomic"
43                   type="completion" selectorid="2"/>
44     </requirements>
45    </service>
46   </services>
47  </bpel−dd>
```

Listing 7.4: A deployment descriptor for the transfer process

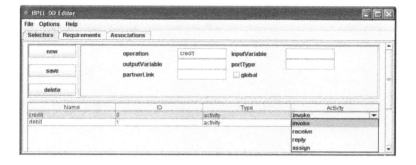

Figure 7.2: The selector view of the GUI tool

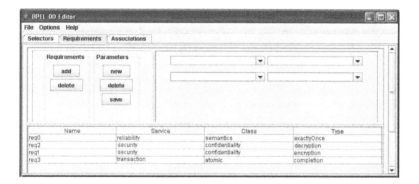

Figure 7.3: The requirement view of the GUI tool

7.4.2 Requirement enforcement

The *process container* and the *middleware services* are responsible for enforcing the non-functional requirements that are specified in the deployment descriptor. Both the container and the middleware services are concepts at the implementation level that the framework users do not have to know about.

The process container

BPEL processes are executed inside a process container, which intercepts the execution of certain activities at well-defined points in order to enforce the non-functional requirements of those activities.

To enforce messaging-level requirements, the container just needs to intercept one messaging activity. For example, to encrypt the request message of an *invoke* activity, the process container intercepts that activity at the point where the request message is created and encrypts it.

To enforce process-level requirements, the container needs to intercept the structured activity and its nested messaging activities. For example, to execute the *sequence* activity *debit_credit* as a transaction, the process container intercepts that activity and its children as follows.

1. When the *sequence* starts, the process container intercepts it and creates a coordination context for the new transaction.

2. When the nested *invoke* activities are executed the container intercepts them and enhances their request messages with a transaction header that contains the coordination context.

3. If a fault was thrown during the execution of the *sequence* activity, the process container rolls back the transaction.

4. When the *sequence* completes, the process container runs the 2-Phase-Commit protocol to decide on the outcome of the transaction.

For modularity reasons the container does not implement middleware functionality such as encrypting a message or creating a coordination context by itself. Instead, the container calls external middleware services, which provide that functionality.

The separation of container and middleware services makes the container light-weight. Moreover, it allows the middleware services to be replaced by other services that provide the same interface. With some appropriate container implementation techniques, it should be possible to add new middleware services to the framework easily.

The middleware services

The middleware services provide the necessary functionality to enforce the non-functional requirements of BPEL processes. Three middleware Web Services were implemented for security, reliable messaging, and transactions.

The security service allows to secure the SOAP messages of messaging activities, e.g., by adding authentication tokens to them, encrypting or signing them, etc. In addition, it supports the creation and cancellation of a secure conversation context as well as the use of that context for encrypting messages, signing messages, etc.

The reliable messaging service allows to send the SOAP messages of messaging activities with a guaranteed delivery assurance such as *exaclty-once*. In addition, it supports the ordered delivery of messages corresponding to messaging activities, even when these messages go to different partners.

The transaction service allows to create a new transaction, add a messaging activity to a transaction, start the 2-Phase-Commit protocol, and roll back a transaction.

7.5   Conclusion

This chapter presented several non-functional requirements of BPEL processes such as security, reliable messaging, and transactions. These requirements were classified into messaging-level requirements and process-level requirements.

After surveying a number of current BPEL engines w.r.t. their support for security, reliable messaging, and transactions, it became clear that process-level requirements such as secure conversations and multi-party ordered message delivery are not supported.

To support the process-level requirements, this chapter introduced a generic, modular, and user-friendly process container framework, which uses a deployment descriptor to specify the non-functional requirements declaratively. Moreover, the framework uses a process container and several middleware services to enforce those requirements.

This chapter presented the framework components at the conceptual level only. The next chapter will describe the implementation of the framework. The container is implemented by a set of AO4BPEL aspects that are generated automatically from the deployment descriptor using XSLT. The middleware services are implemented as Web Services by extending Open Source implementations of WS-* specifications. The middleware Web Services are called from the advice of container aspects to enforce the non-functional requirements of the activities.

Implementing the Process Container Framework

8.1 Introduction

The previous chapter presented a process container framework that supports the non-functional requirements of BPEL processes. This chapter[1] will present the implementation of that framework.

The process container is implemented as a light-weight and aspect-based container using a set of AO4BPEL aspects. With appropriate pointcuts, the container intercepts the execution of the process activities at well-defined points. At these points, the container uses appropriate advice to call the middleware services, which are implemented as Web Services.

The framework users do not have to write the container aspects manually. They define a deployment descriptor, from which the container aspects will be generated automatically using XSLT. This makes the process container framework user-friendly.

The process container does not provide the middleware functionality by itself. For modularity reasons, this functionality is provided by the middlware Web Services, which are not part of the BPEL engine. Hence, these services can be replaced easily by other ones and new services can be added.

This chapter will also present three middleware Web Services: for security, reliable messaging, and transactions. These middleware Web Services extend Open Source implementations of WS-Security, WS-ReliableMessaging, and WS-AtomicTransaction. The implementation of the reliable messaging Web Service is especially challenging because current WS-* specifications for reliable messaging do not support reliable messaging between more than two endpoints.

The remainder of this chapter is organized as follows. Section 8.2 presents the container implementation using AO4BPEL aspects and the automatic generation of the container aspects. Section 8.3 presents the security Web Service. Section 8.4 presents the reliable messaging Web Service. Section 8.5 presents

---

[1]Parts of this chapter were published in the paper *Reliable, Secure, and Transacted Web Service Compositions with AO4BPEL*, ECOWS 2006 [41].

the transaction Web Service. Section 8.6 discusses the limitations of the current implementation. Section 8.7 reports on related work. Section 8.8 concludes this chapter.

8.2 An AO4BPEL-based Container

This section shows the advantages that an aspect-based implementation of the process container brings. Moreover, it presents the different types of container aspects and gives some examples. In addition, it explains how the automatic generation of these aspects works.

8.2.1 Container aspects

The container aspects intercept the execution of the process activities at well-defined points using appropriate pointcuts, which capture either activity join points or internal join points. Then, these aspects call the middleware Web Services with appropriate advice, e.g., to create a secure conversation context, encrypt or sign a message, add a reliable messaging header to some message, start an atomic transaction, etc.

Examples

In the following, three examples of container aspects are presented. These aspects are generated from the deployment descriptor that was shown in Listing 7.4 in Chapter 7.

A security aspect Listing 8.1 shows a security aspect, which enforces the confidentiality requirement of the *invoke* activity that calls the operation *debit*. This aspect declares the security Web Service as partner (line 3). Moreover, it defines two variables (lines 6–7), which contain the input and output data of the *invoke* activity that calls the operation *encryptMessage* on the security Web Service (lines 37–39).

The pointcut of this aspect (lines 10–12) selects the *invoke* activity that calls the operation *debit*. It intercepts the point during the execution of that activity, where the SOAP request message has been created and it is about to be sent out. This join point is selected by using the advice type *before soapmessageout* together with a cross-layer pointcut.

The advice of this aspect is executed before reaching the internal join point that is selected by the pointcut. The advice activity is a *sequence* activity (lines 14–46) that contains an *assign* activity (lines 15–36) for setting the different input parameters of the call to the operation *encryptMessage*, an *invoke* activity for calling that operation on the security Web Service (lines 37–39), and another *assign* activity (lines 40–45) for overriding the request message of the join point activity with the encrypted message that is returned by the security Web Service.

In this advice, the request message of the join point activity (i.e., the *invoke* activity that calls the operation *debit*) is accessed by means of the AO4BPEL context collection variable *soapmessage* (line 17). The special context collection variable *newsoapmessage* is used to pass data from the middleware Web Service

125

```
 1  <aspect name=" debit_confidentiality_encryption ">
 2   <partnerLinks>
 3    <partnerLink name="securityService" partnerLinkType="SecServPLT" />
 4   </partnerLinks>
 5   <variables>
 6    <variable messageType="encryptMessageRequest" name="inMsg" />
 7    <variable messageType="encryptMessageResponse" name="SecMsg" />
 8   </variables>
 9   <pointcutandadvice>
10    <pointcut name="debit" type="internal" designator="soapmessageout">
11     //invoke[@operation="debit"]
12    </pointcut>
13    <advice type="before soapmessageout">
14     <sequence>
15      <assign>
16       <copy>
17        <from part="message" variable="soapmessage" />
18        <to part="msg" variable="inMsg" /></copy>
19       <copy>
20        <from expression="'http://www.w3.org/2001/04/xmlenc#tripledes−cbc'" />
21        <to part="symmetricEncAlgorithm" variable="inMsg" />
22       </copy>
23       <copy>
24        <from expression="'http://www.w3.org/2001/04/xmlenc#rsa−1_5'" />
25        <to part="keyEnc" variable="inMsg" />
26       </copy>
27       <copy>
28        <from expression="'16c73ab6−b892−458f−abf5−2f875f74882e'" />
29        <to part="transportKeyId" variable="inMsg" />
30       </copy>
31       <copy>
32        <from expression="'−1'" />
33        <to part="keyIdentifierType" variable="inMsg" />
34       </copy>
35       ...
36      </assign>
37      <invoke name="ssencryptInvoke" partner="securityService"
38          operation="encryptMessage" portType="SecurityServicePT"
39          inputVariable="inMsg" outputVariable="SecMsg" />
40      <assign>
41       <copy>
42        <from part="encryptMessageReturn" variable="SecMsg" />
43        <to part="newmessage" variable="newsoapmessage" />
44       </copy>
45      </assign>
46     </sequence>
47    </advice>
48   </pointcutandadvice>
49  </aspect>
```

Listing 8.1: A container aspect for encryption

to the process. In the encryption advice, this variable is used to override the SOAP message of the current join point activity by the encrypted message that was returned by the security Web Service (line 43). Consequently, when the join point activity executes after advice completion, it sends the encrypted message instead of the original one.

A reliable messaging aspect   Listing 8.2 shows a reliable messaging aspect, which enforces the exactly-once delivery assurance for the *invoke* activity that calls the operation *credit*.

This aspect declares one partner, which is the reliable messaging Web Service (line 3) and two variables (lines 6–7), which contain the input and output data for the *invoke* activity that calls the operation *sendWithExactlyOnceSemantics* on the reliable messaging Web Service (lines 29–31).

The pointcut of this aspect (lines 10–12) intercepts the *invoke* activity that calls the operation *credit* at the same internal join point as the encryption advice shown in Listing 8.1. This join point is captured by using the advice type *around soapmessageout* in conjunction with a cross-layer pointcut. The effect of the *around soapmessageout* advice is to execute the advice activity instead of the internal join point that is selected by the pointcut.

Unlike the encryption aspect, the usage of the *around soapmessageout* advice in this aspect is necessary because the reliable messaging Web Service must send the SOAP message on behalf of the process to ensure the reliable delivery. That is, the advice of the reliable messaging aspect must be executed instead of the internal join point during the execution of the *invoke* activity that calls the operation *credit*. This activity should complete without sending the SOAP message once more. In the encryption aspect, the advice just overrides the request message of the join point activity by an encrypted message. Sending the message is done by the *invoke* activity itself and not by the security Web Service.

The advice of the reliable messaging aspect (lines 13–39) consists of a *sequence* that contains three activities: an *assign* activity for setting the input parameters of the call to the reliable messaging Web Service (lines 15–28), an *invoke* activity for calling the operation *sendWithExactlyOnceSemantics* on the reliable messaging Web Service (lines 29–31), and another *assign* activity to pass the response message of the operation *credit* from the reliable messaging Web Service back to the process (lines 32–37). This is necessary because the reliable messaging Web Service, which has sent the request message of the operation *credit*, receives the response message of that operation and not the process.

In this advice, the request message of the join point activity is accessed by means of the AO4BPEL context collection variable *soapmessage* (line 17). The values of the input parameters of the operation *sendWithExactlyOnceSemantics* are accessed using the AO4BPEL reflective variable *ThisJPActivity* (lines 21 and 25). This operation takes two input parameters: a boolean indicating whether the message that will be sent corresponds to a one-way interaction and the endpoint of the partner that the message will be sent to. To pass the response message of the operation *credit* from the reliable messaging Web Service to the process, the context collection variable *newsoapmessage* is used (line 35).

```
1  <aspect name="credit_semantics_exactlyOnce">
2   <partnerLinks>
3    <partnerLink name="rmService" partnerLinkType="RMService" />
4   </partnerLinks>
5   <variables>
6    <variable messageType="sendExactlyOnceReq" name="inMsg" />
7    <variable messageType="sendExactlyOnceRes" name="outMsg" />
8   </variables>
9   <pointcutandadvice>
10   <pointcut name="credit" type="internal" designator="soapmessageout">
11    //invoke[@operation="credit"]
12   </pointcut>
13   <advice type="around soapmessageout">
14    <sequence>
15     <assign>
16      <copy>
17       <from part="message" variable="soapmessage" />
18       <to part="message" variable="inMsg" />
19      </copy>
20      <copy>
21       <from part="isInonly" variable="ThisJPActivity" />
22       <to part="inonly" variable="inMsg" />
23      </copy>
24      <copy>
25       <from part="partnerEndpoint" variable="ThisJPActivity" />
26       <to part="endpoint" variable="inMsg" />
27      </copy>
28     </assign>
29     <invoke operation="sendWithExactlyOnceSemantics" name="rmInvoke"
30             partner="rmService" portType="RMService"
31             inputVariable="inMsg" outputVariable="outMsg" />
32     <assign>
33      <copy>
34       <from part="sendExactlyOnceReturn" variable="outMsg" />
35       <to part="newmessage" variable="newsoapmessage" />
36      </copy>
37     </assign>
38    </sequence>
39   </advice>
40  </pointcutandadvice>
41 </aspect>
```

Listing 8.2: A container aspect for reliable messaging

A transaction aspect Listing 8.3 shows a container aspect for transaction rollback. This aspect declares one partner, which is the transaction Web Service (line 3) and two variables (lines 6–7), which contain the input and output data for the *invoke* activity that calls the operation *rollback* on the transaction Web Service (lines 23–25).

The pointcut of this aspect selects the *sequence* activity *debit_credit*. This pointcut is associated with an around advice (lines 13–32) that embeds that activity using the *proceed* activity (line 29) in a *scope* that has a compensation handler. When a fault occurs during the execution of the *sequence* activity, which is selected by the pointcut, the default fault handler calls implicitly that compensation handler. Consequently, the operation *rollback* is called on the transaction Web Service. The part *scopeid* of the reflective variable *ThisJPActivity* is used in the compensation handler as an identifier for the transaction (line 19).

```
 1  <aspect name="transaction_rollback">
 2   <partnerLinks>
 3    <partnerLink name="transactionService" partnerLinkType="txServicePLT" />
 4   </partnerLinks>
 5   <variables>
 6    <variable name="inMessage" messageType="rollbackRequest" />
 7    <variable name="outMessage" messageType="rollbackResponse" />
 8   </variables>
 9   <pointcutandadvice>
10   <pointcut name="transactivity">
11    /process//sequence[@name="debit_credit"]
12   </pointcut>
13   <advice type="around">
14    <scope>
15    <compensationHandler>
16    <sequence>
17     <assign>
18      <copy>
19       <from part="scopeid" variable="ThisJPActivity" />
20       <to part="id" variable="inMessage" />
21      </copy>
22     <assign>
23     <invoke name="trans_rollback" operation="rollback"
24            inputVariable="inMessage" outputVariable="outMessage"
25            partner="transactionService" portType="TXService" />
26    </sequence>
27    </compensationHandler>
28    <sequence>
29     <proceed/>
30    </sequence>
31    </scope>
32   </advice>
33   </pointcutandadvice>
34  </aspect>
```

Listing 8.3: A container aspect for transaction rollback

Execution order of container aspects

A process activity may be matched by more than one container aspect. For example, the *invoke* activity that calls the operation *debit* in the transfer process can be matched by pointcuts that are defined in container aspects for message encryption, message decryption, message sending with exactly-once semantics, and participation in a transaction.

When several container aspects match the same join point activity, the AO4BPEL engine executes them in the following order according to the advice type: *before → around → before soapmessageout → around soapmessageout → around soapmessagein → after soapmessagein → after*.

In the case of a synchronous *invoke* activity such as the one that calls the operation *debit*, the advice type based execution order ensures that the encryption aspect, which has the advice type *before soapmessageout* is executed before the decryption aspect, which has the advice type *after soapmessagein*.

The advice type based execution order also ensures that the encryption aspect and the transaction participation aspect are executed before the reliable messaging aspect, which sends the message of the join point activity with exactly-once semantics. The first two aspects have the advice type *before soapmessageout*, whereas the third has the advice type *around soapmessageout*.

If there are two container aspects that are executed at the same join point and they also have the same advice type, the *order* attribute of the *advice* element can be used to define the advice execution order.

For example, both the encryption aspect and the aspect for participating in a transaction use advice of the type *before soapmessageout*. If one wants to first add a transaction header to the request message of the *invoke* activity and then encrypt that message, one has to set the *order* attribute of the transaction advice to a lower value than the *order* attribute of the encryption advice. Thus, the transaction aspect will be executed before the encryption aspect. If one wants to add a transaction header to the encrypted message, one sets the values of the *order* attributes in reverse order.

8.2.2 Generation of container aspects

The container aspects are generated automatically from the deployment descriptor because the advice used for integrating the middleware Web Services follow well-defined patterns. For instance, for security, there are recurring patterns for adding authentication tokens to messages, signing messages, starting a secure conversation, etc. For reliable messaging, there are recurring patterns for sending a message with exactly-once semantics, creating a reliable messaging sequence, etc. For transactions, there are recurring patterns for starting a transaction, adding a messaging activity to a transaction, committing a transaction, etc. These recurring patterns are called *aspect types*.

Aspect types

There is at least one aspect type for each non-functional requirement that can be specified in the deployment descriptor. Tables 8.1, 8.2, and 8.3 show the aspect types that are generated automatically. The first column shows the aspect type, the second column shows where the aspect takes effect, the third column shows the advice execution order. The join point activities that can be selected by these aspects and their advice types are also shown in these tables.

Aspect type	Join point	Advice type
message encryption	invoke/reply	before soapmessageout
message decryption	invoke/receive	after soapmessagein
message signature	invoke/reply	before soapmessageout
checking message signature	invoke/receive	after soapmessagein
message authentication	invoke/reply	before soapmessageout
checking authentication token	invoke/receive	after soapmessagein
creating a conversation context	sequence	before
canceling a conversation context	sequence	after
message encryption with context	invoke/reply	before soapmessageout
message decryption with context	invoke/receive	after soapmessagein
message signature with context	invoke/reply	before soapmessageout
checking signed message with context	invoke/receive	after soapmessagein

Table 8.1: Aspect types for security

Aspect type	Join point	Advice type
sending a message exactly-once	invoke/reply	around soapmessageout
sending a message at-most-once	invoke/reply	around soapmessageout
sending a message at-least-once	invoke/reply	around soapmessageout
creating a new RM sequence	sequence	before
adding a message to an RM sequence	invoke/reply	around soapmessageout

Table 8.2: Aspect types for reliable messaging

Aspect type	Join point	Advice type
starting an atomic transaction	sequence/flow/scope	before
adding a message to a transaction	invoke/reply	before soapmessageout
committing a transaction	sequence/flow/scope	after
rolling back a transaction	sequence/flow	around

Table 8.3: Aspect types for transactions

Container aspects that correspond to the same aspect type have advice that follow well-defined patterns. They only vary in their pointcut expressions and in the values of the input parameters that are passed to the middleware Web Service. Because of this high similarity, aspects that have the same aspect type share a common skeleton. The variable parts of these aspects can be set using the data of the deployment descriptor.

For these reasons, the generation of container aspects is implemented as a transformation of some parts of the deployment descriptor into AO4BPEL aspects. The generation instructions for each aspect type are specified in an *aspect template*, which is implemented by an XSLT style sheet. That is, there is an XSLT style sheet for each requirement type that can be specified in the deployment descriptor.

The generation process is illustrated in Figure 8.1. The aspect generator tool takes the deployment descriptor as input, looks for XSLT style sheets in a predefined directory, and then runs each of them against the deployment descriptor. If a style sheet finds a matching requirement type in the deployment descriptor, it generates one or more container aspects.

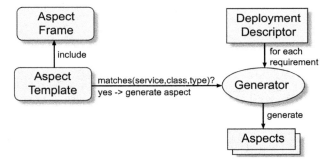

Figure 8.1: Aspect generation

The common parts of the style sheets of a given middleware concern are factored out into an *aspect frame*, which is included in each style sheet. For instance, there is an aspect frame for all security aspects. This frame emits parts that are shared by all security aspects such as the partner link to the security Web Service.

The specific parts of each aspect are defined in each XSLT style sheet using templates that are called by the aspect frame to generate the variable parts of the aspect. This approach is necessary because the advice code that copies the input parameters in an encryption advice for instance is different from the advice code that copies the input parameters in a message signing advice. Consequently, each aspect template must define its own template for copying input parameters and the latter is called from the shared aspect frame for security.

Listing 8.4 shows the aspect template for generating message encryption aspects. This template configures the security aspect frame to match the message encryption requirement type by setting the variables *serviceName* (line 3), *reqClass*(line 8), and *reqType* (lines 9) to the triple (*security, confidentiality, encryption*). This aspect template includes the security aspect frame (line 13) and defines a template (lines 14–35) for generating the BPEL code that sets the input and output parameters of the call to the security Web Service in the advice of the encryption aspect.

```
1  <xsl: stylesheet  xmlns: xsl =" http://www.w3.org/1999/XSL/Transform"...>
2   <xsl: variable  name=" partnerName" select=" 'securityService'" />
3   <xsl:variable name="serviceName" select="'security '"/>
4   <xsl: variable  name=" partnerLinkType" select=" 'SecurityServicePLT'" />
5   <xsl: variable  name=" inputMessageType" select=" 'encryptMessageRequest'" />
6   <xsl: variable  name=" outputMessageType" select=" 'encryptMessageResponse'" />
7   <xsl: variable  name=" serviceOperationName" select=" 'encryptMessage'"  />
8   <xsl:variable name="reqClass" select="'confidentiality'"/>
9   <xsl:variable name="reqType" select="'encryption'"/>
10  <xsl: variable  name=" inputMessagePartToCopyIn" select=" 'msg'" />
11  <xsl: variable  name=" responsePartToCopy" select=" 'encryptMessageReturn'" />
12  <xsl: variable  name=" aspectAdviceType" select=" 'before soapmessageout'" />
13  <xsl:include href="aspectframes/securityaspectframe.xsl"/>
14  <xsl:template name=" copyParameters" >
15   <xsl: call −template name=" copyParameter" >
16    <xsl:with−param name=" parametername" select=" 'key'"  />
17   </xsl: call −template>
18   <xsl: call −template name=" copyParameterWithDefaultValue" >
19    <xsl:with−param name=" parametername" select=" 'symmetricEncAlgorithm'"  />
20   <xsl:with−param name=" default−value"
21             select =" 'http://www.w3.org/2001/04/xmlenc#tripledes−cbc'" />
22   </xsl: call −template>
23   <xsl: call −template name=" copyParameterWithDefaultValue" >
24    <xsl:with−param name=" parametername" select=" 'keyEnc'"  />
25   <xsl:with−param name=" default−value"
26             select =" 'http://www.w3.org/2001/04/xmlenc#rsa−1_5'" />
27   </xsl: call −template>
28   <xsl: call −template name=" copyParameter" >
29    <xsl:with−param name=" parametername" select=" 'transportKeyId'"  />
30   </xsl: call −template>
31   <xsl: call −template name=" copyParameterWithDefaultValue" >
32    <xsl:with−param name=" parametername" select=" 'keyIdentifierType'"  />
33   <xsl:with−param name=" default−value" select="'−1'"  />
34   </xsl: call −template>
35  </xsl:template>
36 </xsl: stylesheet >
```

Listing 8.4: Aspect template for message encryption

Listing 8.5 shows an excerpt of the security aspect frame. This frame uses the variables that are defined in the aspect template that includes it. The first template (lines 2–6) is triggered by the element *services* of the deployment descriptor. For each *requirement* element, this template calls a second template (lines 7–45), which matches only when the values of the attributes *class* and *type* of the requirement element match those defined by the including aspect template. In such a case, an aspect will be generated provided that a non empty selector is associated with the requirement (line 9).

```
1   <xsl: stylesheet  xmlns: xsl ="http://www.w3.org/1999/XSL/Transform"...>
2   <xsl:template match="dd:services">
3    <!-- generate security aspect-->
4    <xsl:apply-templates select="dd:service[@name=$serviceName]//dd:requirement
5    [@class=$reqClass and @type=$reqType]" />
6   </xsl:template>
7   <xsl:template match="dd:requirement[@class=$reqClass and @type=$reqType]">
8    <xsl: variable  name="selectorid" select ="@selectorid" />
9    <xsl: if  test ="//dd:selector[@id=$selectorid]">
10   <xsl:text  disable -output-escaping="yes"><aspect name="
11   <xsl:value-of select ="concat(
12   //dd: selector [@id=$selectorid]/@name,'_',@class ,'_', @type)" />">
13   </xsl:text>
14   <partnerLinks>
15    <partnerLink name="{$partnerName}" serviceLinkType="{$SLType}"/>
16   </partnerLinks>
17   <variables>
18    <variable name="inMsg" messageType="{$inMsgType}"/>
19    <variable name="SecMsg" messageType="{$outMsgType}"/>
20   </variables>
21   <pointcut name="{//dd:selector[@id=$selectorid]/@name}">
22    <xsl:value-of select ="//dd:selector[@id=$selectorid]" />
23   </pointcut>
24   <advice type="{$aspectAdviceType}">
25   <sequence>
26    <assign>
27     <copy>
28      <from variable="soapmessage" part="message"/>
29      <to variable ="inMsg" part="{$requestMsgPart}"/>
30     </copy>
31     <xsl: call -template name="copyParameters" />
32    </assign>
33    <invoke name= "{$serviceName}_{$serviceOpName}" partner="{$partnerName}"
34         portType="{$serviceName}" operation="{$serviceOpName}"
35         inputVariable ="inMsg" outputVariable="SecMsg" />
36   <assign>
37    <copy>
38     <from variable="SecMsg" part="{$responseMsgPart}"/>
39     <to variable ="newsoapmessage" part="newmessage"/>
40    </copy>
41   </assign>
42   </sequence>
43   </advice>
44   <xsl:text  disable -output-escaping="yes"></aspect></xsl:text>
45   </xsl:template>
46   <xsl:template name="copyParameter">
47   <xsl:param name="parametername" />
48   <copy>
49    <from expression="'{dd:parameters/dd:parameter[@name=$parametername]}'"/>
50    <to variable="inputMessage" part="{$parametername}" />
51   </copy>
52   </xsl:template>
53   <xsl:template name="copyParameterWithDefaultValue">
54    ...
55   </xsl:template>
56    ...
57   </xsl: stylesheet >                    134
```

Listing 8.5: Aspect frame for security aspects

The generation of the aspect code starts by emitting the *aspect* element (line 10). The partner and variable declarations are generated and set using the variables that are defined in the including aspect template (lines 14–20). The content of the *pointcut* element is set to the activity selector of the current requirement (lines 21–23).

After that, the advice code is generated (lines 24–43). The first *copy* statement of the *assign* activity that sets the input data of the call to the security Web Service is generated by the aspect frame (lines 27–30). The other *copy* statements are aspect type specific. Therefore, they are generated by the aspect template, which provides a template called *copyParameters* (lines 14–35). The latter calls recursively some templates of the aspect frame such as *copyParameter* (lines 46–52). The *invoke* activity that calls the security Web Service is generated by the aspect frame (lines 33–35) followed by an *assign* activity, which overrides the original SOAP message with the secured one (lines 36–41).

Integration with the AO4BPEL engine

The generation of container aspects is integrated with the process deployment tool of the AO4BPEL engine. The process deployment interface of the AO4BPEL engine was extended with an input field for the deployment descriptor file.

For example, to deploy the bank transfer process, the user specifies the BPEL file, the WSDL file of the composite Web Service (i.e., the transfer Web Service), and the deployment descriptor file as shown in Figure 8.2.

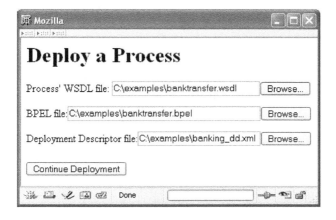

Figure 8.2: Deploying the transfer process

In the next step, the user specifies the WSDL files of the partner Web Services of the transfer process. Then, the process deployment is completed and the composite Web Service can serve client requests. Moreover, the container aspects are generated from the deployment descriptor and they are deployed automatically on the AO4BPEL engine.

135

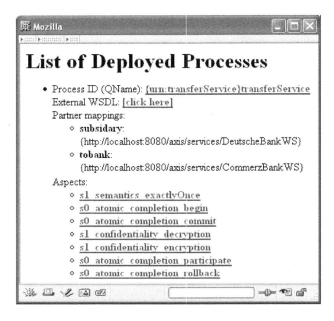

Figure 8.3: The process view of the AO4BPEL engine

The user can see the container aspects by switching to the process list view of the AO4BPEL engine. This view visualizes the aspects that affect each deployed process as shown in Figure 8.3. Alternatively, the user can switch to the aspect view, which shows all aspects that are currently deployed in the AO4BPEL engine. The user can modify or extend the container by undeploying some container aspects and/or deploying new ones.

8.2.3 Advantages of the aspect-based container

The aspect-based implementation of the process container results in a lightweight, extensible, open, and dynamically configurable container.

First, this implementation is modular because the container and the BPEL engine are two separate and independent components. Whilst the programmer has no access to the implementation of the BPEL engine, he has full access to the aspects that implement the process container. Consequently, one can easily understand and extend the container implementation. Moreover, the container itself is modular as each non-functional concern is implemented by separate aspects. In this way, the container logic that is responsible for security for instance can be understood and maintained independently of the container logic that is responsible for reliable messaging and transactions.

Second, the aspect-based container is extensible. That is, other non-functional concerns such as persistence or notification can be supported by writing appropriate AO4BPEL aspects. In particular, no changes to the BPEL engine are required for such an extension.

The aspect-based container does not only provide extensibility points but its entire implementation is exposed in the advice of the container aspects. Thus, the programmer can see how a certain requirement is enforced and which middleware Web Services are called at what points during the activity execution.

Third, the container can be modified at runtime according to the needs of the applications. The programmer can add or remove aspects to/from the container of a given process without redeploying that process. This feature is especially useful in the highly dynamic context of Web Service composition because the policies of some partner Web Service may change after the process deployment.

For example, the security policy of some partner Web Service can be updated to require X.509 tokens for authentication instead of username tokens. In that case, the container can be reconfigured by undeploying the authentication aspects that add username tokens to the message and deploying authentication aspects that add X.509 tokens. This reconfiguration can also be done at runtime because the AO4BPEL engine supports the dynamic composition of aspects and processes.

8.3 The Security Web Service

The security Web Service[2] provides operations to enforce the security requirements of BPEL activities.

8.3.1 The interface

The operations of the security Web Service are grouped in two port types: one for *secure messaging* (according to WS-Security) and one for *secure conversations* (according to WS-SecureConversation).

```
String addToken(String msg, String tokenid, String tokentype,
                boolean encrypted, String actor, int timetolive)
boolean checkToken(String msg, string tokentype)
String  signMessage(String msg, String algorithm, String name,
boolean useSingleCert, int keyIdType, String actor, int timetolive)
boolean checkSignature(String msg, String algorithm)
String  encryptMessage(String msg, String key, String symEncAlgorithm,
                String keyEnc, String transportKeyId, int keyIdType,
                String actor, int timetolive)
String  decryptMessage(String msg, String symEncAlgorithm)
```

Listing 8.6: The secure messaging port type

Secure messaging port type

Listing 8.6 shows the operations of the secure messaging port type. This port type provides operations for adding a user name or a binary token to a message, checking an authentication token, adding a signature to a message, checking

---

[2]Parts of this section were published in the Paper *Using Aspects for Security Engineering of Web Service Compositions*, ICWS 05 [37].

a signed message, encrypting a message, and decrypting a message. All these operations take the SOAP message as the first parameter. Some of them return a String representation of the SOAP message after processing it according to WS-Security. The operations *checkSignature* and *checkToken* return a boolean indicating whether the authentication token or the signature is valid.

The operation *addToken* takes several parameters in addition to the SOAP message. The parameter *tokenid* can be either a user name (in the case of user name tokens) or an identifier of an X.509 certificate (in the case of binary tokens). The parameter *tokentype* is a URI that uniquely identifies the type of the authentication token. The parameter *encrypted* specifies whether the password should be encrypted in case of a user name token. It is ignored in the case of an X.509 certificate.

The passwords for username tokens and for accessing a certificate from the keystore are not passed to the operation *addToken* as parameter. Instead, they are retrieved from the password store component of the security Web Service. In this way, the deployer does not have to specify sensitive information such as passwords in the deployment descriptor.

The parameters *actor* and *timetolive* appear in the signature of several operations of the security Web Service. The parameter *actor* defines which role is allowed to process the security header. The parameter *timetolive* defines a validity period for the security header.

The operation *checkToken* verifies whether the authentication token that is contained in the security header of a SOAP message is valid. The parameter *tokentype* allows the security Web Service to find out which handler should be used to validate the token (e.g., the X.509 handler). Without this parameter, the security Web Service would have to parse the entire SOAP message to find the corresponding handler.

The parameters of the operation *signMessage* have the following meaning: The parameter *algorithm* specifies the algorithm that should be used to sign the message. The parameter *name* identifies the key or certificate that should be used to generate the signature. The parameter *useSingleCert* specifies whether one certificate or a certificate chain should be used to generate the signature. The parameter *keyIndentifierType* determines how the key or certificate that is used to sign the message is referenced in the secured SOAP message.

In addition to the SOAP message, the operation *checkSignature* takes a parameter called *algorithm*, which allows the security Web Service to find the appropriate handler for verifying the signature without parsing the entire SOAP message.

Secure conversation port type

Listing 8.7 shows the operations of the secure conversation port type. This port type provides operations for establishing and canceling security contexts using the Security Token Service (STS) of a partner Web Service. Moreover, it includes operations for using a security context to encrypt messages, decrypt messages, sign messages, and check signed messages.

In these operations, the parameter *partner* is an identifier for a security context that is established between the client (e.g., the BPEL process) and the Web Service (e.g., the partner). The parameter *partnerSTSURI* is the URI of the Security Token Service (STS) of that Web Service. The security Web Service interacts with the STS to create and to cancel a security context.

```
boolean  createContext( String  partner ,  String  partnerSTSURI, String  keyType,
          String  keySize ,  String  signWith,  Sring  encryptWith,
          String  responseSignatureAlgo ,  String  responseEncryptionAlgo,
          String  requestSignatureAlgo ,  String  username)
boolean  cancelContext( String  partner ,  URI  partnerSTSURI)
String   signWithContext(String  partner ,  String  message,
                         boolean  useDK,  int  generation )
boolean  checkSignatureWithContext(String  message)
String   encryptWithContext(String  partner ,  String  message,
                            boolean  useDK,  int  generation )
String   decryptWithContext (String  message)
```

Listing 8.7: The secure conversation port type

The operation *createContext* takes several parameters that allow an advanced and flexible configuration of the security context that will be created. The parameters *keyType* and *keySize* respectively define the type and the length of keys in the security context that will be established. The parameters *signWith* and *encryptWith* specify the signature and the encryption algorithms that should be used for this context. The parameters *responseSignatureAlgo* and *responseEncryptionAlgo* specify whether the response of the Security Token Service should be signed or encrypted and what algorithms to use for that. If the request message to the Security Token Service has to be signed, the parameter *requestSignatureAlgo* should be set to the name of the algorithm for signing and the parameter *username* should specify the certificate that will be used for signing.

The operations *signWithContext* and *encryptWithContext* take a parameter *useDK*, which specifies whether derived keys should be used. These derived keys are generated from the keys that were exchanged during context creation. They make the interactions between the client and the Web Service more secure. The generation of derived keys can be done in several steps and the parameter *generation* specifies the step that should be used.

8.3.2 Usage by the process container

To secure a messaging activity, the process container intercepts the point where the SOAP message corresponding to that activity is received or is about to be sent out. In the AO4BPEL-based implementation of the container, this interception is done by the cross-layer pointcut designators *soapmessageout* and *soapmessagin*, which are used together with messaging activities. Then, the container calls the appropriate operation on the security Web Service (the secure messaging port type), which modifies or verifies the SOAP message according to WS-Security. In the AO4BPEL-based implementation of the container, this invocation is done by the advice activity.

In Figure 7.1, the container intercepts the execution of the *invoke* activity that calls the operation *credit* (arrow 2). Then, it calls the operation *encryptMessage* on the security Web Service to encrypt the corresponding SOAP message (arrow 3). The security Web Service returns the encrypted message to the BPEL engine (arrow 4), which resumes the suspended *invoke* activity. The latter sends the encrypted message instead of the original one (arrow 5).

Figure 8.4 illustrates how the container interacts with the security Web Service to execute a structured activity and its nested messaging activities using a secure conversation. In that figure, the process contains a *sequence* activity, which has two nested *invoke* activities that interact with the same partner.

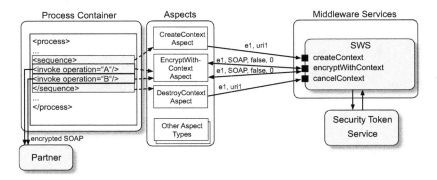

Figure 8.4: Interaction of the container and the security service

Figure 8.4 shows that three aspect types are involved in the execution of a structured activity using a secure conversation: the aspect type for creating a security context, the aspect type for destroying a context, and the aspect type for encrypting a message with a context (cf. Table 8.1).

When the *sequence* activity starts, a container aspect calls the operation *createContext* on the security Web Service. The parameter *e1* identifies the security context that should be established and the parameter *uri1* is the URI of the Security Token Service of the partner Web Service. Then, for each nested *invoke* activity, another container aspect calls the operation *encryptWithContext* on the security Web Service. This operation takes the context identifier *e1* as a parameter in addition to the SOAP message, a boolean indicating whether a derived key should be used, and the generation step. When the *sequence* completes, the process container calls the operation *cancelContext* to remove the context *e1*.

8.3.3 The implementation

The security Web Service consists of three main components:

- The *security manager* is the central component of the security Web Service. It manages the different handlers and stores that are available.

- The *stores* contain sensitive security information of a given type. There is a store for passwords, a store for keys and certificates, and a store for security contexts.

- The *handlers* provide the core functionality of the security Web Service. For example, there is a handler for message encryption, a handler for message signature, a handler for user name tokens, etc. Through a configuration file, new handlers can be added easily to the security Web Service.

The implementation of the security Web Service is based on Apache WSS4J [8], which is an Open Source implementation of WS-Security. WSS4J contains the necessary interfaces for WS-Trust and WS-Conversation but it does not provide any implementation of these interfaces.

To secure SOAP messages according to WS-Security, the handlers of the security Web Service use methods of WSS4J, e.g., to encrypt or to sign messages. The implementation of the secure messaging port type with WSS4J was straightforward.

To support secure conversations, it was necessary to implement a conversation handler to tackle tasks such as context creation, context cancellation, encryption with context, etc. That is, the interfaces that WSS4J provides for trust and secure conversation had to be implemented. In addition, it was necessary to implement an Axis handler, which should be deployed at the partner side. This handler processes the messages that were secured by the container aspects using the secure conversation port type. The secure conversation port type is implemented as follows.

When the operation *createContext* is called, the security Web Service stores the parameters of that operation in a *secureContextStore* that is indexed by the context identifier. Then, the security Web Service uses the secure conversation handler to send a request to the Security Token Service (STS) of the partner Web Service. If the STS can create a security context, it returns a positive response that contains information about the created context and a unique context identifier. The security Web Service stores this context information for later use in the *secureContextStore*.

When the operation *signWithContext* or *encryptWithContext* is called, the security Web Service retrieves the context information from the *secureContextStore* using the parameter *partner*, which identifies the secure conversation context. Then, it uses the algorithms and keys of that context together with the encryption and signature methods of WSS4J to perform the necessary functionality.

When the operation *cancelContext* is called, the secure conversation handler sends a request message to the Security Token Service of the partner to destroy the security context. Once the partner confirms that the context was deleted, the security Web Service removes the corresponding entry from the *secureContextStore*.

8.4 The Reliable Messaging Web Service

The reliable messaging Web Service[3] provides operations to support the reliable messaging requirements of the process activities, as shown in Listing 8.8.

8.4.1 The interface

The first three operations in the interface of this Web Service send a SOAP message with a certain delivery assurance. They take three input parameters: the SOAP message, the endpoint reference of the partner, and a boolean indicating whether the messaging activity is a one-way or a request-response interaction. To ensure the required delivery assurance, the SOAP message is sent by the reliable messaging Web Service and not by the client.

```
String sendWithExactlyOnceSemantics(
              String message, String endpoint, boolean inonly)
String sendWithAtMostOnceSemantics(
              String message, String endpoint, boolean inonly)
String sendWithAtLeastOnceSemantics(
              String message, String endpoint, boolean inonly)

boolean startNewSequenceWithExactlyOnce(
              String [] end points, boolean [] inonly, String seqId)
boolean startNewSequenceWithAtLeastOnce(
              String [] end points, boolean [] inonly, String seqId)
boolean startNewSequenceWithAtMostOnce(
              String [] end points, boolean [] inonly, String seqId)

String addToReliableSequence(String message, String seqId)
```

Listing 8.8: The interface of the reliable messaging Web Service

The subsequent three operations start a multi-party reliable messaging sequence with a certain delivery assurance. These operations support the ordered delivery of messages to more than one endpoint. They take the following parameters: an array with the partner endpoints (i.e., the partners that are used by the messaging activities), an array of booleans indicating the message exchange pattern of each messaging activity, and a string identifier for the multi-party reliable messaging sequence that will be created.

The operation *addToReliableSequence* is used to add the SOAP message of a messaging activity to a previously created multi-party reliable messaging sequence. This operation takes two parameters: the SOAP message and the identifier of the reliable messaging sequence (previously created using one of the operations *startNewSequenceWith...*).

8.4.2 Usage by the process container

To enforce a certain delivery assurance for a messaging activity, the process container intercepts the internal join point where the SOAP request message corresponding to that activity is about to be sent out. Then, the process container passes that message to the reliable messaging Web Service by calling one

---

[3]This section is based on the Paper *Reliable Messaging for BPEL Processes*, ICWS 06 [42].

of the operations *sendWith*.... A container aspect with an *around soapmessage-out* advice is used to call the reliable messaging Web Service because the join point activity should not send the message once more.

Figure 8.5 illustrates how the process container interacts with the reliable messaging Web Service to enforce the requirements of structured BPEL activities. In this figure, a *sequence* activity contains two one-way *invoke* activities for interacting with two different partners. This figure shows that two aspect types are involved in the execution of a structured activity with multi-party ordered message delivery: the aspect type for starting a multi-party reliable messaging sequence with a certain assurance and the aspect type for adding a message to a multi-party reliable messaging sequence (cf. Table 8.2).

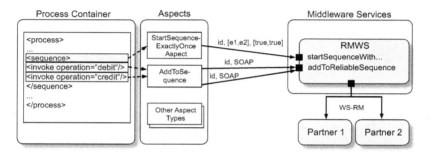

Figure 8.5: Interaction of the container and the reliable messaging service

To guarantee ordered message delivery for this *sequence*, a container aspect calls the operation *startNewSequenceWithExactlyOnce* when the *sequence* activity starts. This operation takes the following parameters: the sequence identifier *id*, the endpoints of the partners as an array [*e1,e2*], and an array of booleans indicating that both activities are one-way interactions.

Then, for each *invoke* activity, an appropriate container aspect calls the operation *addToReliableSequence* to send the SOAP message of that activity as part of the ordered reliable messaging sequence *id*. The partner endpoint and the message exchange pattern are not needed because they were already passed to the reliable messaging Web Service at sequence creation time.

After the last call to the operation *addToReliableSequence*, the reliable messaging Web Service terminates implicitly the multi-party sequence by using the length of the array parameters that were passed at sequence creation. Therefore, the process container does not have to call any operation on the reliable messaging Web Service for sequence termination.

8.4.3   The implementation

The reliable messaging Web Service is based on Apache Sandesha [7], which is an Open Source implementation of WS-RM [45].

The enforcement of a delivery assurance for a messaging activity using Sandesha is straightforward. In contrast, the enforcement of multi-party ordered message delivery [42] is more challenging because both WS-RM and WS-

Reliability do not support reliable messaging between more than two endpoints. In the following, the problems that arise when using WS-RM with more than two endpoints are discussed. To solve these problems, three approaches for multi-party reliable messaging are proposed and one of them is implemented in the reliable messaging Web Service.

Problems in using WS-RM with more than two endpoints

To illustrate the problems that arise when using WS-RM with more than two endpoints consider the following scenario: An endpoint A sends three messages 1,2,3 to two endpoints B and C. Message 1 and 3 should be delivered to the endpoint B and Message 2 should be delivered to the endpoint C.

The messages should be received by B and C in the order in which they were sent by A. That is, first Message 1 is received by B, then Message 2 is received by C, and finally Message 3 is received by B. When using WS-RM for this scenario, the following problems arise:

- *Problem 1: Sequence creation and identification*
  The first problem is that the sequence creation message is sent only to one receiver in WS-RM. In the current scenario, endpoint C has to be informed about the sequence creation (in addition to B). Otherwise, C will not be able to handle the messages of that sequence.

  Even if both B and C receive sequence creation messages, there is still another problem with the *sequence identifier*. B and C may produce different sequence identifiers, which leads to an ambiguous identification of the sequence. Hence, the sender would not know which identifier to use to relate a message to a certain reliable messaging sequence.

- *Problem 2: Message numbering*
  Assume that Problem 1 is solved and that Message 2 arrives to C. Having the first ever arriving message at C be numbered 2 breaks the following invariant of WS-RM: *The RM Source MUST assign each reliable message a sequence number [...], beginning at 1 and increasing by exactly 1 for each subsequent reliable message* [45]. The constraint of incrementing message numbers by one is also broken when Message 3 is sent after Message 1 to endpoint B.

- *Problem 3: Missing acknowledgment information*
  When endpoint B receives Message 3, it can acknowledge message reception but it does not know whether it can move that message from the buffer to the application because it is waiting for Message 2, which will never arrive.

- *Problem 4: Sequence termination*
  Sequence termination messages should also be sent to all receivers (i.e., B and C) and not only to one receiver, as WS-RM does. This is necessary to ensure that all receivers free the resources that are allocated to the reliable messaging sequence.

144

In the following, three approaches are proposed for supporting multi-party reliable messaging. Then, these approaches will be compared.

Approach 1: Extending the WS-RM protocol In this approach, minimal extensions are introduced to the protocol of WS-RM to solve the four problems mentioned earlier. These extensions require new logic at the sender and the receiver.

To solve Problem 1, the sequence creation message must be sent to all receivers that take part in the ordered sequence. In WS-RM, the sequence identifier is generally defined by the receiver but the sender could also propose an identifier by using the element `/CreateSequence/Offer/Identifier` in the sequence creation message. Once all receivers accept the identifier proposed by the sender Problem 1 is solved.

However, the identifier suggested by the sender may be already in use by one of the receivers. Consequently, that receiver refuses the proposal and returns another sequence identifier in its `CreateSequenceResponse` message. To handle this problem, the WS-RM protocol could be extended as follows: The sender waits for the `CreateSequenceResponse` messages from all receivers. If one of them contains a sequence identifier that is different from the one proposed by the sender, the latter transmits a `TerminateSequence` message to all receivers. Then, the sender restarts sequence creation by sending a `CreateSequence` message with a different sequence identifier. This process is repeated until all receivers agree on the sequence identifier. To solve Problem 2, the numbering invariant of WS-RM should be relaxed.

Next, some extensions to WS-RM are proposed to solve Problem 3. These extensions are explained using the example scenario, in which A sends three messages to B and C: Message 1 to B, Message 2 to C, and Message 3 to B.

Endpoint B receives Message 1 and 3. Once B receives Message 3 it acknowledges Message 1 and Message 3 because the latter contains the *lastMessage* element. B is not allowed to deliver Message 3 to the application as long as Message 2 is not received. Therefore, B must put Message 3 into the buffer to keep the messages in order. As Message 2 will be sent to C, B needs to know that that message has been delivered successfully to C. However, since B is not aware of C, B will never get this information. The only party which knows whether a certain message has been acknowledged is the sender.

To solve Problem 3 from the perspective of B, the sender must forward the acknowledgment received from C (for Message 2, with *ackRequested* element) to B. After receiving that acknowledgment, B can deliver Message 3 to the application because it knows that Message 2 was successfully delivered. The acknowledgment forward message contains an additional *ackRequested* element, which forces receiver B to acknowledge all received messages (1,3, and 2). Thus, the sender can be sure that the acknowledgment forward is received by B.

From the view point of C the only message that arrives is Message 2. As this message contains a *lastMessage* element, C acknowledges it immediately and holds it in the buffer waiting for Message 1 that will never arrive. Here again the sender must forward the acknowledgment of Message 1 received from B to C with an additional *ackRequested* element. Once C receives this message, it can deliver Message 2 to the application. C also acknowledges all yet received messages. Thus, the sender can be sure that the acknowledgment forward message is received by C.

In this extended version of WS-RM, if the sender waits passively for the acknowledgment messages from the receivers then the whole sequence would be blocked because the acknowledgment messages are usually sent after the last message is received. The timing of acknowledgment messages depends also on the configuration of the receivers. To improve performance, the sender should pull acknowledgments from the receiver actively using the element *ackRequested*.

To solve Problem 4, the sender sends the sequence termination message to all receivers. The sender should only send this message after it receives acknowledgments for all messages of the multi-party reliable messaging sequence.

In Figure 8.6 the complete message exchange for the extended WS-RM protocol is shown. The sender suggests the sequence identifier 123. The sequence creation message is sent to both endpoints B and C. Then the sequence messages are sent with Message 3 and Message 2 containing the *lastMessage* element. When these messages are received, B and C acknowledge all received messages. The sender forwards the acknowledgment of Message 1 and 3 to C and gets an acknowledgment of Message 1, 2 and 3. Then the sender forwards the acknowledgment of Message 1, 2 and 3 to B, which acknowledges all messages again. Finally, A sends a *TerminateSequence* message to B and C.

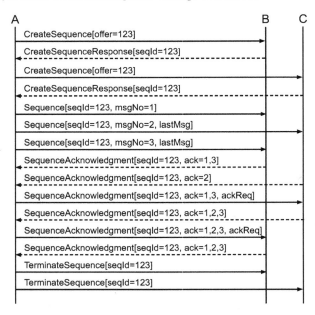

Figure 8.6: The extended reliable messaging protocol

Approach 2: Implementing the extension at the sender As explained earlier, the main problem of reliable messaging with multiple receivers is the lack of acknowledgment information. That is, the receivers cannot process the messages instantly because they do not know if the preceding messages have been already delivered to the other endpoints.

In WS-RM, the only party that is aware of this information is the sender, which must coordinate the delivery of acknowledgment messages. This is done by forwarding these messages in Approach 1.

In Approach 2, the main idea is that the sender splits a big sequence containing messages going to different endpoints into *subsequences*, so that each subsequence contains continuously numbered messages and involves two parties: the sender and exactly one receiver. In this approach, a subsequence can be sent using an ordinary WS-RM sequence because it involves two parties only. Moreover, the subsequences are handled one after the other.

The sender needs to be extended with additional logic to split a sequence into subsequences. It must wait for the completion of one subsequence before it starts processing the next one. Therefore, the sender must buffer the remaining messages of the sequence.

To understand the splitting mechanism, consider a scenario with the endpoints A, B, C and six messages M1 to M6. The required delivery order is as follows: M1, M2, M5 to A, M3 to B, and M4 and M6 to C. The sender would split the parent sequence into five subsequences: SS1 (M1,M2) delivered to A, SS2 (M3) delivered to B, SS3 (M4) to C, SS4 (M5) to A, and SS5 (M6) to C.

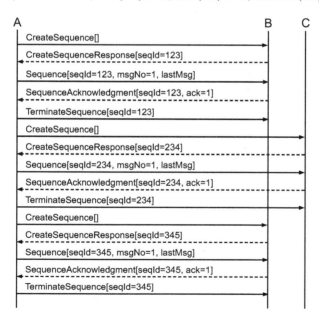

Figure 8.7: Extending the sender

Figure 8.7 depicts the simple scenario that was mentioned above with Message 1 and 3 to B and Message 2 to C. This figure shows that there are three subsequences. Each of them is handled with an ordinary WS-RM sequence that is started when the previous sequence completes successfully.

The advantage of this approach is that the extension is implemented completely and only at the sender, which has the additional task of splitting the sequence into subsequences. Each subsequence can be delivered by the ordinary WS-RM protocol, because it involves exactly two endpoints. Moreover, the configuration of the partner Web Services must not be changed because they already support the WS-RM protocol.

Approach 3: Defining an entirely new protocol This approach defines a new protocol, which is optimized for multi-party reliable messaging.

For solving Problem 1, the concept of *implicit sequence creation* of WS-Reliability can be reused. The sender specifies a unique sequence identifier in the first application message. When this message arrives, the receiver either creates a new sequence or returns a fault if the identifier is already in use.

Problem 2 can be solved by using the idea of subsequences as explained in Approach 2. A multi-party reliable sequence is decomposed into continuously numbered *subsequences* that target exactly one receiver. Moreover, in this new protocol, each message carries a subsequence number in addition to the sequence number. Thus, a message is encoded as a triple (*SequenceNumber, SubsequenceNumber, MessageNumber*), whereby the message number is unique only in the context of its sequence number and its subsequence number.

For illustration, reconsider the simple scenario with the three endpoints A, B, and C. In approach 3, the messages of this example would be numbered as follows: Message 1 (S1, SS1, M1), Message 2 (S1, SS2, M1), Message 3 (S1, SS3, M1).

In addition, the new protocol defines a new *lastSubMsg* element that the sender should embed in the last message of a subsequence. This element has a similar semantics to the element *lastMessage* of WS-RM. When the receiver gets a message with this new element, it acknowledges all received messages of the subsequence.

To solve Problem 3, the acknowledgment strategy can be taken either from Approach 1 or from Approach 2.

First, the acknowledgment forward idea of Approach 1 can be integrated in the new protocol by using a new *ackForward* message instead of the sequence acknowledgment message of WS-RM. The *ackForwad* message contains all already acknowledged subsequence numbers and it will be forwarded by the sender to all other receivers. The resulting message exchange for the simple example of the three messages and the endpoints A, B, and C is shown in Figure 8.8.

Second, one could use the idea of Approach 2 to solve Problem 3. That is, the sender processes each subsequence completely before proceeding with the next one. In this way, each receiver can be sure that the preceding subsequences were delivered successfully. Consequently, it can process all incoming messages immediately. The advantage of this alternative is that message acknowledgment forward is not needed. The disadvantage of this approach is that the messages must be buffered at the sender until the previous subsequence is acknowledged. This derivate of Approach 3 is called the blocking variant as opposed to the other

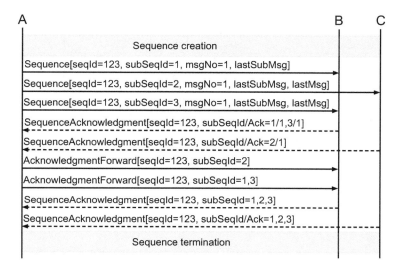

Figure 8.8: The entirely new reliable messaging protocol (non-blocking)

non-blocking variant that was presented in the last paragraph. The message exchanges for the simple scenario using the blocking variant of Approach 3 are shown in Figure 8.9.

Problem 4 can be solved as in WS-Reliability using *implicit sequence termination*. The receiver terminates the sequence when the message with the *lastMessage* element is received and all preceding messages have been received. As there is more than one receiver, the *lastMessage* element must be put in the last message that goes to each receiver.

Comparison Approach 3 is definitely the most complex solution but it has the advantage of providing a completely redesigned reliable messaging protocol that is optimized for multi-party conversations. In Approach 3, the usage of new constructs such as the *ackForward* message raises the understandability of the protocol. Moreover, mechanisms such as implicit sequence creation and termination improve the efficiency.

Instead of defining a completely new protocol, Approach 1 defines the necessary minimal extensions that make WS-RM support multi-party reliable messaging. Approach 1 requires new logic to be added to both the sender and the receiver.

Unlike Approach 1 and Approach 3, Approach 2 extends only the logic of the sender. As the WS-RM protocol is unchanged, no configuration changes are required for the partner Web Services that already support WS-RM. In fact, partner Web Services are typically provided by other parties that would not easily agree to change their configuration. Another advantage of Approach 2 is

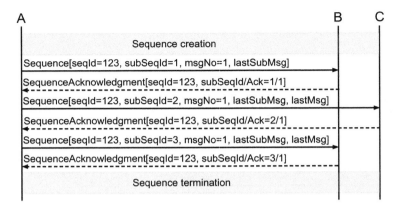

Figure 8.9: The entirely new reliable messaging protocol (blocking)

that it can be easily implemented by reusing existing implementations of WS-RM. For these reasons, the reliable messaging Web Service uses this approach to support multi-party reliable messaging.

Implementing the reliable messaging Web Service

The reliable messaging Web Service is based on Approach 2. In the following some details on the implementation of the different operations of that Web Service are given.

When the container calls the operation *startNewSequenceWith...* to start a reliable multi-party sequence, the reliable messaging Web Service stores the information about the endpoint and message exchange pattern of each messaging activity in a map with the sequence identifier parameter as key.

When the operation *addToReliableSequence* is called, the reliable messaging Web Service loads the context for the multi-party sequence using the sequence identifier. This context contains the number of the current message, which is used to retrieve the corresponding message exchange pattern, the partner endpoint, and the reliable messaging context provided by Sandesha.

If the current message exchange pattern differs from that of the next call (which is a limitation of Sandesha), or the next endpoint differs from that of the current call (which is a limitation of WS-RM), the reliable messaging Web Service marks the current message as being the last of a subsequence and terminates the reliable messaging context of Sandesha.

If the current message is not the last of the context[4], a new reliable messaging sequence is established and it is added to the context. If the current message is the last of the whole sequence, the current reliable messaging sequence is terminated and the context is removed from the map.

---

[4]This can be determined by comparing the current message number with the length of the endpoint array.

8.5 The Transaction Web Service

The transaction Web Service[5] provides operations to enforce the transaction requirements of BPEL activities.

8.5.1 The interface

The transaction Web Service provides a port type for *atomic transactions* [139] as shown in Listing 8.9.

```
boolean begin( String transactionID )
String participate ( String transactionID , String soapMsg)
boolean commit(String transactionID )
void rollback ( String transactionID )
```

Listing 8.9: The atomic transaction port type

The operation *begin* starts a new transaction and creates a new coordination context as defined in WS-Coordination [65]. This operation takes a parameter *transactionID* that is used to relate messaging activities to the created transaction. The returned boolean signals if the creation of the transaction succeeded.

The operation *participate* allows a messaging activity to participate in a previously created transaction. This operation takes the transaction identifier and the SOAP message of the messaging activity as input parameters. It returns the SOAP message after enhancing it with a transaction header that includes the coordination context.

The operation *commit* runs the completion protocol of WS-AtomicTransaction to commit the transaction that is passed as parameter. The operation *rollback* rolls back the transaction.

8.5.2 Usage by the process container

To enforce the transactional requirements of a structured activity, the process container intercepts the start and termination of that activity as well as the execution of its nested messaging activities. At these points, the container calls appropriate operations on the transaction Web Service.

Figure 8.10 illustrates the interaction of the process container and the transaction Web Service to execute the *sequence* activity *debit_credit* as an atomic transaction.

Four aspect types are involved in the execution of this *sequence* activity as an atomic transaction: the aspect type for creating a transaction, the aspect type for adding a message to a transaction, the aspect type for transaction commit, and the aspect type for transaction roll back (cf. Table 8.3).

When the *sequence* activity starts, the begin transaction aspect calls the operation *begin* on the transaction Web Service and uses the name of the parent scope (the parameter id) of that *sequence* as a transaction identifier.

Then, for each *invoke* activity, a container aspect calls the operation *participate* and passes the SOAP message of each activity as parameter in addition

---

[5]This section is based on the Paper *Transactional BPEL Processes with AO4BPEL Aspects*, ECWOS 07 [43].

151

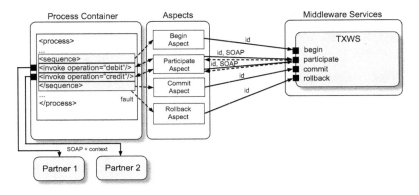

Figure 8.10: Interaction of the container and the transaction service

to the transaction identifier. The transaction Web Service enhances that message with a transaction header, which includes the coordination context of the transaction that has the identifier *id*.

When the *sequence* activity completes, a commit aspect calls the operation *commit* on the transaction Web Service. Consequently, the *coordinator* of the atomic transaction initiates the 2-Phase-Commit protocol to decide on the outcome of the transaction.

When a fault is raised during the execution of a transactional activity (e.g., in the execution of the *invoke* activity that calls the operation *credit*), a container aspect catches that fault and calls the operation *rollback* on the transaction Web Service to undo the transaction (as shown in Listing 8.3).

8.5.3 The implementation

The transaction Web Service consists of two main components: the *coordination framework*, which implements WS-Coordination and WS-AtomicTransaction and the *transaction framework*, which manages the transactions internally.

Apache Kandula [10] is used for the coordination framework. It is an Open Source implementation of WS-Coordination and WS-AtomicTransaction on top of Axis. Kandula provides a set of Web Services such as the activation service, the registration service, and the coordinator. Apache Geronimo [9] is used for the transaction framework. Apache Geronimo implements the package *javax.transaction*.

When the operation *begin* is called, the transaction Web Service creates a transaction object using the transaction framework. Moreover, it creates a new distributed activity using the activation Web Service of Kandula. Then, it stores the coordination context returned by the activation service in the created transaction object, which is put into a map with the transaction identifier as key.

When the operation *participate* is called, the transaction Web Service retrieves the transaction object from the map. Moreover, it enhances the SOAP message parameter with the coordination context of that transaction.

When the partner Web Service receives the enhanced SOAP message, it registers as *participant* for Durable2PC at the registration service. The latter returns a reference to the coordinator.

When the operation *commit* is called, the transaction Web Service retrieves the transaction object and uses Kandula to register for the completion protocol. The registration service returns a reference to the coordinator, to which the transaction Web Service sends a commit message. Once the coordinator receives that message, it runs the 2-Phase-Commit protocol with all previously registered participants. After that, either all participants commit or the transaction is aborted. Finally, the transaction object is removed from the map so that the respective transaction identifier can be used by other transactions.

8.6 Limitations of the Current Implementation

Some activities may require support for more than one non-functional concern. For example, an *invoke* activity that requires confidentiality and exactly-once semantics could also participate in an atomic transaction. In such a case, a combined usage of the three middleware Web Services is necessary.

When transaction and security are combined, the security Web Service can be called either before (e.g., to send an encrypted message with a plain coordination context header) or after the transaction Web Service (e.g., to encrypt a message that was previously enhanced with a coordination context).

The other two combinations of reliable messaging with transaction or security are not supported in the current implementation because of problems that arise when Sandesha is used together with WSS4J or Kandula.

In fact, Sandesha and WSS4J cannot work together unless all messages of the WS-RM protocol have security headers, because the message handler of WSS4J discards all messages that do not have a security header. To solve this problem, sequence creation messages and acknowledgment messages should have security headers and not only the application messages. However, the protocol specific messages of WS-RM are not accessible to the process container, which can only intercept application messages.

Moreover, Sandesha and Kandula use WS-Addressing [26] handlers. Kandula requires these handlers not only at the Web Service side but also at the client side. When these handlers are added at the client side, Sandesha can no longer send the messages of the WS-RM protocol because this causes an error in the addressing handler. This problem is currently being addressed by the developers of Kandula and Sandesha.

Another limitation of the AO4BPEL container is that aspects can be only applied to application messages, i.e., it is not possible to use a container aspect to send messages of the transaction protocols in a reliable way for example. That is, the combination of transaction protocols with reliable messaging is not supported. The transaction Web Service cannot use the reliable messaging aspects because there is no possibility to define aspects on the middleware Web Services.

8.7 Related Work

This section first presents some research works that use aspects to modularize middleware services and to implement light-weight containers. Then, it reports on other works that address non-functional concerns in the context of Web Service compositions.

8.7.1 Works on light-weight containers

The process container is inspired by the Spring framework [116], which uses Aspect-Oriented Programming to provide J2EE services such as transaction management to plain old Java objects (so-called POJOs). Spring AOP uses method interception to insert custom behaviour before or after method invocations. Together with Java 1.5 annotations, Spring can be used to provide transaction support declaratively as the AO4BPEL process container framework does for BPEL processes.

In [75], an approach to the design of component middleware frameworks is presented. This approach, which is called Alice, combines Aspect-Oriented Programming and annotations. In Alice, business logic is implemented in POJO classes and the crosscutting middleware services are implemented using aspects.

The Java Aspect Components framework (JAC) [154] also uses aspects to modularize the implementation of middleware services such as persistence and transactions. The programmer works with POJOs and the middleware services of EJB are replaced by loosely coupled dynamically pluggable aspect components. JBoss AOP [28] is another aspect-based container framework, which provides an aspect library for supporting non-functional concerns such as security and transaction.

In [159], the container model is generalized to mobile computing environments, where applications join or leave the network spontaneously. Using dynamic AOP, a spontaneous container allows the nodes of a network to dynamically acquire support for non-functional concerns such as transactions, orthogonal persistence, logging, and access control.

The process container framework is different from the works mentioned above in several regards. First, the process container framework targets BPEL workflow processes whilst the works mentioned above target Java objects. Second, AO4BPEL container aspects intercept join points across the process layer and the SOAP messaging layer, rather than points in the execution of object-oriented Java programs. Third, the process container framework is tailored to the specific requirements of BPEL workflows and to the Web Service middleware, which operates on SOAP messages according to the WS-* specifications. Fourth, the whole AO4BPEL process container is a set of aspects and there is no kernel as in Alice or JAC. The BPEL engine itself can be seen as the kernel.

8.7.2 Works on non-functional concerns in BPEL

Colombo [60] is a light-weight platform for service-oriented applications, which supports transactional, reliable, and secure Web Service interactions. The messaging-level requirements are expressed indirectly by attaching policies to local copies of the WSDL files of partner Web Services. At deployment time, the policy component parses the policies that are attached to the different WS-DLs and configures a handler chain for each incoming or outgoing message.

As already said, Colombo supports the messaging-level requirements of BPEL activities. In a joint work with the group of the Colombo project, the author extended the Colombo platform with support for process-level requirements by attaching external policies to BPEL processes [33]. To enforce such requirements, the BPEL engine of Colombo was modified to notify the policy component about various events in the process execution.

In [179], an approach to transactions in the context of BPEL compositions is presented. This approach uses WS-Policy [115] and WS-PolicyAttachment [47] to specify the transactional requirements of scopes and partner links.

To enforce the transactional requirements of the coordinated scopes and partner links, the BPEL process, which is annotated with transaction policies, is compiled to Java using a special compiler. The complied Java code uses an implementation of WS-AtomicTransaction and WS-BusinessActivity to enforce the transaction requirements of the BPEL scope. Both atomic transactions and business activities are supported.

Whilst the purpose of the process container and the transaction Web Service is also to support transactions in BPEL processes, there are several differences between the AO4BPEL process container framework and the approach proposed in [179] with respect to requirement specification and requirement enforcement.

With respect to requirement specification, WS-Policy is too declarative and does not provide means to specify the necessary parameters for enforcing non-functional requirements such as security keys and certificates (*what* and not *how*), unlike the deployment descriptor of the AO4BPEL process container framework.

Moreover, when using the internal policy attachment mechanism of WS-PolicyAttachment as done in [179], one has to annotate each transactional activity in the BPEL process with an appropriate transactional policy using the WSDL extensibility attribute `wsp:PolicyRefs`. In contrast, the deployment descriptor uses XPath-based activity selectors, which eliminates the need to attach policies to BPEL activities in a point-wise fashion. Another advantage of the deployment descriptor over the internal policy attachment mechanism is the separation between the specification of the non-functional properties and the specification of the functional composition (i.e., the BPEL process).

With respect to requirement enforcement, a special compiler is used in [179] to generate a Java stub that contains the necessary calls to the transaction middleware. As a result, it is not possible to exchange the transaction middleware by another one or to integrate further middleware services such as security and reliable messaging without changing the implementation of the compiler. Such extensions are supported easily in the AO4BPEL container framework by writing appropriate aspects.

Moreover, with WS-Policy based approaches such as [179], the logic for enforcing the transaction requirements is hidden, e.g., a coordination context is implicitly created when a transactional scope starts. Thus, people who want to extend the container cannot do that because they do not understand the interaction of the BPEL interpreter with the middleware services. They also cannot understand the interactions and dependencies between the different middleware services, e.g., which service is called before another. In the AO4BPEL-based process container the logic for enforcing the non-functional requirements is available explicitly in container aspects.

In the context of security of BPEL processes, the work described in [30] presents a brokered architecture for security conscious Web Service composition. In that proposal, each Web Service describes its security constraints (using the WSDL extensibility mechanism) and capabilities (using the Security Markup Assertion Language (SAML)). Moreover, a security broker assigns specific Web Services to the activities of a BPEL process by matching the requirements and capabilities of the process with those of the partner Web Services. That work is concerned only with the specification of the security requirements of the process activities, but it is not concerned with the enforcement of those requirements, unlike the AO4BPEL process container framework. Moreover, process-level security requirements such as secure conversations and federations are not addressed in that work.

In [22], Berbner et. al. address other non-functional properties in Web Service composition such as cost, availability, and throughput. That work assumes that there is a set of alternative Web Services with similar functionality for each activity in the workflow process and that these Web Services have different QoS properties. It presents a heuristic-based approach to solve the QoS-aware Web Service composition problem, i.e., how to select Web Services so that the overall QoS requirements of the workflow process are satisfied.

8.8 Conclusion

This chapter presented a modular and extensible implementation of the process container using AO4BPEL aspects. In that implementation, container aspects are generated automatically from the deployment descriptor using XSLT.

Moreover, three middleware services for BPEL were presented. These services were implemented as Web Services to allow the AO4BPEL container aspects to call them. For each middleware Web Service, this chapter presented the interface, the mode of interaction with the process container, and some implementation details. For implementing the middleware Web Services, open-source implementations of WS-* specifications were reused and extended to support the process-level requirements.

Chapter 6 has shown that AO4BPEL aspects improve the modularity of BPEL processes and increase their flexibility. The current chapter has shown that AO4BPEL aspects support the process-level non-functional requirements of BPEL processes, which is an unsolved problem in all current BPEL implementations. The process container framework allows for secure, reliable, and transactional BPEL processes. Thus, this framework enables Web Service based *production workflows*.

The ultimate message of this chapter to BPEL implementors is: *engines that support AO4BPEL aspects provide not only modularity and flexibility but also support for security, reliable messaging, and transactions.*

CHAPTER 9

Implementing Business Rules with AO4BPEL

9.1 Introduction

This chapter[1] presents a second application of AO4BPEL in the context of business rules in BPEL processes.

Several business domains are inherently policy- and decision-intensive such as the finance and insurance sectors. In these domains, an important part of the business knowledge is available in the form of policies, recommendations, and preferences. Business rules are declarative statements capturing that kind of business knowledge.

When software applications are developed using object-oriented programming languages or process-oriented workflow languages such as BPEL, the business rules are embedded in the application code and they no longer exist explicitly as separate first-class entities. This poses several problems with respect to modularity and flexibility. First, the business rules are intertwined with the process business logic, which leads to complex processes that are hard to understand and to maintain. Second, the business rules cannot be reused across different processes. Reusability is, however, crucial especially for organization-wide business rules. Third, business rules cannot be changed independently of the business process although they are the more volatile part of the composition logic. Consequently, changing business rules involves expert programmers and cannot be done by business analysts.

To solve these problems, this chapter proposes a hybrid composition approach that separates the business rules from the business processes. In this approach, the core business logic is defined in the BPEL process, whereas decisions and policies are defined in well-modularized and separated business rules.

To implement this hybrid approach, one needs a business rule implementation technology, a workflow engine for executing the processes, and a technology for integrating the business rule implementation technology and the workflow

---

[1]This chapter is based on the paper *Hybrid Web Service Composition: Business Processes Meet Business Rules*, ICSOC 2004 [36].

157

engine. In this chapter, AO4BPEL aspects are used for implementing the business rules and the AO4BPEL engine is used as an integration technology for the business rules implementation (i.e., the AO4BPEL aspects) and the business process implementation (i.e, the BPEL process).

To the best of the author's knowledge, the work presented in this chapter is the first to address the problem of business rules in BPEL processes. One year after presenting this work [36], research proposals such as the work presented in [164] and industrial products such as Oracle BPEL Process Manager [148] adopted similar approaches. The Oracle BPEL Process Manager was integrated with the ILOG rule engine [111] and the process modeling tool ARIS was recently integrated with Corticon's business rules [109].

The remainder of this chapter is organized as follows. Section 9.2 defines business rules and introduces the Business Rules Approach. Section 9.3 highlights the problems that arise when business rules are embedded in BPEL processes. Section 9.4 presents a novel hybrid approach to Web Service composition and its implementation with AO4BPEL. Section 9.5 reports on related work and Section 9.6 concludes this chapter.

9.2 Business Rules

This section defines business rules and presents a classification schema for them. Then, the Business Rules Approach is introduced and its principles are explained.

9.2.1 Definition

According to the Business Rules Group, "a business rule is a statement that defines or constrains some aspect of the business. It is intended to assert business structure or to control the behavior of the business" [182]. Business rules are usually expressed either as *constraints* or in the form *if conditions then action*.

In the travel agency scenario used throughout this book, there are several business rules that need to be integrated into the different BPEL processes, for example:

- *R1: if no flight is found for the dates given in the client request, do not search for accommodation*

- *R2: if more than two persons travel together, the third one pays only half price*

A *business rule system* is a software system that puts special emphasis on the expression, management, and automation of the rules. According to [182], "a business rule system is an automated system in which the rules are separated logically and perhaps physically from the other parts of the application". Business rule systems focus on the separation of rule-based knowledge throughout the different phases of the software development cycle (analysis, design, implementation).

The *business rule engine* is the main part of a business rule system. It controls the selection and the activation of the business rules. The business rule engine consists of three components:

- The *knowledge base* contains declarative business rules in the form *if conditions then action*. It encapsulates the rule-based domain knowledge.

- The *working memory* is a store that contains the facts, on which the business rules are defined. It includes the application data that will be used to evaluate the rule conditions. The state of the working memory may change when a rule action is executed.

- The *inference engine* decides which rules are ready to fire by applying the rules of the knowledge base to the facts contained in the working memory. The *pattern matcher* is a component of the inference engine that matches rules with facts.

9.2.2 Classification

In lack of a standard classification for business rules, several classification proposals have emerged [182, 191, 192]. In [191], four kinds of business rules are distinguished:

- A *constraint* rule is a statement that expresses an unconditional circumstance that must be true or false, e.g., *a vacation request must specify a departure city and a destination city (R0)*.

- An *action enabler* rule is a statement that checks conditions and upon finding them true initiates some action, e.g., *if no flight is found for the dates given by the customer, do not look for accommodation (R1)*.

- A *computation* rule is a statement that checks a condition and when the result is true, provides an algorithm to calculate the value of a term, e.g., *if more than 2 persons travel together, the third pays only half price (R2)*.

- An *inference* rule is a statement that tests conditions and upon finding them true, establishes the truth of a new fact, e.g., *if a customer is a frequent customer, he gets a discount of 5 % (R3)*. This kind of rules is also known as deduction or derivation rules.

9.2.3 The Business Rules Approach

The Business Rules Approach is a software development approach, in which business rules are expressed in a declarative form and managed as separate entities. This approach brings several benefits such as decoupling business rules from the application code, making maintenance and changes easier, allowing non-programmers to manage rules, and increasing rule reusability. The Business Rules Approach has four so-called *STEP* principles [191]:

- *Separate:* Business rules must be separated from the rest of the application.

- *Trace:* A connection should be maintained from the business rule to its origin in the business organization (such as a business policy or a decision) and to its implementation (i.e., all places in the implementation where the rule is executed).

- *Externalize:* Business rules should be expressed in a form that business people, which are generally non-programmers, can understand easily.

- *Position:* Business rules should be implemented using a technology that supports easy and non-invasive changes.

9.3   Integrating Business Rules in BPEL

The only way to integrate a business rule with a BPEL process is by adding appropriate activities, variables, and partners to that process. To do that, the programmer can proceed as follows.

First, the programmer has to find the activities, the variables, and the partners that are related to the rule condition. Then, at all activities that might enable the rule condition, the programmer has to add a *switch* activity for evaluating the rule condition. The *switch* activity must contain a *case* branch with the necessary activities for executing the rule action when the rule condition evaluates to true. Moreover, it might be necessary for the programmer to add partners and variables that are needed to evaluate the rule condition and/or to execute the rule action.

In the following, the integration of some business rule examples with the travel package process is illustrated. Then, the shortcomings of this integration approach are discussed.

9.3.1   Examples

The travel package process that was presented in Chapter 3 is extended with price calculation logic as shown in Listing 9.1. A *sequence* activity is added to that process for price calculation (lines 46–53). This activity determines the total price of a travel package offer by summing up the flight price and the hotel price and multiplying that sum by the number of passengers. This *sequence* activity contains an *assign* activity for setting the part *totalprice* of the variable *clientresponse*, which is used by the *reply* activity (lines 54–55).

In order to integrate the action enabler rule R1 in this travel package process, the programmer can proceed as follows. First, he finds the activities that perform the flight search (this is the *invoke* activity on lines 25–27). Then, he inserts a *switch* activity after that *invoke* and defines a *case* branch, which uses the variable *flightresponse* to check whether a flight has been found. If no flight is found, the programmer terminates the process instance by using the *terminate* activity in the respective *case* branch. The programmer can also throw some fault (using the *throw* activity) or send a message to the client (using a *reply* activity) before terminating the process instance. The integration of the constraint rule R0 can be done in a similar manner.

To integrate the computation rule R2 with the travel package process, the programmer proceeds as described in the last paragraph. The number of passengers is available to the process immediately after the execution of the *receive* activity (lines 16–18). This data is stored in the part *numOfPassengers* of the variable *clientrequest* and does not change in the rest of the process. Then, the programmer integrates the rule action into the process by adding a *switch* activity after the price calculation activity. The *switch* activity should have a *case* branch that executes if the part *numOfPassengers* is bigger than 2.

```
1   <process name="travelPackage" .../>
2   <partnerLinks>
3    <partnerLink name="client" partnerLinkType="clientPLT" .../>
4    <partnerLink name="flight" partnerLinkType="flightPLT" .../>
5    <partnerLink name="hotel" partnerLinkType="hotelPLT" .../>
6   </partnerLinks>
7   <variables>
8    <variable name="clientrequest"  messageType="findPackageRequest" />
9    <variable name="clientresponse" messageType="findPackageResponse" />
10   <variable name="flightrequest"  messageType="findAFlightRequest"/>
11   <variable name="flightresponse" messageType="findAFlightResponse" />
12   <variable name="hotelrequest"   messageType="findARoomRequest" />
13   <variable name="hotelresponse"  messageType="findARoomlResponse" />
14  </variables>
15  <sequence name="packageSequence">
16   <receive name="receiveClientRequest" partnerLink="client"
17           portType="travelServicePT" operation="getTravelPackage"
18           variable ="clientrequest" createInstance ="yes" />
19   <assign>
20    <copy>
21    <from variable=" clientrequest" part="deptDate">
22    <from variable=" flightrequest" part="DepartOn">
23    ...
24   </assign>
25   <invoke name="invokeFlightService" partnerLink="flight"
26           portType="flightPT" operation="findAFlight"
27           inputVariable =" flightrequest" outputVariable =" flightresponse" />
28   <invoke name="invokeHotelService" partnerLink="hotel"
29           portType="HotelPT" operation="findARoom"
30           inputVariable ="hotelrequest" outputVariable ="hotelresponse" />
31   <assign>
32    <copy>
33    <from variable=" flightresponse" part=" flightDetails " />
34    <to variable ="clientresponse" part=" flightInfo" />
35    </copy>
36    <copy>
37    <from variable="hotelresponse" part=" roomDetails" />
38    <to variable ="clientresponse" part="hotelInfo" />
39    </copy>
40    <copy>
41    <from expression="concat(getVariableData(' flightresponse ',' flightnum '),
42                            getVariableData (' hotelresponse ',' id'))" />
43    <to variable ="clientresponse" part="offerid" />
44    </copy>
45   </assign>
46   <sequence name="price calculation">
47   <assign><copy>
48    <from expression="(getVariableData(' flightresponse ',' flightprice ') +
49                       getVariableData (' hotelresponse ',' hotelprice '))*
50                       getVariableData (' clientrequest ',' numOfPassengers')" />
51    <to variable ="clientresponse" part=" totalprice" />
52   </copy></assign>
53   </sequence>
54   <reply name="replyToClient" partnerLink="client" portType="travelServicePT"
55          operation="getTravelPackage"   variable ="clientresponse" />
56  </sequence>
57 </process>
```
161

Listing 9.1: The extended travel package process

The body of the *case* branch should use an *assign* activity to recalculate the price according to R2 and to modify the part *totatprice* of the variable *clientresponse*.

Next, the integration of inference rules such as R3 is discussed. The condition part of the rule R3 (*if a customer is frequent*) cannot be associated directly with activities and variables as it is the case for R1 and R2. To decide whether a customer is frequent, some additional computation and/or logical derivation is needed, as elaborated below.

As an example for additional computation, one may need to call a customer information Web Service that takes the customer id and returns the frequency grade of the customer. It may also be necessary to do logical derivation together with computation. For example, there may be another business rule R4, which states that a customer, who has bought products for a total sum exceeding 4000 Euros is a frequent customer. In that case, resolving the condition of R3 would require a call to the customer information Web Service to get the total value of purchases of a customer. Moreover, the business rule R4 should be used to derive whether the customer is frequent using the return data of the customer information Web Service.

Assuming that only an additional computation is needed to resolve the condition of R3, the programmer integrates R3 in the travel package process as follows. After the price calculation activity, he adds a *sequence* activity that contains an *invoke* to call the customer information Web Service and a *switch* activity to decide whether a customer is frequent. He also has to add a partner link to the customer information Web Service and two variables for holding the input and output of the *invoke* activity that calls that Web Service. The *switch* activity should have a *case* branch, which uses the output variable of that *invoke* to decide whether the customer is frequent. This *case* branch uses an *assign* for recalculating the price and modifying the part *totalprice* as explained for R2.

9.3.2 Problems

Considering the business rule examples R0 to R3 and the way they are integrated in the travel package process, one observes that the problems of implementing business rules in procedural and object-oriented languages [114, 71] also exist in process-oriented workflow languages such as BPEL. These problems are:

1. Conditional statements are ordered into the application flow manually.
2. Rule identity is lost.
3. The impact of changing a single rule is not localized.

Two further problems are observed:

4. Business rules are expressed in a non-natural way.
5. It is not possible to change the business rules dynamically.

Problem 1 arises when one tries to integrate the business rules R1, R2, and R3 with the travel package process. These rules have to be integrated manually in the process flow using the conditional activity *switch* as explained above. One also has to understand where and when to merge the conditional activities with the process flow, e.g., the integration of R2 and R3 has to be done after the price calculation activity. Moreover, one has to resolve the rule conditions manually, which requires a thorough understanding of the whole process: which activities implement a given functionality, which activities use or modify which variables, which variables contain what data, etc. As the process of integrating R3 indicated, resolving the condition part of inference rules is quite complex.

Problem 2 is caused by the lack of a module concept for expressing business rules separately. The whole business logic underlying the Web Service composition is expressed in the BPEL process. Consequently, when business rules are integrated in BPEL they are embedded in the process code. Thus, the *Separate* principle of the Business Rules Approach is violated. Moreover, the business rules loose their identity and no longer exist as *first-class* entities. Business rules are valuable pieces of knowledge about the business. Therefore, it is inappropriate to bury that knowledge deep in code where no one can identify it as such [191]. Due to the loss of identity, the *Trace* principle of the Business Rules Approach is also violated, i.e., matching the business rules with their implementation in the BPEL process becomes difficult.

Problem 3 arises because the *Position* principle of the Business Rules Approach is violated. This problem is tightly related to Problems 1 and 2. The business rules cannot be changed easily because they are buried in the process code and they do not exist as separate entities. To change a single business rule, one has to find all places where a rule is buried in the process code and modify them consistently and correctly.

For example, if the travel agency changes its discount policy, the programmer needs to extract all the business logic related to discounts out of the different workflow process specifications. Moreover, he has to integrate the new rules or alter existing rules and ensure that each process is still working correctly. Obviously, this requires understanding and changing the whole workflow process specifications. Such an approach is inappropriate because business rules tend to change more often than the rest of the application [15, 165]. As noted in [165], "The most significant changes do not come from re-engineering the workflow, but from rethinking rules".

Problem 4 arises because business rules must be expressed in terms of BPEL constructs (activities, variables, partners) before their integration into the process code. Thus, they are not expressed in the declarative if/then form. The *Externalize* principle of the Business Rules Approach is violated. Consequently, non-programmers cannot understand and manage the business rules.

Problem 5 follows from Problems 2 and 3. As the rule implementation is not decoupled from the process code, it cannot be changed dynamically. The support for dynamic changes is a key requirement in the highly dynamic context of Web Service composition. In fact, organizations that are involved in a Web Service composition may often change their rules to react to changes in the business environment, e.g., new regulations, new partnerships, changing strategies, mergers, etc. Supporting the dynamic modification of business rules would allow organizations to react more rapidly and adequately to such changes.

9.3.3 Discussion

The previous subsection illustrated the modularity and flexibility problems that arise when business rules are embedded into the process code and explained how the STEP principles of the Business Rules Approach are violated.

Problems 1,2, and 4 can be traced down to the lack of modularity in the implementation of business rules. There is no module concept for encapsulating the business rule implementation and separating it from the process. Consequently, the implementation of a business rule is not only tangled with the process logic, but may also be scattered across different processes (in the case of crosscutting business rules).

For example, the rule R3, which gives a discount of 5 % to frequent customers, is a crosscutting business rule. It spans several processes in the travel agency scenario such as the travel package process and the flight process. Hence, when the programmer tries to implement that business rule, he will have to modify not only the travel package process as explained above, but also the flight process. In addition, it might be necessary to add the implementation of a business rule several times to the same process, e.g., in a more complex travel package process where several activities are used for price calculation.

Implementing business rules affects in general sets of points in the execution of several processes. The implementation of business rules cannot be modularized because it cuts across the modular process-based structure of the travel package process and the flight process. That is, business rules are also crosscutting concerns. As BPEL does not provide concepts for crosscutting modularity, the implementation of business rules leads to the tangling and scattering problems that were mentioned in Chapter 3.

To avoid these problems, business rules need to be encapsulated in separate modules. Moreover, the decision about "where" and "when" to trigger the evaluation of the rule condition and the execution of the rule action during the execution of a BPEL process must also be encapsulated in a separate unit.

The flexibility problems 3 and 5 are related to the lack of modularity: if one could break down the business logic underlying the composition into several modules with well-defined interfaces, the composition becomes more flexible because each module can evolve independently of the rest. With appropriate tool support, well-modularized business rules can be activated, modified, and deactivated at runtime.

9.4   Hybrid Web Service Composition

The previous section motivated the need for a modular implementation of business rules in the context of Web Service compositions. However, a pure rule-based approach to engineering Web Service compositions is also not appropriate because understanding a composition that is defined using a multitude of business rules is complex. Moreover, business rules are not suited for specifying certain aspects of the Web Service composition such as control and data flow.

To solve the problems that were discussed in the last section, a hybrid approach to Web Service composition is proposed. This approach combines process-oriented Web Service composition with the Business Rules Approach. The control and data flow between the Web Services of the composition are defined primarily in the BPEL process, whereas decisions and policies are defined in well-modularized and separated business rule modules.

In this approach, business rules are considered as parts of the internal implementation of a composite Web Service. Thus, they are not visible to external partners. They are also not intended to be published among partners.

Assuming a methodology for Web Service composition, which distinguishes an analysis phase and an implementation phase, the idea of hybrid Web Service composition is illustrated in Figure 9.1.

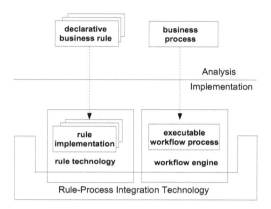

Figure 9.1: A hybrid approach to Web Service composition

The analysis phase is out of the scope of this work. The author merely presumes that the Web Service composition is specified as a business process and business rules are expressed in a declarative way in the analysis phase.

In the implementation phase, the separation between processes and business rules is kept. This separation can be achieved by using an integration technology that combines some workflow engine and some rule implementation technology, as shown schematically in the bottom of Figure 9.1.

For the implementation of this hybrid approach, one has to select a concrete workflow language for implementing the business process and a concrete rule technology for implementing the business rules. For example, one could choose BPEL and a compliant orchestration engine to implement the process. For implementing the business rules, two alternatives will be discussed.

In the first alternative, the aspect-orientation paradigm is used for modularizing the implementation of business rules. As explained in the discussion, the implementation of business rules tends to be crosscutting and aspects provide means to modularize crosscutting concerns. Aspect-Oriented Programming has been already found valuable for modularizing business rules in object-oriented software [69]. Along the same lines, AO4BPEL aspects can be used for modularizing business rules in BPEL processes.

In the second alternative, the idea is to combine the workflow language BPEL with a rule-based language. This alternative would provide native business rule support for BPEL processes in a similar manner to the support provided by rule-based systems such as Jess [86] and JRules [110] to Java applications. At the implementation level, this alternative requires the integration of a rule engine with the BPEL orchestration engine. This alternative will not be implemented in this work.

Independently of the chosen implementation alternative, a key point in the hybrid composition approach is that business rules should be well-modularized parts of the composition logic in the analysis and implementation phases as shown in Figure 9.1.

9.4.1 Implementing business rules with AO4BPEL

Aspect-Oriented Programming is a suitable vehicle for modeling business rules because of their crosscutting nature and also because of the similarities between aspects and business rules.

In fact, aspects have the *if/then* flavor of business rules. An aspect basically answers three questions: *when/where* and *what*: join points and pointcuts specify when and where crosscutting functionality should be executed during the execution of the base program; the advice define what crosscutting functionality to execute. Business rules also answer these three questions. The condition part of the rule specifies *when/where* to execute the rule action (the *what*).

There is also an analogy between the *base program* in AOP and the *working memory* in the Business Rules Approach: conditions are statements over the facts that are contained in the working memory like pointcuts, which are statements over the static or dynamic structure of the base program. When a pointcut matches a join point in the base program execution, the advice is executed in a similar way to the rule's action, which is executed when the rule condition matches some facts in the working memory.

In the following, AO4BPEL aspects are used as a rule implementation technology and the AO4BPEL engine is used as an integration technology for the BPEL engine and the business rule implementation. The implementation of the different types of business rules with AO4BPEL will be illustrated using the business rule examples *R0* to *R3*.

Constraints

To implement a constraint rule in AO4BPEL, the programmer has to identify the activities where the target data is modified, i.e., where the constraint may be violated. For example, to implement the constraint rule R0 (*a vacation request must contain a departure city and a destination city*) using an AO4BPEL aspect, the programmer searches in the travel package process for the activities, variables, and partners that are related to the condition part of R0. These are the *receive* activity (lines 16–18), the partner *client* (line 3), and the variable *clientrequest* (line 8).

Then, the programmer implements *R0* using an AO4BPEL aspect as shown in Listing 9.2. The pointcut of this aspect (lines 3–5) selects the *receive* activity of the travel package process. An after advice (lines 6–14) is associated with this pointcut. This advice uses a *switch/case* branch (lines 7–13) to terminate the process if the constraint R0 is not fulfilled (line 11). In order to access the variable *clientrequest* of the travel package process, the advice uses the context collection construct *ThisProcess(clientrequest)* (lines 9–10).

In this implementation, the rule R0 is reformulated to "if the part *deptcity* or the part *destcity* of the variable *clientrequest* is an empty string after the completion of the *receive* then terminate the process".

166

```
1  <aspect name="R0">
2    <pointcutandadvice>
3    <pointcut name="receive request">
4    //process[@name="travelPackage"]//receive[@operation="getTravelPackage"]
5    </pointcut>
6    <advice type="after">
7     <switch>
8      <case condition=
9          "getVariableData('ThisProcess( clientrequest )',' deptcity')= ''  or
10          getVariableData('ThisProcess( clientrequest )',' destcity')= ''">
11     <terminate/>
12     </case>
13    </switch>
14   </advice>
15  </pointcutandadvice>
16  </aspect>
```

Listing 9.2: The constraint rule R0 as an aspect

The advice of all constraint rules can be built according to the pattern shown in Listing 9.2. It consists of a *switch* activity that has a *case* branch with a nested *terminate* activity to terminate the process if the constraint is violated.

```
1  <aspect name="R1">
2    <pointcutandadvice>
3    <pointcut name="Berlin Air Invocations">
4    //process[@name="travelPackage"]//invoke[@operation="findAFlight"]
5    </pointcut>
6    <advice type="after">
7     <switch>
8      <case condition="getVariableData(
9          'ThisProcess( flightresponse )',' findAFlightReturn')= ''">
10     <!-- Here the action implementation of the action enabler -->
11     <sequence>
12      <assign>
13      <copy>
14       <from expression="'no flight is found for the selected dates'">
15       <to variable="clientresponse" part="flightInfo">
16      </copy>
17      </assign>
18      <reply partnerLink="client" portType="travelServicePT"
19             operation="getTravelPackage" variable="clientresponse" />
20      <terminate/>
21     </sequence>
22     </case>
23    </switch>
24   </advice>
25  </pointcutandadvice>
26  </aspect>
```

Listing 9.3: The action enabler rule R1 as an aspect

Action enablers

To implement the action enabler rule (*R1: if no flight is found for the dates given by the client, do not look for accommodation*), the programmer searches for the activities, variables, and partners that are related to the condition part of R1. These are the *invoke* activity that calls Berlin Air Web Service (lines 25–27), the variable *flightresponse* (line 11), and the partner *flight* (line 4).

The aspect that implements R1 is shown in Listing 9.3. The pointcut of this aspect selects the *invoke* activity that calls Berlin Air Web Service. The after advice of this aspect uses a *switch* activity with a *case* branch to test whether the part *findAFlightReturn* of the variable *flightreponse* equals the empty string. The *case* branch contains a *sequence* activity, which contains three activities: an *assign* activity (lines 12–17) to set the message that will be returned to the customer, a *reply* activity (lines 18–19) to send that message, and a *terminate* activity (line 20) to terminate the process instance.

In this implementation, the rule R1 is reformulated to "if the response of the flight Web Service equals the empty string then send a message to the client and terminate the process".

```
1  <aspect name="R2">
2    <pointcutandadvice>
3      <pointcut name="price calculation">
4      //process[@name="travelPackage"]//sequence[@name="price calculation"]
5      </pointcut>
6      <advice type="after">
7       <switch>
8        <case condition=
9          "getVariableData('ThisProcess( clientrequest )',' numOfPassengers')>2">
10         <!-- Here comes the action implementation of the computation rule -->
11         <sequence name="price recalculation">
12          <assign>
13           <copy>
14            <from expression="
15            ((getVariableData('ThisProcess( clientresponse )',' totalprice ') * 2) /
16            getVariableData('ThisProcess( clientrequest )',' numOfPassengers')) +
17            (getVariableData('ThisProcess( clientresponse )',' totalprice ') /
18            (getVariableData('ThisProcess( clientrequest )',' numOfPassengers') * 2) *
19            (getVariableData('ThisProcess( clientrequest )',' numOfPassengers')- 2)"/>
20            <to variable="clientresponse" part="totalprice"/>
21           </copy>
22          </assign>
23         </sequence>
24        </case>
25       </switch>
26      </advice>
27    </pointcutandadvice>
28  </aspect>
```

Listing 9.4: The computation rule R2 as an aspect

Computation rules

To implement the computation rule R2 (*if more than two persons travel together, the third pays only half price*), the programmer proceeds as explained for R0 and R1. He finds that the *receive* activity of the travel package process is the activity where the number of passengers becomes known. That information is stored in the part *numOfPassengers* of the variable *clientrequest* and does not change in the rest of the process.

The aspect that implements R2 is shown in Listing 9.4. The pointcut of this aspect (lines 3–5) selects the price calculation activity in the travel package process. The action part R2 is implemented using an *after* advice, which contains a *switch* with a *case* branch (lines 8–24) for recalculating the price when more than two persons travel together. This *case* branch uses an *assign* activity (lines 12–22) to write the new price to the part *totalprice* of the variable *clientresponse*.

The algorithm *alg* for recalculating the total price according to R2 is as follows. Given x the already calculated total price and n the number of passengers, the new price according to R2 is $(2 * (x/n)) + ((n\text{-}2) * (x/2n))$. This means that 2 persons pay the full price x/n and the others $(n\text{-}2)$ pay half price $x/2n$.

In this implementation, the rule R2 is reformulated to "if the part *numOf-Passengers* of the variable *clientrequest* is bigger than 2 recalculate the total price according to the algorithm *alg* and override the part *totalprice* of the variable *clientresponse* with the new value".

When implementing action enabler rules and computation rules, the choice of the pointcut depends not only on the activities that are related to the rule condition, but also on the rule semantics, the rule's action, and the process activities that are affected by that action. For this reason, the pointcut of the aspect shown in Listing 9.4 does not select the *receive* activity where the number of passengers becomes known, but rather the price calculation activity. This is necessary because the price should be updated according to R2 after the price calculation and not before that.

Inference rules

Inference rules are more difficult to implement, because resolving their conditions requires logical derivation and/or additional computations. For example, to implement the rule *R3: if a customer is frequent, he gets a discount of 5 %*, the programmer has to look for the activities, variables, and partners in the BPEL process that are related to the rule condition, but he will not find any.

Assume that there is another business rule R4, which specifies that *if a customer has bought products for a sum exceeding 4000 euros, he is a frequent customer (R4)*. Thus, the condition part of the rule R3 can be resolved using R4 and an additional computation that calls some customer information Web Service to get the total of the previous purchases for a given customer. After resolving the condition of R3, this rule can be written as an action enabler rule, which can be implemented as explained for R2.

Listing 9.5 shows the aspect, which implements the rule R3. This aspect declares the customer information Web Service as a partner (line 3) and two variables (lines 6–7) for the input and output data of the *invoke* activity, which calls that Web Service (lines 20–22). The pointcut of this aspect, which captures the price calculation activity, is associated with an after advice that contains an *assign* activity (line 16–19) for setting the input variable *getTotalPurchasesIn* and an *invoke* activity for calling the operation *getTotalPurchases* on the customer information Web Service (lines 20–22). For implementing the action part of R3, a *switch* activity (lines 24–35) recalculates the price in a similar manner to the advice of R2.

This aspect shows that the advice of aspects that implement inference rules such as R3 contain activities for resolving the rule condition, whereas the advice of aspects for the other rule types contain only activities that implement the rule action.

```
1   <aspect name="R3">
2     <partners>
3       <partner name="customerInfo" partnerLinkType="cInfoPLT" .../>
4     <partners>
5     <variables>
6       <variable name="tPurchasesIn" messageType="getTPRequest"/>
7       <variable name="tPurchasesOut" messageType="getTPResponse"/>
8     </variables>
9     <pointcutandadvice>
10    <pointcut name="price calculation">
11      //process[@name="travelPackage"]//sequence[@name="price calculation"]
12    </pointcut>
13    <advice type="after">
14      <sequence>
15      <!-- condition resolution -->
16      <assign><copy>
17        <from variable="ThisProcess(clientrequest)" part="customerId">
18        <to variable="getTotalPurchasesIn" part="customerNr" >
19      </copy></assign>
20      <invoke name="invokeCIWS" partnerLink="customerInfo"
21              portType="cInfoPT" operation="getTotalPurchases"
22              inputVariable="tPurchasesIn" outputVariable="tPurchasesOut"/>
23      <!-- action implementation -->
24      <switch>
25        <case condition=
26            "getVariableData('tPurchasesOut','total') > 4000">
27          <assign>
28            <copy>
29            <from expression="
30            getVariableData('ThisProcess(clientresponse)',' totalprice')*0.95"/>
31            <to variable="clientresponse" part="totalprice"/>
32            </copy>
33          </assign>
34        </case>
35      </switch>
36    </advice>
37    </pointcutandadvice>
38  </aspect>
```

Listing 9.5: The inference rule R3 as an aspect

The implementation of R3 using an aspect would be more difficult if there were other rules specifying when a customer is frequent, e.g., if there is another rule *R5: if a customer has bought more than 5 travel packages, he is a frequent customer* in addition to R4. If R4 and R5 were inference rules resolving R3 would be more complex.

Discussion

The examples presented so far show that the four types of business rules can be implemented with AO4BPEL aspects in a modular way. In the analysis phase, business rules are expressed declaratively. Thus, the *Externalize* principle of the Business Rules Approach is supported. In the implementation phase, each business rule is mapped to an aspect that is defined in a separate file. Thus, the *Separate* principle of the Business Rules Approach is fulfilled. Moreover, the *Trace* principle can be supported by having a mapping between the business rule and the aspect that implements it. As the business rules are well-modularized in aspects, they can be changed easily and the impact of changing them is localized. Hence, the *Position* principle of the Business Rules Approach is supported.

When using AO4BPEL as an implementation technology for business rules, four of the five problems that were mentioned above are solved.

Problem 2 is solved as the business rules do not loose their identity, neither in the analysis phase nor in the implementation phase. Problem 3 is solved as the business rules are encapsulated in separate aspect modules and they can be changed easily. Problem 4 is solved because the business rules are expressed in a declarative form in the analysis phase. Problem 5 is solved since the AO4BPEL engine supports the dynamic composition of aspects and processes.

Problem 1 remains unsolved because the implementation of the business rules with AO4BPEL requires programmer knowledge. In fact, the programmer has to understand the BPEL process and how the rule affects it (which activities, variables, and partners are related to the business rule, where to test the condition, which process activity should be the pointcut, how to implement the action, etc). However, it should be possible to have a tool that generates the business rule aspect from a high-level declarative specification of the business rule, because the advice of these aspects follow well-defined patterns. In this way, Problem 1 will be solved.

Nevertheless, even if the business rule aspects are generated automatically, the user would not have support for rule management. Tasks such as handling rule dependencies, checking rule consistency, combining rules, solving rule conflicts, and handling inference rules would still have to be done manually. For instance, if there are two business rule aspects for *Ra: if A then B* and *Rb: if B then C*, the user will have to manually derive the rule *Rc: if A then C*.

To solve these problems, a *rule engine* should be used. The rule engine not only generates the rule implementation, but also controls the activation and execution of the business rules, manages the rule dependencies and conflicts, and handles logical inference. Thus, it relieves the user from managing the business rules and let his focus on the implementation of the BPEL process.

9.4.2 Issues in using a rule engine

The second alternative for implementing business rules in BPEL processes consists in using a rule engine that is integrated with the orchestration engine. Such a hybrid system is not in the scope of this work. In what follows, some issues that should be considered when undertaking such an endeavor are presented shortly.

At the language level, BPEL should be integrated with a rule-based language in a similar approach to the one taken by systems such as Jess [86] and JRules [110], which integrate the object-oriented language Java with rule-based languages.

This integration can be achieved by extending the rule-based language with BPEL constructs. In this way, activities, partners, and variables can be used in the condition and/or action of the business rule. Extending BPEL with features of the rule-based language is not an option because this would inhibit the portability of BPEL processes.

The integration of a rule-based language with BPEL will, however, confront BPEL programmers with a paradigm mismatch as they will have to understand and use constructs of a rule-based language. In this regard, an implementation of the hybrid composition approach by a hybrid system integrating a rule-based language with BPEL is inferior to the aspect-based implementation.

In fact, using AO4BPEL to implement the business rules as discussed above has the advantage of consistency for process programmers. Thus, the verification of the properties of the resulting Web Service composition can be done more easily because the same paradigm is used for the specification of the process and the business rules, i.e., BPEL activities are used for implementing the process and the advice of the business rule aspects.

Aspects may be useful even for the integration of a rule-based language with BPEL. As argued in [70], hybrid systems that integrate object-oriented programming and rule-based reasoning lack seamless integration. For a better integration of both paradigms, hybrid aspects were introduced [71]. A similar approach to hybrid aspects in the context of BPEL and rule-based languages is probably worth considering.

At the implementation level, the rule engine needs to be integrated with the BPEL orchestration engine. This can be done in two ways: by calling the business rule engine explicitly from inside the BPEL process, or by wrapping the business rule engine around the BPEL orchestration engine.

This first alternative was implemented recently in Oracle BPEL process Manager [147], which allows the BPEL process to access the rule engine and invoke rules. To do that, a special *decide* activity is used and the rules are exposed as a decision service.

The second alternative can be implemented by extending the orchestration engine with a component that updates the working memory of the rule engine according to the process execution. Once a rule matches, the control should be passed over from the orchestration engine to the component of the rule engine, which is responsible for executing the rule action. After that, the control should be returned to the orchestration engine to proceed with the execution of the process.

9.5 Related Work

In [205], a rule-based approach to the development of Web Service compositions is presented. The objective of that work is to make the life cycle of Web Service composition development more flexible. In that approach, several phases are differentiated, such as abstract definition, scheduling, construction, execution and evolution. That approach proposes specifying the composition using a process-oriented language such as BPEL. Unlike the work presented in this chapter, it considers only business rules that are related to the development process of a Web Service composition (e.g., business rules for resource selection or runtime constraints) and not business rules that are part of the composition logic.

In [49], AspectJ aspects are used to encapsulate the connection of the business rule to the core application. This connection denotes the events that trigger the business rules in the execution of the core application and the necessary data to execute these rules. In a similar way, AO4BPEL aspects modularize the connector code of the business rules to the BPEL process.

In [69], a survey of current approaches to the integration of object-oriented languages and rule-based languages is presented. That survey revealed that both paradigms are not well integrated and that the programs written using those approaches are tightly coupled. To solve these limitations, *hybrid aspects* are proposed. Hybrid aspects are characterized by two join point models: one for the object-oriented language and one for the rule-based language, and hybrid advice, which can activate a rule or call a method. Moreover, hybrid aspects provide a generic way for passing context from one language to the other in a unified way.

As already mentioned, it is worthwhile to investigate in how far the aspect-based integration approach presented in [69] can be adopted to the needs of business rules in the context of Web Service compositions. Supporting hybrid aspects in AO4BPEL can be achieved by defining appropriate extensions to the join point model and advice language.

In [51], Cilia et. al. compare Event Condition Action rules (ECA) in the area of active databases with aspects in AspectJ and identify several commonalities. However, business rules are quite different from ECA rules, because business rules do not require a database. Business rules are present in other contexts such as object-oriented applications and workflow management systems [21]. They also come in various flavors either as production rules, integrity rules in SQL, ECA-rules, logic rules like in Prolog, etc. ECA rules are not adequate to express inference rules.

In the following, some more recent research works on business rules in Web Service composition are presented shortly.

In [50], Cibran et. al. present example categories of business rules that are applicable in the context of Web Service composition. In that work, business rules are implemented using the JAsCo language, which is an extension to Java. JAsCo supports stateful pointcuts, which allow the implementation of business rules based on the execution history. Moreover, JAsCo supports dynamic weaving, which allows the aspects implementing business rules to be plugged in and out. The interesting feature of this work is that temporal relationships can be used to express the rule condition. The major limitation is however, that JAsCo aspects work only with Java, i.e, they cannot be used for integrating business rules in BPEL, which is the standard for Web Service composition.

In [164], a service-oriented approach to integrating business rules in BPEL processes is presented. That proposal uses a *rule interceptor service*, which intercepts incoming and outgoing messages that come from or go to the BPEL engine, and calls a *business rule broker* to apply the business rules. The mapping of business rules to BPEL activities is defined by the BPEL programmer in an XML mapping document, which specifies before and after interceptors for certain process activities. In this approach, the working memory of the rule engine is not updated when the process executes. Moreover, rule inference is not supported. As this approach is based on intercepting SOAP messages, it can be used only for business rules that affect messaging activities, unlike AO4BPEL business rule aspects, which can be triggered by any BPEL activity.

The idea of hybrid systems integrating business processes and business rules has been incorporated recently in several commercial products such as Oracle BPEL Process Manager and the process modeling platform ARIS.

In 2005, Oracle BPEL Process Manager has been extended with support for business rules [147]. In a first stage, it was integrated with ILOG's JRules rule-based system, which includes a rule editor, a rule builder, a rule debugger, etc [111]. In a later stage, Oracle BPEL Process Manager will be integrated with a new and native business rule engine that will be developed by Oracle as part of a future release of Oracle Fusion Middleware.

In May 2006, IDS Scheer and Corticon announced that Corticon Studio, which is a rule-based system, was integrated with the ARIS platform for process modeling [109]. Unlike ILOG JRules, which are specified in a technical language, Corticon rules are specified in a graphical way. Therefore, Corticon rules are well-suited for complementing the graphical process specifications of ARIS.

9.6 Conclusion

This chapter presented a second application of AO4BPEL in the context of business rules in BPEL processes. In this application, a hybrid approach to Web Service composition was proposed to separate business rules and their implementation from the business process and the BPEL workflow process that implements it.

In the analysis phase, business rules are expressed declaratively and the business process is specified at a high abstraction level. In the implementation phase, the process is specified using a workflow language such as BPEL and the business rules are implemented with some technology that needs to be integrated appropriately with the BPEL orchestration engine.

Driven by the similarities between business rules and aspects and also by the crosscutting nature of business rules, the hybrid composition approach was implemented using AO4BPEL aspects. This chapter has shown how the four types of business rules can be implemented in AO4BPEL. In addition, it explained how this aspect-based implementation fulfills the STEP principles of the Business Rules Approach. Thus, business rules, which embody valuable business knowledge, are no longer buried and hidden in the BPEL process code. Moreover, as AO4BPEL supports dynamic composition, business rules can be changed at runtime.

CHAPTER 10

Conclusions

10.1 Summary

The objective of this work was to solve the problems of current workflow languages with respect to *crosscutting concern modularity* and *change modularity* and to design and implement a workflow language, which incorporates that solution.

After implementing examples of crosscutting concerns in a travel agency scenario with a visual graph-based workflow language and the BPEL language, scattering and tangling problems were observed. The lack of constructs for modularizing crosscutting concerns leads to complex workflow process specifications that are hard to understand, to maintain, to reuse, and to change.

Moreover, a study on the expression of workflow changes in static and adaptive workflow management systems revealed that these systems lack a module concept for encapsulating the workflow constructs that implement a workflow change and the decision about where and when the change should be applied. In addition, these systems do not support workflow changes as first-class entities. Consequently, understanding, tracing, and managing workflow changes becomes a complex task.

The central thesis of this work is that Aspect-Oriented Software Development can be applied in the context of workflow languages to solve the problems that were mentioned above.

After studying the decomposition mechanisms of current workflow languages, this book proposed a *concern-based decomposition* of workflow process specifications. This decomposition technique is incorporated in a new type of workflow languages that are called *aspect-oriented workflow languages*. These languages introduce concepts from Aspect-Oriented Software Development to workflow languages and provide means to modularize crosscutting concerns and workflow changes.

To illustrate the concepts of aspect-oriented workflow languages, this book presented *aspectual workflow graphs*, which are an extension to the graph-based language that was mentioned above with constructs that represent graphically aspect-oriented concepts such as pointcuts and advice.

Moreover, this book presented several requirements on the join point models, pointcut languages, advice languages, and composition mechanisms of aspect-oriented workflow languages. It also presented the design of AO4BPMN, which supports aspect-oriented business process modeling as well as the design and implementation of AO4BPEL, which can be considered as a proof-of-concept for aspect-oriented workflow languages.

With AO4BPMN and AO4BPEL this book puts the foundations for a novel aspect-oriented workflow management approach. This approach supports the modularization of crosscutting concerns and changes in business processes and workflow processes throughout their entire lifecycle, i.e., from the design and modeling phase to the implementation and execution phase.

To show the usefulness of workflow aspects, this book explained through several examples how workflow aspects allow to modularize crosscutting concerns and workflow changes. In addition, two applications of AO4BPEL were presented:

The first application introduced a *process container framework*, which supports the specification and enforcement of non-functional requirements in BPEL such as security, reliable messaging, and transactions. In this application, an automatically generated AO4BPEL-based process container enforces the non-functional requirements of the process activities by calling dedicated middleware Web Services. This application not only demonstrates the usefulness of AO4BPEL aspects, but also provides support for process-level non-functional requirements in BPEL such as secure conversations, multi-party ordered message delivery, and transactional structured activities.

In the second application, AO4BPEL aspects are used to implement the different types of business rules according to the principles of the Business Rules Approach. In this aspect-based implementation, business rules are separate, traceable, easy to change, and first-class pieces of business knowledge.

The following conclusions can be drawn from the experiences that were gained during this work.

- The aspect-orientation paradigm is not only applicable in the context of programming languages, but also in other contexts such as business process management and workflow management.

- Workflow aspects are not only useful at the modeling level as shown by aspectual workflow graphs and AO4BPMN but also at the process implementation and execution levels as shown by AO4BPEL.

- Workflow aspects allow the modularization of several crosscutting concerns, which range from simple ones such as data collection for billing and activity execution time measurement to more complex concerns such as security, reliable messaging, and transactions.

- Aspects can be used for expressing workflow changes in a modular way. They encapsulate all workflow constructs that implement a certain change as well as the decision about when and where the change should be applied during the process execution. Moreover, in aspect-aware workflow engines, workflow changes are treated as first-class entities, which eases change management significantly.

- AO4BPEL and its applications show that aspect-oriented workflow languages are feasible and useful. This is also confirmed by recent proposals for aspect-oriented workflow languages such as Padus [27].

- Through the dynamic composition mechanism of the AO4BPEL engine, aspects allow to change BPEL processes dynamically. This shows how the modular expression of workflow changes together with an appropriate composition mechanism enhance the flexibility of workflows. Thus, AO4BPEL aspects make BPEL processes more flexible and adaptable at runtime, which is especially important in the highly dynamic context of Web Services.

- The concepts of aspect-oriented workflow languages are generic, i.e., they are applicable to any workflow language. AO4BPMN and AO4BPEL incorporate these concepts in the context of process design and process execution.

- Whereas aspect-oriented workflow languages and aspect-oriented programming languages define similar constructs, they differ in their join point models, pointcut languages, advice types, and advice languages. Moreover, the composition mechanisms of aspects and processes in aspect-oriented workflow languages are also different from the weaving mechanisms that are used in aspect-oriented programming languages.

- When designing an aspect-oriented extension to an existing workflow language, the constructs of the base workflow language must be understood in depth. In particular, the effect of aspects on language mechanisms such as fault handling and compensation handling should be defined carefully.

- The process container framework shows that container architectures are applicable in workflow management. The process container enables BPEL-based production workflows by supporting non-functional requirements such as security, reliable messaging, and transactions. Moreover, the aspect-based implementation results in a light-weight, modular, open, and extensible container.

  In addition, the process container framework shows that AO4BPEL aspects can be used as an internal implementation technology that the framework end users do not have to know about.

- The aspect-based implementation of the hybrid approach to business rules in Web Service compositions shows that AO4BPEL can implement all types of business rules in a separate and modular way according to the principles of the Business Rules Approach.

10.2   Future work

In the following, some directions for future work are outlined. They span three different areas: AO4BPMN and supporting tools, AO4BPEL and its implementation, and AO4BPEL applications.

1. Works on AO4BPMN

   To improve the adoption of AO4BPMN appropriate tools should be provided. These tools include a visual editor for AO4BPMN, which could be based on existing open source editors for BPMN. Moreover, a composition mechanism based on model transformation can also be implemented. Another possible direction for future work could focus on the transformation of AO4BPMN aspects into AO4BPEL aspects.

2. Works on AO4BPEL

   The AO4BPEL language can be improved in several regards as explained in the following.

   - Extensions to the pointcut language
     The pointcut language of AO4BPEL can be extended with support for XQuery in addition to XPath. Currently, perspective-oriented pointcut expressions such as *//partner* and *//variable* are handled internally by the AO4BPEL engine, which transforms them into activity-based pointcut expressions. As already shown in the work of Eichberg et. al. [76], XQuery would make the pointcut language of AO4BPEL more open and extensible so that AO4BPEL programmers can define their own pointcut designators by using appropriate XQuery functions.

     Currently, the pointcut language of AO4BPEL does not support temporal pointcuts such as *when activity a is executed after activity b*. These pointcuts are needed, e.g., in Web Service composition management aspects, which express crosscutting functionality such as *when an activity invokes a partner P and the previous invocation of that partner has failed then use an alternative partner Web Service*. AO4BPEL can be extended with constructs that allow the expression of temporal relationships between the activities. A logic-based approach such as the one adopted in ALPHA [152] will work also for AO4BPEL.

   - Extensions to the advice language
     The advice language of AO4BPEL can be extended with a construct for deploying other aspects. This is especially important for supporting self-adaptive and self-healing BPEL processes, where some monitoring aspects deploy other adaptation aspects dynamically to ensure some policies or some service level agreements.

     For example, an AO4BPEL monitoring aspect may wait for the response of a partner Web Service for a predefined period of time. If the response is not received after that period, the monitoring aspect deploys a redirection aspect to replace the bad performing partner by an alternative partner Web Service.

   - AO4BPEL update to support WS-BPEL 2.0
     The AO4BPEL language can be updated according to the new WS-BPEL 2.0 standard of OASIS. The implementation of AO4BPEL for WS-BPEL 2.0 can be based on Open Source BPEL engines such as ActiveBPEL 2.0 [129], which already supports most elements of the WS-BPEL 2.0 standard.

3. Works on AO4BPEL applications

Further applications of AO4BPEL can be considered, e.g., in the context of Web Service composition management and in self-adaptive and self-healing systems. In addition, the two applications presented in this book can be improved in several ways.

- Extensions to the process container framework

  The process container framework can be enhanced with a policy management component for supporting policies. Currently, the policies of the partner Web Services are not taken in consideration when the BPEL process is deployed. For example, it is possible that the deployment descriptor of some process requires authentication through X.509 certificates, whereas the partner Web Service supports only username tokens. In such a scenario, the process will be deployed successfully but at runtime a fault will be raised when the partner Web Service is called.

  To avoid such mismatches, the process deployer has to check the policies of the partner Web Services and ensure that they are compatible with the deployment descriptor. A better solution would be to automate these checks by supporting *policy-based process deployment*. In this advanced deployment concept, a policy management component checks automatically whether the requirements specified in the deployment descriptor are compatible with the policies of partner Web Services. This component should detect conflicts and incompatibilities and signal them to the deployer. It may also assist him in solving them.

  The BPEL middleware Web Services can also be extended. The transaction Web Service can be extended with support for business activities as soon as the support for WS-BusinessActivity is completed in Apache Kandula. The security Web Service can also be extended with support for federation [3].

- Extensions to the hybrid Web Service composition approach

  This book explained how the different types of business rules can be implemented using AO4BPEL aspects. So far, the aspects implementing business rules are written manually. One could investigate to what extent these aspects can be generated automatically as already done for the process container aspects. Moreover, one can use aspects as part of the container to integrate the process execution by the workflow engine with a business rule engine.

  Another possible extension to this approach would be the design and implementation of hybrid AO4BPEL aspects to integrate a rule-based language with BPEL, in a similar approach to [71].

Bibliography

[1] Gustavo Alonso, Divyakant Agrawal, Amr El Abbadi, and C. Mohan. Functionality and Limitations of Current Workflow Management Systems. *IEEE Expert,Special Issue on Cooperative Information Systems*, 12(5), 1997.

[2] Gustavo Alonso, Fabio Casati, Harumi Kuno, and Vijay Machiraju. *Web Services: Concepts, Architecture, and Applications*. Springer, 2003.

[3] Anthony Nadalin and Chris Kaler (Eds.). Web Services Federation Language (WS-Federation), July 2003. http://www-128.ibm.com/ developerworks/library/specification/ws-fed/.

[4] Anthony Nadalin and Martin Gudgin (Eds.). Web Services Trust Language (WS-Trust), February 2005. http://www-128.ibm.com/ developerworks/library/specification/ws-trust/.

[5] Apache. Agila BPEL. http://incubator.apache.org/projects/ agila/index.html.

[6] Apache. Xalan-Java 2.6.0. http://xml.apache.org/xalan-j/.

[7] Apache. Sandehsa 1.0. http://ws.apache.org/sandesha/sandesha1. html, July 2005.

[8] Apache. WSS4J 1.1. http://ws.apache.org/ws-fx/wss4j/, March 2005.

[9] Apache. Geronimo 1.0. http://geronimo.apache.org/, January 2006.

[10] Apache. Kandula 0.2. http://ws.apache.org/kandula/, May 2006.

[11] Ivica Aracic, Vaidas Gasiunas, Mira Mezini, and Klaus Ostermann. Overview of CaesarJ. *Transactions on AOSD I*, 3880:135 – 173, 2006.

[12] Assaf Arkin. Business Process Modeling Language (BPML) Version 1.0. http://www.bpmi.org/bpml.esp, June 2002.

[13] Assaf Arkin, Sid Askary, Ben Bloch, et al. Web Services Business Process Execution Language 2.0, Public Review Draft, 23 August 2006. `http://docs.oasis-open.org/wsbpel/2.0/wsbpel-specification-draft.html`.

[14] Assaf Arkin et al. Web Service Choreography Interface (WSCI) 1.0. `http://www.w3.org/TR/wsci/`, August 2002.

[15] Ali Arsanjani. Rule Object 2001: A Pattern Language for Adaptive and Scalable Business Rule Construction. In *Proc. of the 8th Conference on Pattern Languages of Programs (PLoP)*, pages 370–402, Washington DC, USA, September 2001. IEEE Computer Society.

[16] Boris Bachmendo and Rainer Unland. Aspect-based Workflow Evolution. In *Proc. of the Workshop on Aspect-Oriented Programming and Separation of Concerns*, August 2001.

[17] J.-P. Barros and L. Gomes. Activities as Behavior Aspects. In *Proc. of the 2nd Workshop on Aspect-oriented Modeling (held in conjunction with UML 2002)*, September 2002.

[18] Paulo Barthelmess and Jacques Wainer. Workflow Systems: a few Definitions and a few Suggestions. In *Proc. of Conference on Organizational Computing Systems (COCS)*, pages 138–147. ACM Press, August 1995.

[19] BEA and IBM. BPELJ: BPEL for Java, Joint White Paper. `http://www-128.ibm.com/developerworks/library/specification/ws-bpelj/`, March 2004.

[20] Boualem Benatallah, Quan Z. Sheng, and Marlon Dumas. The Self-Serv Environment for Web Services Composition. *IEEE Internet Computing*, 7(1):40–48, 2003.

[21] Benjamin Grosof and Harold Boley. Introduction to RuleML, Talk at the joint US/EU ad hoc Agent Markup Language Committee. `http://ebusiness.mit.edu/bgrosof/paps/talk-ruleml-jc-ovw-102902-main.pdf`, October 2002.

[22] Rainer Berbner, Michael Spahn, Nicolas Repp, Oliver Heckmann, and Ralf Steinmetz. Heuristics for QoS-aware Web Service Composition. In *Proc. of the 4th IEEE International Conference on Web Services (ICWS)*, pages 72–82. IEEE Computer Society, September 2006.

[23] Christoph Bockisch, Michael Haupt, Mira Mezini, and Klaus Ostermann. Virtual Machine Support for Dynamic Join Points. In *Proc. of the 3rd International Conference on Aspect-Oriented Software Development (AOSD)*, pages 83–92. ACM Press, March 2004.

[24] Ron Bodkin. Application Security Aspects, March 2005. Invited talk at the industry track of the 4th International Conference on Aspect-Oriented Software Development (AOSD).

[25] Jonas Bonér and Alexandre Vasseur. AspectWerkz. `http://aspectwerkz.codehaus.org/index.html`, February 2004.

[26] Don Box and Francisco Curbera (Eds.). Web Services Addressing (WS-Addressing). http://www.w3.org/Submission/ws-addressing/, August 2004.

[27] Mathieu Braem, Kris Verlaenen, Niels Joncheere, Wim Vanderperren, Ragnhild Van Der Straeten, Eddy Truyen, Wouter Joosen, and Viviane Jonckers. Isolating Process-Level Concerns using Padus. In *Proc. of the 4th International Conference on Business Process Management (BPM)*, volume 4102 of *LNCS*, pages 113–128. Springer, September 2006.

[28] Bill Burke, Marc Fleury, Adrian Brock, et al. JBoss AOP 1.3.0. http://aop.jboss.org, 2005.

[29] Christoph Bussler. Adaptation in Workflow Management. In *Proc. of the 5th International Conference on the Software Process (ICSP)*, June 1998.

[30] Barbara Carminati, Elena Ferrari, and Patrick C. K. Hung. Security Conscious Web Service Composition. In *Proc. of the 4th IEEE International Conference on Web Services (ICWS)*, pages 489–496. IEEE Computer Society, September 2006.

[31] Fabio Casati, Stefano Ceri, Barbara Pernici, and Giuseppe Pozzi. Workflow Evolution. *Data & Knowledge Engineering*, 24(3):211–238, 1998.

[32] Fabio Casati, Ski Ilnicki, Li jie Jin, Vasudev Krishnamoorthy, and Ming-Chien Shan. Adaptive and Dynamic Service Composition in eFlow. In *Proc. of the 12th International Conference on Advanced Information Systems Engineering (CAiSE)*, volume 1789 of *LNCS*, pages 13–31. Springer, June 2000.

[33] Anis Charfi, Rania Khalaf, and Nirmal Mukhi. QoS-aware Web Service Compositions Using Non-Intrusive Policy Attachment to BPEL. In *Proc. of the 5th International Conference on Service Oriented Computing (IC-SOC), Industry track, to appear*. Springer, September 2007.

[34] Anis Charfi and Mira Mezini. Aspect-Oriented Web Service Composition. In *Student Extravaganza of the 3rd International Conference on Aspect-Oriented Software Development (AOSD), Poster Session*, March 2004.

[35] Anis Charfi and Mira Mezini. Aspect-Oriented Web Service Composition with AO4BPEL. In *Proc. of the 2nd European Conference on Web Services (ECOWS)*, volume 3250 of *LNCS*, pages 168–182. Springer, September 2004.

[36] Anis Charfi and Mira Mezini. Hybrid Web Service Composition: Business Processes Meet Business Rules. In *Proc. of the 2nd International Conference on Service Oriented Computing (ICSOC)*, pages 30–38. ACM Press, November 2004.

[37] Anis Charfi and Mira Mezini. Using Aspects for Security Engineering of Web Service Compositions. In *Proc. of the 3rd IEEE International Conference on Web Services (ICWS)*, pages 59–66. IEEE Computer Society, July 2005.

[38] Anis Charfi and Mira Mezini. Aspect-Oriented Web Service Composition in AO4BPEL, Demo at the 5th International Conference on Aspect-Oriented Software Development (AOSD). http://aosd.net/2006/demos/index.php, March 2006.

[39] Anis Charfi and Mira Mezini. Aspect-Oriented Workflow Languages. In *Proc. of the 14th International Conference on Cooperative Information Systems (CoopIS)*, volume 4275 of *LNCS*, pages 183–200. Springer, November 2006.

[40] Anis Charfi and Mira Mezini. AO4BPEL: An Aspect-Oriented Extension to BPEL. *World Wide Web Journal: Recent Advances in Web Services (special issue)*, March 2007.

[41] Anis Charfi, Benjamin Schmeling, Andreas Heizenreder, and Mira Mezini. Reliable, Secure and Transacted Web Service Composition with AO4BPEL. In *Proc. of the 4th IEEE European Conference on Web Services (ECOWS)*, pages 23–34. IEEE Computer Society, December 2006.

[42] Anis Charfi, Benjamin Schmeling, and Mira Mezini. Reliable Messaging for BPEL Processes. In *Proc. of the 4th IEEE International Conference on Web Services (ICWS)*, pages 293–302. IEEE Computer Society, September 2006.

[43] Anis Charfi, Benjamin Schmeling, and Mira Mezini. Transactional BPEL Processes with AO4BPEL Aspects. In *Proc. of the 5th IEEE European Conference on Web Services (ECOWS)*, pages 149–158. IEEE Computer Society, November 2007.

[44] Ruzanna Chitchyan, Awais Rashid, Pete Sawyer, Alessandro Garcia, Mónica Pinto Alarcon, Jethro Bakker, Bedir Tekinerdogan, Siobhán Clarke, and Andrew Jackson. Report synthesizing state-of-the-art in aspect-oriented requirements engineering, architectures and design. Technical report, Lancaster University, AOSD-Europe Deliverable D11, AOSD-Europe-ULANC-9, May 2005.

[45] Chris Ferris and David Langworthy (Eds.). Web Services Reliable Messaging Protocol (WS-ReliableMessaging). http://www-128.ibm.com/developerworks/library/specification/ws-rm/, February 2005.

[46] Chris Kaler and Anthony Nadalin (Eds.). Web Services Security Policy Language (WS-SecurityPolicy) Version 1.1. http://www-128.ibm.com/developerworks/library/ws-secpol/, July 2005.

[47] Chris Sharp (Eds.). Web Services Policy Attachment (WS-PolicyAttachment). ftp://www6.software.ibm.com/software/developer/library/ws-polat.pdf, September 2004.

[48] Christoph Ferris. Critical Comparison of WS-RM and WS-R, OASIS Symposium: Reliable Infrastructures for XML. http://www.oasis-open.org/events/symposium/slides/ferris.ppt, April 2004.

[49] Maria A. Cibran, Maja D'Hondt, and Viviane Jonckers. Aspect-Oriented Programming for Connecting Business Rules. In *Proc. of the 6th International Conference on Business Information Systems (BIS)*, March 2005.

[50] Maria A. Cibran and Bart Verheecke. Dynamic Business Rules for Web Service Composition. In *Proc. of the Dynamic Aspects Workshop (DAW) in conjunction with AOSD*, March 2005.

[51] Mariano Cilia, Michael Haupt, Mira Mezini, and Alejandro P. Buchmann. The Convergence of AOP and Active Databases: Towards Reactive Middleware. In *Proc. of the 2nd International Conference on Generative Programming and Component Engineering (GPCE)*, volume 2830 of *LNCS*, pages 169–188. Springer, September 2003.

[52] James Clark and Steve DeRose. XML Path Language (XPath) 1.0. `http://www.w3.org/TR/xpath`. W3C Recommendation 16 November 1999.

[53] Cape Clear. Cape Clear Enterprise Server Bus 6.5. `http://www.capeclear.com/products/cc6.shtml`.

[54] Cape Clear. Cape Clear Orchestrator 6.5. `http://www.capeclear.com/products/orchestrator.shtml`.

[55] Adrian Colyer, Andy Clement, George Harley, and Matthew Webster. *Eclipse AspectJ: Aspect-Oriented Programming with AspectJ and the Eclipse AspectJ Development Tools*. Addison Wesley, 2005.

[56] AOSD Community. Aspect-Oriented Software Development Community and Conference. `http://www.aosd.net`.

[57] Thomas Cottenier and Tzilla Elrad. Dynamic and Decentralized Service Composition with Aspect-Sensitive Services. In *Proc. of the 1st International Conference on Web Information Systems and Technologies (WEBIST)*, pages 56–63, May 2005.

[58] Carine Courbis and Anthony Finkelstein. Towards an Aspect-weaving BPEL-engine. In *Proc. of the 3rd Workshop on Aspects, Components, and Patterns for Infrastructure Software (ACP4IS)*, March 2004.

[59] Carine Courbis and Anthony Finkelstein. Towards Aspect Weaving Applications. In *Proc. of the 27th International Conference on Software Engineering (ICSE)*, pages 69–77. ACM Press, May 2005.

[60] Francisco Curbera, Matthew Duftler, Rania Khalaf, William Nagy, Nirmal Mukhi, and Sanjiva Weerawarana. Colombo: Lightweight Middleware for Service-Oriented Computing. *IBM Systems Journal*, 44(4):799–820, 2005.

[61] Francisco Curbera, Yaron Goland, Johannes Klein, et al. Business Process Execution Language for Web Services (BPEL4WS) Version 1.1. `http://www-106.ibm.com/developerworks/library/ws-bpel/`, May 2003.

[62] Francisco Curbera, Rania Khalaf, Nirmal Mukhi, Stefan Tai, and Sanjiva Weerawarana. The Next Step in Web Services. *Commun. ACM*, 46(10):29–34, 2003.

[63] Francisco Curbera, Rania Khalaf, William Nagy, and Sanjiva Weer-awarana. Implementing BPEL4WS: The Architecture of a BPEL4WS Implementation. In *Proc. of the 10th GGF Workshop on Workflow in Grid Systems*, March 2004.

[64] Bill Curtis, Marc I. Kellner, and Jim Over. Process Modeling. *Commun. ACM*, 35(9):75–90, 1992.

[65] David Langworthy (Eds.). Web Services Coordination (WS-Coordination). `ftp://www6.software.ibm.com/software/developer/library/WS-Coordination.pdf`, November 2004.

[66] Pierre Delisle, Jan Luehe, and Mark Roth. Java Server Pages Specification, Version 2.1. `http://java.sun.com/products/jsp/`.

[67] Linda G. DeMichiel et al. Enterprise JavaBeans Specification, Version 2.0. `http://java.sun.com/products/ejb/docs.html`, August 2001.

[68] Frank DeRemer and Hans Kron. Programming-in-the-Large versus Programming-in-the-Small. *IEEE Transactions on Software Engineering*, 2(2):80–86, 1976.

[69] Maja D'Hondt. *Hybrid Aspects for Integrating Rule-based Knowledge and Object-Oriented Functionality*. PhD thesis, Vrije Universit Brussel, Brussel, Belgium, 2004.

[70] Maja D'Hondt, Kris Gybels, and Viviane Jonckers. Seamless Integration of Rule-based Knowledge and Object-oriented Functionality with Linguistic Symbiosis. In *Proc. of the 19th ACM Symposium on Applied Computing (SAC)*, pages 1328–1335, Nicosia, Cyprus, March 2004. ACM Press.

[71] Maja D'Hondt and Viviane Jonckers. Hybrid Aspects for Weaving Object-oriented Functionality and Rule-based Knowledge. In *Proc. of the 3rd International Conference on Aspect-Oriented Software Development (AOSD)*, pages 132–140. ACM Press, March 2004.

[72] Digite. Enterprise BPM 4.2. `http://www.digite.com/products/digite_ent_business-process.htm`.

[73] Remco M. Dijkman and Marlon Dumas. Service-Oriented Design: A Multi-Viewpoint Approach. *International Journal of Cooperative Information Systems*, 13(4):337–368, 2004.

[74] Frederic Duclos, Jacky Estublier, and Philippe Morat. Describing and Using Non-functional Aspects in Component Based Applications. In *Proc. of the 1st International Conference on Aspect-Oriented Software Development (AOSD)*, pages 65–75. ACM Press, April 2002.

[75] Michael Eichberg and Mira Mezini. Alice: Modularization of Middleware using Aspect-Oriented Programming. In *Proc. of the 5th International Workshop Software Engineering and Middleware (SEM)*, volume 3437 of *LNCS*, pages 47–63. Springer, March 2005.

[76] Michael Eichberg, Mira Mezini, and Klaus Ostermann. Pointcuts as Functional Queries. In *Proc. of the 2nd Asian Symposium on Programming Languages and Systems (APLAS)*, volume 3302 of *LNCS*, pages 366–382. Springer, November 2004.

[77] Clarence Ellis, Karim Keddara, and Gzregorz Rozenberg. Dynamic Change within Workflow Systems. In *Proc. of the Conference on Organizational Computing Systems (COCS)*, pages 10–21. ACM Press, August 1995.

[78] Abdelkarim Erradi, Piyush Maheshwari, and Vladimir Tosic. Policy-driven Middleware for Self-Adaptation of Web Service Compositions. In *Proc. of the 7th International Middleware Conference (Middleware)*, volume 4290 of *LNCS*, pages 62–80. Springer, November 2006.

[79] Onyeka Ezenwoye and Sayed Sadjadi. TRAP/BPEL: A Framework for Dynamic Adaptation of Composite Services. Technical Report FIU-SCIS-2006-06-02, Florida International University, June 2006.

[80] Johan Fabry and Thomas Cleenewerck. Aspect-Oriented Domain Specific Languages for Advanced Transaction Management. In *Proc. of the 7th International Conference on Enterprise Information Systems (ICEIS)*, pages 428–432, May 2005.

[81] Donald F. Ferguson, Brad Lovering, Tony Storey, and John Shewchuk. Secure, Reliable, Transacted Web Services: Architecture and Composition. http://www-106.ibm.com/developerworks/webservices/library/ws-transpec/, 2003.

[82] Andrea Ferrara. Web Services: a Process Algebra Approach. In *Proc. of the 2nd International Conference on Service Oriented Computing (ICSOC)*, pages 242–251. ACM Press, November 2004.

[83] Robert E. Filman and Daniel P. Friedman. Aspect-Oriented Programming is Quantification and Obliviousness. In *Proc. of the Workshop on Advanced Separation of Concerns in conjunction with OOPSLA*, pages 21–35, October 2000.

[84] Tony Flechter, Peter Furniss, Alastair Green, and Robert Haugen. BPEL and Business Transaction Management, Choreology submission to OASIS, 2003.

[85] Patric Fornasier and Pawel Kowalski. Bexee - BPEL Execution Engine. http://bexee.sourceforge.net/.

[86] Ernest Friedmann-Hill. JESS: The Java Expert System Shell. http://www.jessrules.com.

[87] Dimitrios Georgakopoulos, Mark F. Hornick, and Amit P. Sheth. An Overview of Workflow Management: from Process Modeling to Workflow Automation Infrastructure. *Distributed and Parallel Databases*, 3(2):119–153, 1995.

[88] Gregor Kiczales and Andreas Paepcke. Open Implementations and Metaobject Protocols. http://www2.parc.com/csl/groups/sda/publications/papers/Kiczales-TUT95/for-web.pdf, 1996.

[89] Object Management Group. CORBA Component Model 3.0. Specification formal/02-06-65, OMG, June 2002.

[90] Martin Gudgin and Anthony Nadalin (Eds.). Web Service Secure Conversation Language (WS-SecureConversation) 1.0. http://specs.xmlsoap.org/ws/2005/02/sc/WS-SecureConversation.pdf, February 2005.

[91] Kris Gybels and Johan Brichau. Arranging Language Features for more Robust Pattern-based Crosscuts. In *Proc. of the 2nd International Conference on Aspect-Oriented Software Development(AOSD)*, pages 60–69. ACM Press, March 2003.

[92] Hugo Haas and Allen Brown. UDDI Version 3.0, UDDI Spec Technical Committee Draft 19 October 2004. http://www.oasis-open.org/committees/uddi-spec/doc/tcspecs.htm#uddiv3.

[93] Hugo Haas and Allen Brown. Web Services Glossary, W3C Working Group Note 11 February 2004. http://www.w3.org/TR/ws-gloss/.

[94] Rachid Hamadi and Boualem Benatallah. A Petri net-based Model for Web Service Composition. In *Proc. of the 14th Australasian Database Conference (ADC)*, pages 191–200, February 2003.

[95] Yanbo Han and Amit Sheth. On Adaptive Workflow Modeling. In *Proc. of the 4th International Conference on Information Systems Analysis and Synthesis (ISAS)*, pages 108–116, July 1998.

[96] Yanbo Han, Amit Sheth, and Christoph Bussler. A Taxonomy of Adaptive Workflow Management. In *Proc. of the Workshop Towards Adaptive Workflow Systems in conjunction with CSCW*, November 1998.

[97] David Harel. On Visual Formalisms. *Communications of the ACM*, 31(5), 1988.

[98] Erik Hilsdale and Jim Hugunin. Advice Weaving in AspectJ. In *Proc. of the 3rd International conference on Aspect-oriented software development(AOSD)*, pages 26–35. ACM Press, March 2004.

[99] Robert Hirschfeld and Katsuya Kawamura. Dynamic Service Adaptation. In *Proc. of the 4th International Workshop on Distributed Auto-adaptive and Reconfigurable Systems (DARES)*, Tokyo, Japan, March 2004.

[100] Charles Antony Richard Hoare. *Communicating Sequential Processes*. Prentice-Hall, 1985.

[101] Pavel Hruby. Specification of Workflow Management Systems with UML. In *Proc. of the Workshop on Implementation and Application of Object-oriented Workflow Management Systems in conjunction with OOPLSA*, October 1998.

[102] Michael N. Huhns and Munindar P. Singh. Service-Oriented Computing: Key Concepts and Principles. *IEEE Internet Computing*, 09(1):75–81, 2005.

[103] IBM. WebSphere Enterprise Service Bus. `http://www-306.ibm.com/software/integration/wsesb/`.

[104] IBM. WebSphere MQ Workflow. `http://www-306.ibm.com/software/integration/wmqwf/`.

[105] IBM. WebSphere Process Server Version 6.0. `http://www-306.ibm.com/software/integration/wps/`.

[106] IBM. BPWS4J: A Platform for Creating and Executing BPEL4WS Processes. `http://www.alphaworks.ibm.com/tech/bpws4j`, August 2002.

[107] IBM and Microsoft. Security in a Web Services World: A Proposed Architecture and Roadmap.

[108] IBM and SAP. WS-BPEL Extension for People - BPEL4People. `http://www-128.ibm.com/developerworks/webservices/library/specification/ws-bpel4people/`, July 2005.

[109] IDS Scheer. Integrated Process and Rules Modeling with ARIS Platform. `http://www.ids-scheer.com/belgium/profile/86648`, May 2006.

[110] ILOG. JRules. `http://www.ilog.com/products/jrules`.

[111] ILOG. Press Release. `http://ilog.com/corporate/releases/us/050706_oracle.cfm`, July 2005.

[112] Intalio. Process eXecution Engine (PXE). `http://pxe.fivesight.com`.

[113] Stefan Jablonski. MOBILE: A Modular Workflow Model and Architecture. In *Proc. of the 4th International Working Conference on Dynamic Modelling and Information Systems (DYNMOD)*, pages 1–30, September 1994.

[114] Peter Jackson. *Introduction to Expert Systems*. Addison-Wesley, 1986.

[115] Jeffry. Schlimmer (Eds.). Web Services Policy Framework (WS-Policy). `ftp://www6.software.ibm.com/software/developer/library/ws-policy.pdf`, September 2004.

[116] Rod Johnson. Introduction to the Spring Framework. `http://www.theserverside.com/articles/article.tss?l=SpringFramework`, May 2005.

[117] Dimka Karastoyanova, Alejandro Houspanossian, Mariano Cilia, Frank Leymann, and Alejandro P. Buchmann. Extending BPEL for Run Time Adaptability. In *Proc. of the 9th IEEE International Enterprise Distributed Object Computing (EDOC)*, pages 15–26. IEEE Computer Society, September 2005.

[118] Rania Khalaf, Nirmal Mukhi, and Sanjiva Weerawarana. Service-Oriented composition in BPEL4WS. In *Proc. of the 12th International World Wide Web Conference (Alternate Paper Tracks)*, May 2003.

[119] Gregor Kiczales. The Fun Has Just Begun. http://aosd.net/archive/ 2003/kiczales-aosd-2003.ppt, March 2003. Keynote at AOSD 2003.

[120] Gregor Kiczales, Erik Hilsdale, Jim Hugunin, Mik Kersten, Jeffrey Palm, and William G. Griswold. An Overview of AspectJ. In *Proc. of the 15th European Conference on Object-Oriented Programming (ECOOP)*, volume 2072 of *LNCS*, pages 327–353. Springer, June 2001.

[121] Gregor Kiczales, John Lamping, Anurag Mendhekar, Chris Maeda, Cristina Lopes, Jean-Marc Loingtier, and John Irwin. Aspect-oriented programming. In *Proc. of the 11th European Conference on Object-Oriented Programming (ECOOP)*, volume 1241 of *LNCS*, pages 220–242. Springer, June 1997.

[122] Gregor Kiczales and Mira Mezini. Aspect-Oriented Programming and Modular Reasoning. In *Proc. of the 27th International Conference on Software Engineering (ICSE)*, pages 49–58. ACM Press, May 2005.

[123] Gregor Kiczales and Mira Mezini. Separation of Concerns with Procedures, Annotations, Pointcut and Advice. In *Proc. of the 19th European Conference on Object-Oriented Programming (ECOOP)*, volume 3586 of *LNCS*, pages 195–213. Springer, July 2005.

[124] Ramnivas Laddad. *AspectJ in Action*. Manning Publications, 2003.

[125] Frank Leymann. Web Services Flow Language (WSFL) 1.0. http:// www-306.ibm.com/software/solutions/webservices/pdf/WSFL.pdf, May 2001.

[126] Frank Leymann and Wolfgang Altenhuber. Managing Business Processes as an Information Resource. *IBM Systems Journal*, 33(2):326–348, 1994.

[127] Frank Leymann and Dieter Roller. Workflow-based Applications. *IBM Systems Journal*, 36(1):102–123, 1997.

[128] Frank Leymann and Dieter Roller. *Production Workflows*. Prentice-Hall, 2000.

[129] ActiveBPEL LLC. ActiveBPEL 2.0. http://www.activebpel.org.

[130] Hidehiko Masuhara and Gregor Kiczales. A Modeling Framework for Aspect-oriented Mechanisms. In *Proc. of the 17th European Conference on Object-Oriented Programming (ECOOP)*, volume 2734 of *LNCS*, pages 2–28. Springer, July 2003.

[131] Mathias Weske and Gottfried Vossen. *Handbook on Architectures of Information Systems*, chapter Workflow Languages, pages 359–379. Springer, Berlin, 1998.

[132] Scott McCready. There is more than one Kind of Workflow Software. *ComputerWorld*, 2, November 1992.

[133] Joao Meidanis, Gottfried Vossen, and Mathias Weske. Using Workflow Management in DNA Sequencing. In *Proc. of the 1st International Conference on Cooperative Information Systems (CoopIS)*, pages 114–123. IEEE Computer Society, June 1996.

[134] Microsoft. BizTalk Server 2006. http://www.microsoft.com/germany/biztalk/default.mspx.

[135] Robin Milner. *A Calculus of Communicating Systems*. Springer, 1982.

[136] OASIS. Web Services Business Process Execution Language (WS-BPEL) Technical Committee. http://www.oasis-open.org/committees/tc_home.php?wg_abbrev=wsbpel.

[137] OASIS. Web Services Reliable Messaging TC WS-Reliability 1.1, 15 November 2004. http://docs.oasis-open.org/wsrm/ws-reliability/v1.1/wsrm-ws_reliability-1.1-spec-os.pdf.

[138] OASIS. Web Services Security: SOAP Message Security 1.0, March 2004. http://docs.oasis-open.org/wss/2004/01/oasis-200401-wss-soap-message-security-1.0.pdf.

[139] OASIS WS-TX TC. Web Services Atomic Transaction (WS-AtomicTransaction) 1.1, Committee Draft 01, March 15, 2006. http://docs.oasis-open.org/ws-tx/wstx-wsat-1.1-spec-cd-01.pdf.

[140] OASIS WS-TX TC. Web Services Business Activity (WS-BusinessActivity) 1.1, Committee Draft 01, March 15, 2006. http://docs.oasis-open.org/ws-tx/wstx-wsba-1.1-spec-cd-01.pdf.

[141] OASIS WSRM TC. Web Services Reliability Options: A Comparison of Web Services Reliable Messaging Specifications. http://www.oasis-open.org/events/symposium/slides/wsrm_notes.pdf, May 2004.

[142] Object Management Group. Object Constraint Language 2.0 Final Adopted Specification. http://www.omg.org/cgi-bin/doc?ptc/2003-10-14, October 2003.

[143] Object Management Group. Meta Object Facility (MOF) 2.0 Query/View/Transformation Specification. http://www.omg.org/docs/ptc/05-11-01.pdf, November 2005.

[144] Object Management Group. Business Process Modeling Notation (BPMN) 1.0, Final Adopted Specification. http://www.bpmn.org/, February 2006.

[145] Martin S. Olivier, Reind P. van de Riet, and Ehud Gudes. Specifying Application-Level Security in Workflow Systems. In *Proc. of the 9th International Workshop on Database and Expert Systems Applications (DEXA)*, pages 346–351, August 1998.

[146] Oracle. An Introduction to Oracle Web Services Manager, Oracle White Paper. http://www.oracle.com/technology/products/webservices_manager/pdf/oracle_wsm_402_wp.pdf, May 2005.

[147] Oracle. BPEL + Business Rules, Feature Preview Webinar. http://www.oracle.com/technology/products/ias/bpel/pdf/ bpelandbusinessrules.pdf, February 2005.

[148] Oracle. BPEL Process Manager 10.1.2. http://www.oracle.com/ technology/products/ias/bpel/index.html, August 2005.

[149] Oracle. Securing BPEL Processes and Services Part 1, Webinar. http://www.oracle.com/technology/products/ias/bpel/htdocs/ webinars.html, September 2005.

[150] Guadalupe Ortiz and Frank Leymann. Combining WS-Policy and Aspect-Oriented Programming. In *Proc. of the International Conference on Internet and Web Applications and Services (ICIW)*, pages 143–148, February 2006.

[151] Guadalupe Ortiz, Juan Hernández Núñez, and Pedro J. Clemente. How to Deal with Non-Functional Properties in Web Service Development. In *Proc. of the 5th International Conference on Web Engineering (ICWE)*, volume 3579 of *LNCS*, pages 98–103. Springer, July 2005.

[152] Klaus Ostermann, Mira Mezini, and Christoph Bockisch. Expressive Pointcuts for Increased Modularity. In *Proc. of the 19th European Conference on Object-Oriented Programming (ECOOP)*, volume 3586 of *LNCS*, pages 214–240. Springer, 2005.

[153] Mike P. Papazoglou. Service-Oriented Computing: Concepts, Characteristics and Directions. In *Proc. of the 4th International Conference on Web Information Systems Engineering (WISE)*, pages 3–12. IEEE Computer Society, December 2003.

[154] Renaud Pawlak, Lionel Seinturier, Laurence Duchien, and Gerard Florin. JAC: a Flexible Solution for Aspect-Oriented Programming in Java. In *Proc. of the 3rd International Conference on Metalevel Architectures and Separation of Crosscutting Concerns (Reflection)*, volume 2192 of *LNCS*, pages 1–24. Springer, 2001.

[155] Chris Peltz. Web Services Orchestration and Choreography. *Computer Journal*, 36(10):46–52, October 2003.

[156] Carl Adam Petri. *Kommunikation mit Automaten*. PhD thesis, Darmstadt University of Technology, Darmstadt, Germany, 1961.

[157] Roman Pichler, Klaus Ostermann, and Mira Mezini. On Aspectualizing Component Models. *Software Practice and Experience*, 33(10):957–974, March 2003.

[158] Andrei Popovici, Gustavo Alonso, and Thomas R. Gross. Just-in-time Aspects: Efficient Dynamic Weaving for Java. In *Proc. of the 2nd International Conference on Aspect-Oriented Software Development (AOSD)*, pages 100–109. ACM Press, March 2003.

[159] Andrei Popovici, Gustavo Alonso, and Thomas R. Gross. Spontaneous Container Services. In *Proc. of the 17th European Conference on Object-Oriented Programming (ECOOP)*, volume 2743 of *LNCS*, pages 29–53. Springer, July 2003.

[160] Awais Rashid and Ruzanna Chitchyan. Persistence as an Aspect. In *Proc. of the 2nd International Conference on Aspect-Oriented Software Development (AOSD)*, pages 120–129. ACM Press, March 2003.

[161] Manfred Reichert, Thomas Bauer, and Peter Dadam. Enterprise-Wide and Cross-Enterprise Workflow-Management: Challenges and Research Issues for Adaptive Workflows. In *Proc. of the Workshop on Enterprise-wide and Cross-enterprise Workflow Management*, pages 56–64, October 1999.

[162] Manfred Reichert and Peter Dadam. ADEPT flex -Supporting Dynamic Changes of Workflows Without Losing Control. *Journal of Intelligent Information Systems*, 10(2):93–129, 1998.

[163] Manfred Reichert, Stefanie Rinderle, and Peter Dadam. ADEPT Workflow Management System: Flexible Support for Enterprise-Wide Business Processes. In *Proc. of the 1st International Conference on Business Process Management (BPM)*, volume 2678 of *LNCS*, pages 370–379. Springer, June 2003.

[164] Florian Rosenberg and Schahram Dustdar. Business Rules Integration in BPEL - A Service-Oriented Approach. In *Proc. of the 7th International Conference on E-Commerce Technology (CEC)*, pages 476–479. IEEE Computer Society, July 2005.

[165] Ronald G. Ross. *Principles of the Business Rules Approach*. Addison-Wesley, 2003.

[166] Wasim Sadiq and Maria E. Orlowska. On Business Process Model Transformations. In *Proc. of the 19th International Conference on Conceptual Modeling (ER)*, volume 1920 of *LNCS*, pages 267–280. Springer, October 2000.

[167] Gwen Salaun, Lucas Bordeaux, and Marco Schaerf. Describing and Reasoning on Web Services using Process Algebra. In *Proc. of the 3rd International Conference on Web Services (ICWS)*, pages 43–51. IEEE Computer Society, June 2004.

[168] Jerome H. Saltzer, David P. Reed, and David D. Clark. End-To-End Arguments in System Design. *ACM Transactions on Computer Systems*, 2(4):277–288, November 1984.

[169] Yoshiki Sato, Shigeru Chiba, and Michiaki Tatsubori. A Selective, Just-in-time Aspect Weaver. In *Proc. of the 2nd International Conference on Generative Programming and Component Engineering (GPCE)*, volume 2830 of *LNCS*, pages 189–208. Springer, September 2003.

[170] Rainer Schmidt and Uwe Assmann. Extending Aspect-Oriented-Programming in Order to Flexibly Support Workflows. In *Proc. of the Aspect-Oriented Programming Workshop in conjunction with ICSE*, pages 41–46, April 1998.

[171] SEEBURGER. Business Integration Server. http://www.seebeyond.com/software/ican.asp.

[172] David Skogan, Roy Gronmo, and Ida Solheim. Web Service Composition in UML. In *Proc. of the 8th International IEEE Enterprise Distributed Object Computing Conference (EDOC)*, pages 47–57. IEEE Computer Society, September 2004.

[173] Lombardi Software. Teamworks Enterprise Edition. http://www.lombardisoftware.com/enterprise-bpm-software.php.

[174] OpenLink Software. Virtuoso Universal Server 4.5. http://www.openlinksw.com/virtuoso/index.htm.

[175] Stefan Jablonski and Christoph Bussler. *Workflow Management: Modeling Concepts, Architecture and Implementation*. International Thomson Computer Press, London, UK, 1996.

[176] Edward A. Stohr and J. Leon Zhao. Workflow Automation: Overview and Research Issues. *Information Systems Frontiers*, 3(3):281–296, 2001.

[177] Davy Suvee, Wim Vanderperren, and Viviane Jonckers. JAsCo: an Aspect-oriented Approach Tailored for Component based Software Development. In *Proc. of the 2nd International Conference on Aspect-Oriented Software Development (AOSD)*, pages 21–29. ACM Press, March 2003.

[178] Clemens Szyperski. *Component Software: Beyond Object-Oriented Programming*. Addison-Wesley Longman Publishing, 2002.

[179] Stefan Tai, Rania Khalaf, and Thomas Mikalsen. Composition of Coordinated Web Services. In *Proc. of the 5th International Middleware Conference (Middleware)*, volume 3231 of *LNCS*, pages 294–310. Springer, October 2004.

[180] Peri Tarr, Harold Ossher, Willliam Harrison, and Stanley M. Sutton. N Degrees of Separation: Multi-dimensional Separation of Concerns. In *Proc. of the 21st International Conference on Software Engineering (ICSE)*, pages 107–119. ACM Press, 1999.

[181] Satish Thatte. XLANG, Services for Business Process Design. http://www.gotdotnet.com/team/xml_wsspecs/xlang-c/default.htm, 2001.

[182] The Business Rules Group. Defining Business Rules, What are they really? . http://www.businessrulesgroup.org, July 2000.

[183] The Workflow Management Coalition. WfMC. http://www.wfmc.org/.

[184] Simon Thompson and Brian Odgers. Aspect-Oriented Process Engineering. In *Proc. of the Workshop on Object-Oriented Technology in conjunction with ECOOP*, June 1999.

[185] Wil van der Aalst and Arthur Hofstede. YAWL: Yet Another Workflow Language. *Information Systems*, 30(4):245–275, 2005.

[186] Wil M. P. van der Aalst. The Application of Petri Nets to Workflow Management. *Journal of Circuits, Systems, and Computers*, 8(1):21–66, 1998.

[187] Wil M. P. van der Aalst. Generic Workflow Models: How to Handle Dynamic Change and Capture Management Information? In *Proc. of the 4th International Conference on Cooperative Information Systems (CoopIS)*, pages 115–126. IEEE Computer Society, September 1999.

[188] Wil M. P. van der Aalst, Arthur H. M. ter Hofstede, Bartek Kiepuszewski, and Alistair P. Barros. Workflow Patterns. *Distributed and Parallel Databases*, 14(1):5–51, 2003.

[189] Bart Verheecke, Maria A. Cibran, Davy Suvee, and Viviane Jonckers. AOP for Dynamic Configuration and Management of Web Services in Client Applications. *International Journal on Web Services Research (JWSR)*, 1(3):25–41, 2004.

[190] Vijay Atluri. Security for Workflow Systems. *Information Security Technical Report*, 6(2):59–68, 2001.

[191] Barbara von Halle. *Business Rules Applied: Building Better Systems Using the Business Rules Approach*. Wiley, 2001.

[192] W3C. OWL Web Ontology Language Overview, W3C Recommendation 10 February 2004. http://www.w3.org/TR/owl-features.

[193] W3C. Simple Object Access Protocol (SOAP) 1.1, W3C Note 08 May 2000. http://www.w3.org/TR/2000/NOTE-SOAP-20000508/.

[194] W3C. Web Services Description Language (WSDL) 1.1, W3C Note 15 March 2001. http://www.w3.org/TR/wsdl.

[195] W3C. XML Query Language (XQuery) Version 1.0, W3C Candidate Recommendation 8 June 2006. http://www.w3.org/TR/xquery/.

[196] W3C. Web Services Choreography Description Language Version 1.0 (WS-CDL). http://www.w3.org/TR/ws-cdl-10/, October 2004.

[197] Sanjiva Weerawarana, Francisco Curbera, Frank Leymann, Tony Storey, and Donald F. Ferguson. *Web Services Platform Architecture : SOAP, WSDL, WS-Policy, WS-Addressing, WS-BPEL, WS-Reliable Messaging, and More*. Pearson Education, 2005.

[198] Mathias Weske. Flexible Modeling and Execution of Workflow Activities. In *Proc. of the 31st Hawaii International Conference on System Sciences (HICSS)-Volume 7*, pages 713–723. IEEE Computer Society, March 1998.

[199] Mathias Weske. Formal Foundation and Conceptual Design of Dynamic Adaptations in a Workflow Management System. In *Proc. of the 34th Hawaii International Conference on System Sciences (HICSS)*, page 7051. IEEE Computer Society, January 2001.

[200] Mathias Weske, Gottfried Vossen, Claudia Bauzer Medeiros, and Fatima Pires. Workflow Management in Geo-processing Applications. In *Proc. of the 6th International ACM symposium on Advances in Geographic Information Systems (GIS)*, pages 88–93, November 1998.

[201] WFMC. Workflow Management Coalition Terminology and Glossary, Document Number WFMC-TC-1011, Version 3. http://www.wfmc.org/standards/docs/TC-1011_term_glossary_v3.pdf, February 1999.

[202] Bart De Win. *Engineering Application-level Security through Aspect-Oriented Software Development*. PhD thesis, Department of Computer Science, K.U.Leuven, Leuven, Belgium, 2004.

[203] Dirk Wodtke, Jeanine Weisenfels, Gerhard Weikum, and Angelika Kotz Dittrich. The Mentor Project: Steps Toward Enterprise-Wide Workflow Management. In *Proc. of the 12th International Conference on Data Engineering (ICDE)*, pages 556–565. IEEE Computer Society, February 1996.

[204] WS-I. Web Services Interoperability Organization. http://www.ws-i.org/.

[205] Jian Yang, Mike P. Papazoglou, and Bart Orriens andWillem-Jan van den Heuvel. A Rule Based Approach to the Service Composition Life-Cycle. In *Proc. of the 4th International Conference on Web Information Systems Engineering (WISE)*, pages 295–298. IEEE Computer Society, December 2003.

[206] Charles Zhang and Hans Arno Jacobsen. Resolving Feature Convolution in Middleware Systems. In *Proc. of the 19th ACM SIGPLAN Conference on Object-Oriented Programming, Systems, Languages, and Applications (OOPSLA)*, pages 188–205. ACM Press, October 2004.

www.ingramcontent.com/pod-product-compliance
Lightning Source LLC
La Vergne TN
LVHW022312060326
832902LV00020B/3412